history of

THEATRE

First published in Great Britain in 2002 by Hamlyn,
a division of Octopus Publishing Group Limited
2–4 Heron Quays, London E14 4JP

Copyright © 2002 Octopus Publishing Group Limited

ISBN 0 600 59632 X

Distributed in the United States and Canada by
Sterling Publishing Co., Inc.
387 Park Avenue South
New York, NY 10016–8810

A catalogue record for this book is available from the
British Library

Produced by Toppan
Printed in China

Executive Editor Julian Brown
Senior Editor Trevor Davies
Creative Director Keith Martin
Senior Designer Peter Burt
Designer Leslie Needham
Picture Research Ellen Root
Senior Production Controller Sarah Scanlon

hamlyn

history of

THEATRE

neil grant

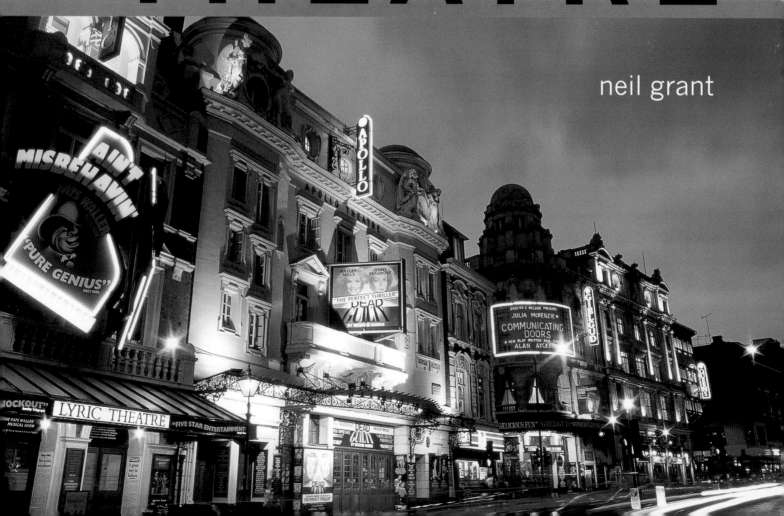

contents

Introduction

The term 'theatre', besides meaning a building where people go to watch a play, in the general sense encompasses a huge range of activities, making it difficult to define exactly. Essentially, theatre is about life, and it is no easier to grasp, classify and confine than life itself. However, it has two constants: a performance and an audience. Those two ingredients alone do not define it, but it does not exist if either is absent. Beyond those essentials, the variations are almost limitless. Theatre may range from religious ritual and poetic drama to ice dancing and sex shows. It includes such relatively modern forms as opera and ballet and employs a multitude of different skills; the core element is the interaction of performers and spectators.

Performers and audience

Its purposes are equally varied. Theatre may be entertainment, but is usually something else besides. It may be didactic or subversive, reassuring or disturbing, stimulating or disgusting. Theatre extends not only to different arts, but also into history, politics, psychology, sociology and many other fields. The peculiar chemistry engendered by live performance lends it a power that cannot be achieved by film, television or books, explaining why theatre in the past has so often fallen foul of authority. For the audience, a live performance is always to some extent unpredictable, a factor that lends it extra excitement. In the same way, as every actor soon learns, an audience is not just a collection of individuals but has an identity of its own, and it too may react in ways unforeseen. The dynamic process through which an audience comes to share an 'act of communion', a coming together of disparate individuals as they form a common interest was described by the director Peter Brook as 'like water coming to the boil . . . a change of state.' And a rehearsal in an empty theatre is an entirely different experience from a performance before a packed audience.

Recovering the past

Theatre is an ephemeral art. Most theatre, though not all, begins with a written script. But a script is not a performance, and although we may still have the scripts of plays written centuries ago, they tell us very little about what it was like to see those plays in their original performances. The script gives us only the basic framework. The historian of the theatre may sometimes feel as though he or she is trying to reconstruct not only the appearance, but also the personality of a human being from the evidence of a skeleton.

It is not as bad as that. There are other sources of evidence – contemporary

accounts, pictures, and the fruits of archaeological research. The authentic
reconstruction of Shakespeare's Globe Theatre in London, which was completed in the 1990s, would have been impossible before excavations had
revealed remains of Elizabethan theatres on the South Bank of the Thames a
few decades earlier. Even so, it is impossible to ever know what it was like to
see Shakespeare performed in the original Globe, with the author in the cast
perhaps, nor, in spite of recent advances made by scholarly research, can we
recreate a performance of Euripides in ancient Greece. The way the actors
moved and spoke, all the incidentals of a live performance, the very smell of
the place – for these we must rely almost exclusively on our
own imagination.

An ancient art

Theatre, or 'performance', seems to be fundamental to human society and it
is common to practically all cultures. Its origins lie so far back in time that
they remain for ever a mystery, although that does not – and should not – stop
scholars searching and advancing many contradictory theories, some rather
improbable, in explanation. Theatre thrives on imagination, and its primary
appeal is to the emotions rather than the mind. It touches inner feelings,
sometimes feelings hardly comprehended, and this too is part of its appeal,
its magic. In the earliest forms of theatre, words were probably unimportant
or absent, and in our theatre at the end of the Second Millennium, when staging, employing all the artifices provided by contemporary technology sometimes achieves primacy over script, perhaps we are seeing a return to an
earlier, more 'magical' concept of theatre.

World Theatre

This book surveys the history of theatre throughout the world from the earliest
times to the present. Of course it is only possible to provide a brief sketch of
so large a subject in a book this size, and some aspects must receive only the
barest mention. The Western tradition, from Athens to Broadway, forms the
core of the book, with most emphasis on the major movements and playwrights. Theatre in other cultures is covered more briefly, and mainly where it
impinges on the Western tradition. Within those limits, the main theme is
what can be called mainstream theatre. Allied performing arts, such as ballet
and opera, are discussed largely inasmuch as they affect that theme.

**Below: A scene from Peter
Shaffer's *Equus*.**

ancient world

chap

Detail showing Dionysus from a Roman Mosaic of *The Drinking Contest* of Dionysus and Heracles.

er1

As nothing is known for certain about the origins of theatre, the subject has attracted a range of theories. One seductive idea draws attention to another apparently ingrained facet of human nature, the desire to play games. The word 'play' itself is common to both activities, and it is suggested that mimicry and performance had roots in the kind of games and contests that children invent for themselves. While no one would deny all parallels between games-playing and theatre, a more widely accepted view looks for the origins of theatre in myth or religion.

dance
drama

Above: Ranga the witch, a grotesquely masked figure who represents Death in the Barong dance-drama, part of a rich and fertile tradition in Indonesia, whose many forms include some of quite recent invention.

Myth and imagination

Human beings are curious, seeking explanations and causes for what they do not understand. Nowadays we expect science to perform this function and, although historically science has seldom provided the right answers (prompting the description of scientific progress as the process of correcting past errors), it does provide answers that are satisfactory and acceptable in their own time. We do not necessarily understand the explanations that science provides, we merely accept them as authoritative. We believe that the Earth circles the Sun, or that volcanoes are caused by geological disturbances, because we are reliably informed that these things are so.

The processes of reason and experiment that provide us with scientific explanations were of course foreign to early human societies. Human beings used reason in a very limited way, partly because they had little data on which to base a reasoning process. They did have, in abundance, another human faculty, imagination. It is tempting to think that early societies had more imagination than we have, though that is probably only a reflection of the comparative absence of the controlling influence of reason. Humanity's greatest achievements have usually involved both. Myth or religion (the distinction between the two is largely a matter of cultural prejudice) provided answers to such questions as: How did life begin? What causes thunder? Why is the Sun hot?

Ritual

The other function of myth was to confirm and reinforce the social behaviour that a particular society had adopted to cope with the world. From both aspects, it gave rise to rituals. By ritual, things could be explained for which

there were no words. Possibly ritual even predates speech. As we may guess from the rituals of preindustrial societies today, the seeds of narrative and of conflict, the prime ingredients of drama, may have been first expressed here. In the earliest surviving paintings, in the Palaeolithic caves of Lascaux and Altamira, we see men disguised as animals. Discarding prosaic and anachronistic explanations that these are hunters who merely employed a practical means of approaching their prey, and with the supporting evidence offered by participants in surviving dance drama (an inadequate term for a complex event) who perform in a state of trance, we may suppose that these hunters sought to achieve a sort of communion with the animals they hunted, in some sense 'becoming' the animals. (In our more rational age we say of a particularly convincing performance that the actor 'is' the character he plays.)

The Barong

In Ronald Harwood's television series on the history of the drama made for the B.B.C. (British Broadcasting Corporation) in the 1980s, the cameras descended upon the island of Bali, a place he described as 'alive with religion, superstition and magic' – in spite of the tourists. They filmed the drama of the Barong, a benign, mythical, dragon-like creature represented by a magnificent mask, which conceals the actor to knee level. The performance was once no doubt a communal affair but is now performed by specialists. The man who represents (or 'is') the Barong is a respected figure, and the role passes from father to son. The magic of the Barong, who is revered by the community, resides in his beard, and strands of the beard are worn by women to prevent illness.

The performance takes place in a circular space and involves music and dance, as well as a long and complicated story with affinities to the classical Hindu epics, in which good, after various vicissitudes, overcomes evil, or Life defeats Death. There are comic episodes, some symbolic violence which is hard for moderns to take (biting the heads off live chickens) and a dramatic climax involving dancers in a state of trance, a remarkable example of actors' commitment to their role, so thorough that self-consciousness is totally abandoned. Audience participation is intense, and it is hard to separate entertainment, which is certainly a feature, from religion.

Masquerade

The Barong drama contains many features characteristic of mythological ritual in many cultures, including the circular 'stage', the importance of dance (and music), the intensity of the involvement of both performers and audience, and of course the mask, which both represents and, when animated by a performer, becomes the character, and is in itself an object of reverence. Sacred masks are similarly employed and cherished in many parts of the world. At Mahekuku in Papua New Guinea, in the annual dance in honour of the River God, performers representing tribal ancestors wear helmet-like masks made of river mud, which are carefully restored and kept year after year.

Below: Hideously extended teeth and fingernails reappear in this 'mudman' from Papua New Guinea, another tradition in which the mask has a sacred or ritualistic character.

origins of

The evidence of Asian cultures, where the ancient traditions generally survived far longer than those in Europe, tends to confirm that dramatic art, as distinct from religious ritual, emerges when a society reaches that stage of development when food production ceases to be the dominant occupation, when trade and crafts develop, when society becomes more sophisticated and more urban. More specifically, it occurs when language rather than dance becomes the medium in which society can more easily express itself, even though the subject matter may remain much the same.

Below: Attic red-figure vase depicting Dionysus playing a lyre. 5th century B.C.

The dramatic 'miracle'

This process seems to have been characteristic of ancient Greece, where drama in an extraordinarily mature form developed in the course of about a hundred years, in the 5th century B.C. The birth of Greek drama has often been described as a 'miracle', and whatever qualifications can be made, it still seems marvellous. But it is not entirely unique. Much the same has been said of the sudden flowering of the Elizabethan theatre, exemplified by Shakespeare, which also seems to have taken place in a moment, with little evident preparation. In both cases, of course, there were antecedents that stretched back centuries. The magnificence of the blossom obscures the seeds and the buds that nourished it.

The Near East

Long before the ancestors of the Greeks had settled in that country, religious dramas were being performed in the older centres of civilization, in Mesopotamia and Egypt. It is impossible to draw a clear line between ritual and drama, but certainly some of the elements of theatre existed in the ancient city-states of Sumer, regarded as the first civilization. They may be detected in the festivals that marked various stages of the calendar, in particular the Spring Festival, when an ordinary person was made make-believe king for a single day, a custom that reminds us of that of the 'Boy Bishop' and the 'Lord of Misrule' in medieval Europe. Similar customs continued in the successor-civilization of Babylon, where mime was a significant ingredient of religious festivals.

Egypt

There is little doubt of the existence of drama in ancient Egypt, where mythological themes of incest, murder, revenge, etc., are remarkably similar to those of Greece. Some writers have referred to thousands of actors performing in battle scenes and to audiences shouting and laughing at rowdy comedy, but they may be viewing the evidence, such as it is, with a rather partial eye. The clearest evidence comes from a tomb at Abydos, where the drama of the apotheosis of Osiris is depicted.

Osiris, whom, it is worth noting, the Greeks were to identify with Dionysus, was one of the leading Egyptian deities, forming a 'trinity' with Isis and Horus. Abydos was a centre of their cult. Originally, Osiris was some kind of nature god, but he achieved his greatest popularity as the god of the dead. Though often pictured as green, he seems to have been dark-skinned and may have been imported at some remote time from a people living to the south of Egypt. Osiris instituted farming and religion and built the first temples and towns.

The drama of Osiris, which was widely performed, probably in mime, by priests and priestesses in the temples, is concerned with his death and resurrection, He is killed by his evil, red-haired brother Set, and hewn into pieces that are scattered far and wide. But the pieces, all except the penis (which has been eaten by a crab), are collected by Osiris's loyal consort (who is also his sister), Isis. She puts them together and restores him to life (or alternatively, performs the first embalming). Osiris resigns his rule on earth to Horus, his son by Isis, and retires to rule over the Kingdom of the Dead, where, thanks to him, his devotees may enjoy a happy existence after death.

The Greeks were acquainted with Egyptian myths, and the cult of Isis later became a major religion of the Roman Empire.

Dionysus

In every little settlement in Archaic Greece, we can imagine annual festivals allied to agriculture and particularly related to the nature-god Dionysus. He is nowadays often described as the god of wine, equivalent to the Roman Bacchus. In reality he was far more than that, a god of fertility and inspiration, distanced from the more conventional Olympian family and associated with orgiastic fertility rites, the Bacchanalia, at an early date involving human sac- rifice, mystic ecstasy – possibly drug-induced hallucination – among his female worshippers. They are memorably captured in art, for instance in the sculpture in Dresden known as the Dancing Maenad of Scopas (a Roman copy of a Greek original).

It is in the Dionysiac revels that we find the roots of Western drama.

Below: *A Dedication to Bacchus* (1889), by Sir Lawrence Alma-Tadema. This rather sedate Victorian view is not intended to reflect the frenzied rites that seem to have characterized the origins of Western drama.

the
Classical theatre

A performance of Classical drama in a painting by Franz von Matsch (1861–1942), now in the Burgtheater, Vienna. The people in the foreground are part of the audience.

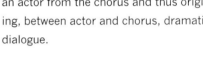

Thespis

The name 'thespian', now a slightly derogatory term for an actor, derives from an Athenian poet of the 6th century B.C. who is traditionally regarded as the founder of the drama. Practically nothing is known about him, but according to legend he arrived in Athens, bringing his own chorus on a cart that could be converted into a kind of stage. He won a prize at the festival of Dionysus, recently much enlarged and formalized by the 'tyrant' Pisistratus, who was responsible for raising Athens from a small country town into a great city. Thespis is said to have been responsible for separating an actor from the chorus and thus originating, between actor and chorus, dramatic dialogue.

The theatre of Dionysus

The Dionysia, the greatest dramatic festival in Classical Athens, took place in spring. Plays by Aeschylus, Sophocles and Euripides were first seen there in the 5th century B.C. For five days the Theatre of Dionysus below the Acropolis was the centre of Athenian life. The festival began with a competition of dithyrambs – songs traditionally sung by a chorus of 50 – for which each of the ten tribes of Athens entered a choir. The winners received a bronze tripod, and there were separate prizes – a bull, a jar of wine, a goat – for the writers.

The rest of the festival was dedicated to drama. The competition for comedies included five plays from different authors, and was completed in a day. The competition for tragedy, the first and most eminent form of the drama according to Aristotle, lasted three days, with three entrants presenting three tragedies, plus a 'satyr play' for light relief. Greek audiences must have had remarkable stamina, though they were not uncritical; at the end of the festival, as well as prizes for the winners, severe penalties were imposed on offenders who jeered.

Stage and audience

Greek theatres were built in the open on a hillside, exploiting the slope to pro-vide a view. At the time of the great tragedians, the audience sat on wooden benches in a semi-circle. Stone theatres were not built until after the time of Euripides. A central block at the front, originally occupied by the priests of Dionysus, was reserved for V.I.P.s, but otherwise the seating arrangements were apparently democratic. Entrance was originally free. Poorer citizens paid nothing, even after the introduction of fees, and attendance at the theatre was an admissible reason to reclaim a day's lost wages. A few bronze 'tickets' have survived.

The performance took place in a large, circular (later semi-circular) space called the orchestra. Originally an altar to Dionysus occupied the centre of this space. It had probably disappeared by the time of Aeschylus, though at the Theatre of Dionysus in Athens, you can still see where it once stood. Behind the orchestra was a permanent structure, somewhat resembling a temple façade, which contained the actors' dressing rooms, the few props and the stage 'machinery', the main item of which was a kind of crane enabling an actor playing a god to descend from the sky (hence the phrase, deus ex machina). It may also have assisted the acoustics, something of a problem in a theatre like that at Syracuse, which held 14,000 people. There was little additional scenery, though some painted backcloths were in use before Sophocles, and virtually no action took place on stage. Sometimes a cart entered at the end of the act presenting a tableau, often of dead bodies, the result of action off-stage.

Actors

Costumes were conventional. In tragedies, actors wore more or less ordinary clothes, perhaps more highly coloured, with boots having raised soles for extra height. In comedy, the actors wore thickly padded garments with (about 400 B.C.) a gigantic phallus made of red leather dangling in front. The chorus might wear some exotic fancy dress, for instance as birds or frogs in Aristophanes' comedies – an extra expense for the wealthy citizens who subsi-dized productions. Just as the stories, drawn from mythology, were familiar to the audience, so in a sense were the actors, because they wore masks, said (improbably) to have been introduced by Thespis, and an excellent device, as in dance drama, for submerging the actor in the role. They were made of wood or cork, and represented different emotions – hate, terror, despair, etc. – in exaggerated form. Over 30 different types are known. It has been sug-gested that masks may have incorporated an acoustic device such as a small trumpet, but there is no conclusive evidence. They made it easier for men to play female roles (there were no actresses) and to play more than one part.

Music

Although some of the ancient theatres, such as that at Epidaurus (4th century B.C.), have been restored to use, and avowedly authentic productions of Classical drama have appeared in many other places, the experience of a per-formance in 5th-century Athens is beyond imagining because we are almost totally ignorant of ancient Greek music. We know that music played an impor-tant part in the drama, which was perhaps closer to opera than a play, but we have no idea how it sounded, nor of the dancing that accompanied it. A sug-gestive comparison posits the revival of a contemporary musical in 2,500 years' time without either the music or the choreography, and with the lyrics spoken not sung.

The Temple of Dionysus at Athens. This is a later, 4th-century B.C. building, but one or two stones remain from the wall of the orchestra in the earlier theatre; the later theatres, which survived due to their stone construction, followed the original pattern.

Greek tragedy

Almost as remarkable as the sudden emergence of Greek drama is the way it evolved in the overlapping careers of the three great tragedians, Aeschylus, Sophocles and Euripides.

Above: The *Oresteia*, performed in full at the National Theatre in London in 1981, is the only surviving trilogy of Aeschylus. Such was his fame that, after his death, the authorities changed the rules permitting only new plays at the festival to allow revivals of Aeschylus.

Aeschylus

So far as we are concerned, narrative drama begins with Aeschylus. There is nothing like starting at the top, for Aeschylus is widely considered the greatest dramatic poet before Shakespeare. His subject matter – the subject matter of all Greek drama – was the rich heritage of Greek mythology enshrined, above all, in the works of the 8th-century B.C. poet Homer. Out of the dynastic and domestic conflicts of ruling families Aeschylus created a mighty epic drama of human civilization.

In the Athenian drama festival, the City Dionysia, founded some years before Aeschylus' birth and attended by people from all over Greece and beyond, the playwright was required to submit three tragedies. Aeschylus therefore wrote trilogies, groups of three plays, self-contained, but forming a greater unity – a towering conception never attempted by his successors. Only one of his trilogies, the overwhelming *Oresteia*, has survived, together with four other complete plays and some fragments. He is said to have written 90 in all.

The competing playwrights in the City Dionysia were also required to submit one satyr-play to win the prize (Aeschylus won it 13 times), so roughly a quarter of Aeschylus' plays must have belonged to this form, of which he was said to be a master, but only odd lines have survived. The satyr-play was a gross comedy, providing light relief after the tragedies and sometimes featuring the same characters – now treated in a ribald way – as well as satyrs, the goatlike creatures who were traditionally the drunken and lecherous companions of Dionysus.

Aeschylus introduced other innovations, the most crucial being the second actor, thus 'turning oratorio into drama'. He also reduced the size of the chorus from 50 to 12. His epitaph (an unlikely story says he was killed when an eagle dropped a tortoise on his bald, rocklike head) does not mention his writing, only his courageous fighting against the Persians in the battle of Marathon (490 B.C.).

Sophocles

Sophocles (496–406 B.C.) was a close contemporary of Pericles, and lived throughout the great period of Athenian history. Living to such a great age, his lifetime overlapped with both Aeschylus and Euripides. Handsome, charming, kindly and a good public servant, he was a highly popular and admired figure in Athens.

Sophocles lacks the cosmic power of Aeschylus, but he is more human, and a more fluent lyricist. His overriding subject is the unavailing struggle of the individual against Fate, often situating the hero in a critical situation – a plague-ridden city in *Oedipus the King*, one ruined by war in *Antigone* – and his characterization is sharper, his plots more complicated than Aeschylus'.

Aristotle, the chief authority on Greek drama (and on practically everything else), seems to have regarded his work as representing the finest form of the drama.

Sophocles introduced the third actor in the drama, an innovation which his older rival, Aeschylus, copied in his later plays. Only seven of his tragedies have survived, including *Oedipus the King*, perhaps the greatest (Aristotle thought so), and the most performed today, together with a large part of one satyr-play.

Euripides

With Euripides (484–406 B.C.) we move a step nearer our own time. Unlike Sophocles, he was reclusive and antisocial, an individualist with none of the great Athenian commitment to service of the state. Success came to him late. A realist, he had little time for the powerful gods who dominate the tragedies of Aeschylus, nor for morality and religion in general. He was more interested in the emotions and psychology of the individual. His plays are less 'classical', in that the characters are more ordinary, more like contemporaries, while some are hardly tragedies at all. Euripides deliberately adopted more every-day language and, apparently, more popular music. Less successful than Sophocles in his own time, though he did win the drama prize five times, he was more popular with later generations, and more of his plays have survived. He is alleged to have written 92, of which we have 17 complete, including one satyr-play.

Euripides followed the basic dramatic form of Sophocles, but it is clear that he found the chorus something of a distraction: it is out of place in a play about private feelings rather than public events. He did not discard it alto-gether, though it disappeared among his successors. Instead, he introduced a prologue, an introduction, often satirical, which explains the background of what is about to happen, delivered by some neutral figure. This device was taken up by the Elizabethans, who confusingly called the speaker of the Prologue the Chorus.

Below: A production of *Antigone* by the Royal Shakespeare Company in 1992. In Sophocles' overwhelmingly powerful drama, tragedy springs from a king's refusal to allow a dead enemy to be honourably buried – a vital matter to the Greeks.

the Greek tragedians

Dates not given are unknown; some others are approximate

Aeschylus
Born: Eleusis 525 B.C.
Died: Sicily 456 B.C.
Surviving plays
The Suppliant Women 490 B.C., *The Persians* 472 B.C., *The Seven Against Thebes* 469 B.C., *Prometheus Bound* 460 B.C., *The Oresteia* (*Agamemnon, The Libation-Bearers and Eumenides*) 458 B.C.

Sophocles
Born: Colonus 496 B.C.
Died: Athens 406 B.C.
Surviving plays
Ajax 442 B.C., *Antigone* 441 B.C., *The Trachiniae* 429 B.C., *Oedipus the King* 429 B.C., *Electra* 409 B.C., *Philoctetes* 409 B.C., *Oedipus at Colonus* (produced posthumously), *The Trackers* (*Ichneutae*, satyr-play)

Euripides
Born: Salamis 484 BC
Died: Macedonia 406 B.C.
Surviving plays
Medea 431 B.C., *Hippolytus* 428 B.C., *The Children of Herakles* 428 B.C., *Hecuba* 426 B.C., *The Trojan Women* 415 B.C., *Iphigenia in Tauris* 414 B.C., *Helen* 412 B.C. *The Phoenician Women* 411 B.C., *Orestes* 408 B.C., *The Madness of Herakles, The Suppliant Women, Ion, Electra, Alcestis, The Bacchae* (produced posthumously), *Iphigenia in Aulis* (produced posthumously), *The Cyclops* (satyr-play)

Greek comedy

It was said that tragedy came before comedy, although this was perhaps a matter of literary priorities rather than chronology, and according to Aristotle tragedy developed from the satyr-play, a different genre from comedy. The Greek words from which we get the word comedy referred to a song sung at revels such as those associated with fertility rites, which involved, besides dancing and singing, coarse jokes and extemporized mocking by-play with spectators. Many of the attributes of Greek comedy are evident in these festivities. Greek comedy does not translate as well as tragedy, because so much of it is purely local, including ferocious (and often completely unfair) satire of contemporary individuals and institutions and Athenian in-jokes that mean little to a modern audience. There is also coarse clowning and unbridled obscenity, as well as brilliant wit, comic ideas and fine poetry. The form followed that of tragedy, part choral singing, part individual dialogue, and there was little plot, the play often taking a contemporary event or situation, with loosely linked scenes dealing with different aspects or effects. However, comedy has one advantage over tragedy in relating to a modern audience: whereas tragedy has changed considerably since the time of Aeschylus and Sophocles, the comic spirit remains the same.

Aristophanes

The plays of only one writer of what was later called the Old Comedy have survived more or less whole, but the fact of their survival, plus the opinion of contemporaries, is proof of their popularity. Aristophanes (c.448–c.380 B.C.) wrote about 40 plays, of which we have 11. Many bear the title of animals (*The Birds*, *The Frogs*), which refers to the costumes worn by the chorus, another custom devised from ancient revels. While capable of wonderful lyric poetry, Aristophanes enthusiastically embraced the 'lowest' forms of comedy, the broadest clowning and farce. Had the ancient Greeks worn trousers, braces would have snapped in Aristophanes as often as in a Whitehall farce. He was prepared to attack everybody, including the gods, and was a savage critic of institutions and individuals, especially politicians and intellectuals. No modern playwright could have written as he did without incurring prosecution; (Aristophanes did find himself in trouble at least once, as a result of his hostility to the Peloponnesian War, and his plays were banned – a remarkable tribute in its way – by the regime of the Colonels in Greece, 1967–74). *The Clouds* contains a parody of Sophocles, and it is said that during the performance Sophocles himself, a hard man to irritate, stood up so that the audience might compare his appearance with the mask worn by the actor.

New Comedy

Between the Old Comedy of Aristophanes and the New Comedy of Menander, literary historians have distinguished a period known as 'Middle Comedy', which begins with the last plays of Aristophanes and spans roughly the first half of the 4th century B.C. The legacy of the ancient revels is less evident, the chorus is downgraded, there is less bawdy humour, more attention to plot and dramatic illusion, and less political satire. But the great period of Greek drama was drawing to a close, along with the decline of Athens itself. In the 4th century, Athens ceased to be the cultural capital of the Western world. It became merely a provincial city, and subject to a foreign power. Freedom of speech was lost and political satire in the manner of Aristophanes was impossible. The playwright had also lost his dominance to the actor, and though masks were still used, the approach of the star performer can be detected.

Menander

The only playwright of the New Comedy whose work has survived is Menander (c.342–293 B.C.), one play and large parts of four others having been discovered in the 20th century. He is said to have written over 100, and in his own time was hugely popular. Menander's New Comedy was essentially a comedy of manners, and his stature as one of the founders of modern comedy is greater than that of Aristophanes, whose influence on the drama, as distinct from literature, was slight.

Menander's characters are not engaged in a tragic conflict with invincible Fate, but are the victims of chance events. The chorus has gone, and so has religion. His subject is the life of ordinary people, specifically of the well-to-do Athenians of his time. Love is a frequent theme, and he employs stock characters, identifiable by their masks, such as the intolerant old man and the crafty

Below: Clay figures of comedy actors, made about the 2nd century B.C.

Right: An 18th-century etching of Greek actors, derived from an antique cameo. Silly old men were a common ingredient of Greek and much subsequent comedy.

In Camei

slave (a tradition exploited in a British television series, *Up Pompeii*, with the comedian Frankie Howerd). Menander is sympathetic to his characters, especially women, but hostile to the aggressive, the greedy, the intolerant and the hypocritical. Though his plots are rather contrived and his characters conventional, he earned praise for his fidelity to life.

Menander has given us some notable aphorisms, among them: 'Evil communications corrupt good manners', quoted by St Paul in his Epistle to the Corinthians; 'Marriage is a necessary evil'; 'He whom the gods love dies young'.

Rome

A mosaic of the 2nd century B.C. from Pompeii, showing a scene of musicians in a contemporary stage performance.

In the words of the Roman poet Horace, Greece was captured by Rome, but Rome was captivated by Greece. The Romans, unlike most conquerors, appreciated the virtues of those (or some of those) they conquered. They recognized that Greek civilization was far superior to their own, and virtually all Roman art was inspired by Greece, though it naturally established a different character in course. Roman art was often even executed by Greeks. The theatre at Syracuse was originally built in the mid-5th century B.C., and must have been familiar to the Romans even before they conquered the Greek colony late in the 3rd century B.C.

Rustic comedy

There were other influences besides the drama of Classical Greece. Southern Italy was also home of a rough type of Italian comedy, the phlyax, knockabout farce, partly extemporized, played in ridiculous padded costumes with over-sized phallus, and depending partly on mime. Our knowledge of it is mainly derived from painted pottery. There was another type of rustic farce associated with Atellana, Campania, based on grotesquely masked stock characters characterized by vulgar vices – drunkenness, obscenity – and engaged in absurd deceits to further their own interests at the expense of others. When it eventually reached Rome, the *fabula atellana*, in which it is tempting to see the remote origins of the commedia dell'arte, was performed by professionals following, more or less, a script. Etruscan traditions originating in the music, dancing, masquerades and clowning associated with religious festivals were probably a still older source. Genuine drama, however, was chiefly to be found in the *fabula palliata*, which consisted of Greek New Comedy adapted for Roman audiences by mostly hack writers who tended to emphasize its less poetic aspects.

Terence and Plautus

Terence (c.190–159 B.C.), an African-born former slave, who worked in this tradition, was an exception, since he was a genuine artist whose plays are original and elegant, have some universal application – they are set in no particular time or place – and contain less coarse clowning and more subtle characterization. No doubt for these reasons, he was increasingly unpopular with Roman audiences, although, like Plautus, he was to have great influence on later ages. Six of Terence's plays have survived, four of which are adaptations of Menander.

Plautus (c.254–184 B.C.), who belonged to the previous generation, introduced stronger characters, though generally stock types (often the crafty slave), and relied more on traditional humour freely mixed with songs, comic by-play and topical reference. In Rome, political or personal satire was dangerous stuff: an earlier playwright, Naevius (died c.199 B.C.), only small fragments of whose work are known, had incurred prison and exile after offending a prominent Roman family. But there appears to have been no restrictions on obscenity, however gross. In spite of sometimes over-complex plots, the plays of Plautus are well crafted, and he is said to have been a former actor, or at least to have had very early experience of the theatre, although practically nothing is known of his life. He was credited with writing 130 plays, most of them probably the work of others, but 21 have survived, in part or in whole. He was also to provide sources for later playwrights, including Shakespeare and Molière, and the American musical, *A Funny Thing Happened on the Way to the Forum* (1962), was based on Plautus.

Tragedy

The main function of the Roman theatre was to provide entertainment for the volatile proletariat whose tastes, notoriously, ran to the spectacular – chariot races, gladiatorial combat, human sacrifice. In the theatre, tragedy took second place to comedy, and although the Romans appreciated the great tragedies of Classical Athens, they liked more action and melodrama. Towards the end of the Republic, fewer plays were written. The writer was losing his ascendancy to the actor and, in the tendency to emphasize the actor behind the mask, there were signs of the emergence of the star performer, though masks were not abandoned. Traditional farce, in particular the *fabula atellana*, crude mime and pantomime held the stage, along with shows whose appeal lay in extravagant scenic effects. Popular taste reached a nadir.

In this situation, serious drama retreated from the public theatre to the private villa. It is doubtful that the ten, or rather nine (one was probably by another writer) surviving tragedies of Seneca (c.4 B.C.–A.D. 65), which were so hugely influential in the Renaissance, were ever performed in public. Modelled on Greek originals, they were probably meant to be read, not acted, and they demand a good deal of knowledge on the part of the audience. The only plays from the period of the Roman Empire which have survived, Seneca's work should be seen not as typical Roman drama but rather as a reaction against what passed for drama in the age of Nero.

Ironically, as drama declined, ever more magnificent theatres were built throughout the Roman Empire. (see page 34).

Some of the finest survivals of late Classical theatres are to be found in North Africa. This splendidly preserved theatre of the 2nd century A.D. is part of the Roman remains at Dougga in Tunisia, originally a Phoenician settlement, about 70 miles south-west of Carthage.

Oriental theatre

chap

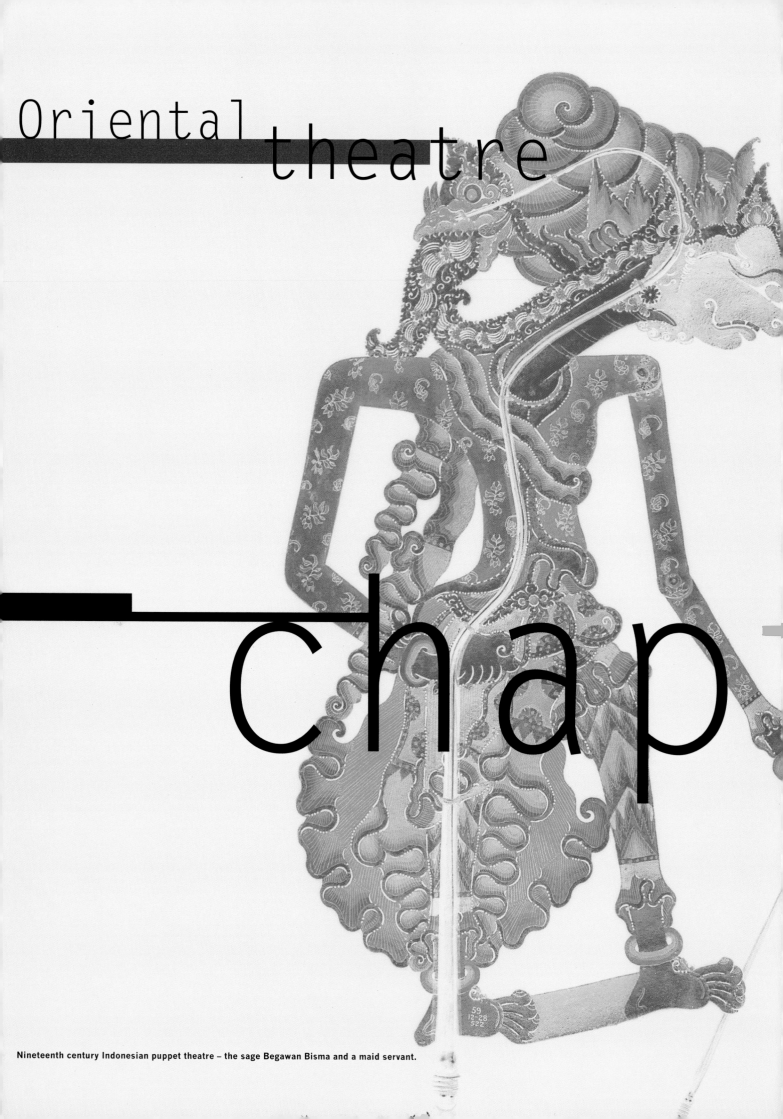

Nineteenth century Indonesian puppet theatre – the sage Begawan Bisma and a maid servant.

er

2

Every country in Asia has its own traditions of theatre, but, for reasons of space, it is necessary to concentrate on the two main regions, India and China, and on that which has stimulated the strongest international interest in modern times, the traditional theatre of Japan.

India

How the drama began

Theatre in south Asia is over 2,000 years old, 3,000 or more if we go back to the earliest temple dance dramas. Its influence was pervasive, conceivably even reaching the Mediterranean, and it is maintained to this day.

The origins of the drama in India are explained by Bharata in the *Natyasastra*, the standard 'manual' written in about the 1st century. In a decadent world, the creator-god Brahma was petitioned to provide a form of entertainment suitable for all castes. Brahma obliged by bringing together song, dance and recitation in a new form, which would both instruct and entertain. After the gods had declined to organize it, the *Natyasastra* was entrusted to Bharata, who set to work on the first play. Its subject, the victory of the gods over the demons, antagonized the latter, and they interfered with rehearsals. Bharata sought divine assistance to create a sacred place where the actors would be safe from these malevolent influences, the sanctified theatre.

The historical evidence is rather sparse. Other references to drama in the ancient writings are few. Unsurprisingly, no theatres (they were probably temporary) have survived from so far in the past, although archaeologists have discovered figurines from the ancient Indus Valley civilization, some 4,000 years old, that are usually identified as dancers.

Sanskrit drama

The first surviving plays in Sanskrit, the classical language of India, were written around A.D. 100, and they suggest that the conventional form was already well established. Both plays and performance were highly stylized and ritualistic. A certain situation required a standard physical response, and voice was less important than mimetic movement and gesture. As actors in

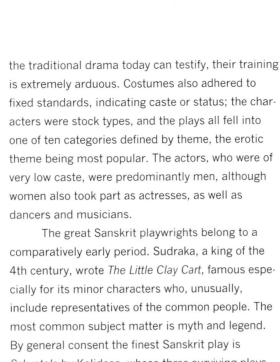

the traditional drama today can testify, their training is extremely arduous. Costumes also adhered to fixed standards, indicating caste or status; the characters were stock types, and the plays all fell into one of ten categories defined by theme, the erotic theme being most popular. The actors, who were of very low caste, were predominantly men, although women also took part as actresses, as well as dancers and musicians.

The great Sanskrit playwrights belong to a comparatively early period. Sudraka, a king of the 4th century, wrote *The Little Clay Cart*, famous especially for its minor characters who, unusually, include representatives of the common people. The most common subject matter is myth and legend. By general consent the finest Sanskrit play is *Sakuntala* by Kalidasa, whose three surviving plays date from the early 5th century and were admired by Goethe.

The theatre was a rectangular building divided equally between audience and performers, the latter including dressing rooms, etc., besides a performance space backed by a curtain. There was little scenery or props and musicians sat at the rear of the stage. According to the *Natyasastra*, the audience space measured only 214 sq.m., so audiences must have been smaller than those in Ancient Greece.

Kutiyattam

Sanskrit drama declined after the Muslim invasions, but for some centuries southern India, where it was well established, notably in Kerala, was little affected. Thanks to the temples to which it is attached, the regional drama known as kutiyattam has survived in Kerala for over 1,000 years within the hereditary caste of temple servants, for whom its performance is a ritual duty. Both the female roles and those who play the large drums (an important part of the ritual in many regional traditions) are also hereditary, although since 1947 kutiyattam has been adopted by non-traditional performers. In kutiyattam, the text is of minor importance; more attention is given to the details of staging, which are preserved in manuals far larger than the scripts. It is a drama not to be hurried, and one act of a single play can take days. Performances start latish in the evening, after the temple rituals, and continue until midnight or beyond. But, for the theatre historian, the most remarkable thing about kutiyattam is the actual buildings. Several theatres survive from the 16th century. In form they are quite similar to those described in the *Natyasastra*, though they vary considerably in size.

Rural traditions

In the 10th century, as in early Christian Europe, the hostility of Islam scattered the performers, but the great Hindu cultural revival in the 15th century, associated with the cult of Krishna, gave rise to a vast number of what can be broadly described as regional dance dramas, proselytizing the faith. There were also tales of more or less historical heroes, notably in that home of heroes, Rajasthan, together with various forms of puppet theatre. These provincial tales, in which dance is often the chief element, are largely inspired by epic literature and legend. Social satire, including indirect comment on contemporary affairs, is another ingredient. This tradition, fertilized (or adulterated) by European influence from the 19th century, carries us up to the present, and in it we see the genesis of 'Bollywood' – the Hindi film industry centred in Bombay, which has had an inimical effect on vernacular 'folk' theatre.

Above: The popular theatre of southern Asia is extraordinarily various and colourful. It includes more forms and styles than can easily be counted, and perhaps reaches its most elaborate in the play cycles of Rama and Krishna in northern India.

Characteristically spectacular make-up for a god in the traditional Chinese theatre known in the West as the Peking Opera. White indicated treachery.

In China and Korea, as in south Asia, drama was originally sponsored by the temples, gradually spreading to the rural festivals linked to the calendar. Professional troupes were hired by towns and villages to enhance the festivities with an entertainment that was adapted to the particular occasion.

China

Tradition

As in most Asian theatre, performance was, if not everything, certainly far the most important ingredient of the theatre and people traditionally watched it to see good acting. For that reason, especially in China, there is no heritage of great dramatic literature. Generally, it was dominated by men and, with some exceptions, women had only a minor function. The old custom of foot-binding may well have been one reason why female actors were unusual and female roles were generally played by men. Actors were, as elsewhere, of low social status, and their morals suspect, although social prejudice could be overcome by quality of performance. Their training was no less demanding than in India. Considerable physical skills were required, and it is no doubt due, at root, to theatre that China is noted for the skill of its acrobats and gymnasts.

The earliest plays were generally about gods and ancestors, although history and public affairs later became chief subjects of the drama. The influence of Confucianism and the generally conservative character of Chinese civilization contributed to the importance of convention. In Chinese theatre we encounter stock figures of a universally familiar sort – the warrior-hero, the crafty peasant, the flighty girl – as well as more typically Chinese stereotypes such as the matriarchal mother-in-law. Masks were originally worn, but, as in India, the alternative of a painted face – green for devils, white for cowards, red for strength – and conventionally coloured costumes became widespread. The traditional Chinese clown wore, instead of a red nose, a white patch. Stories and characters were generally familiar to the audience, and props were minimal owing to the acceptance of symbols such as (in the Peking Opera) an oar for a boat or a whip for a horse.

Zaju

Chinese theatre reached a peak in the Yuan period (13th–14th centuries). The most notable aspect was the *zaju* drama. It consisted of five-act plays, in which each act was devoted to a particular aspect and characterized by songs in a coherent style. The music is lost, but many scripts survive. They are mainly love stories or tales of heroic rebels and tyrants, etc., often based on historical events. In the final act, all wrongs are righted and tranquillity restored. A feature of zaju was that women, usually well-known courtesans, played the female roles.

Kunqu

Drama proliferated in the 16th century under the Ming dynasty. Great landowners and, increasingly, rich merchants maintained private troupes and built private theatres. At the same time, permanent theatres were built in the towns, usually in the red-light district. Performances lasted many hours, and there was a good deal of eating and drinking. The expansion of permanent theatres encouraged the development of regional styles, of which about 300 have been identified. In general, this remained exclusively popular theatre, scorned by intellectuals, but an exception was the classical form of *Kunqu*, in which events take place at the ponderous rate of real life, to the accompaniment of bamboo flutes. A complete drama could take days, and therefore it became common in the private theatres to play a few scenes only. Unlike the more popular forms, the names of Kunqu writers are often known. However, the regional style that eventually gained ascendancy was that of Beijing.

The Peking Opera

The Peking (now Beijing) Opera began in the late 18th century with the arrival of the Anhui companies from the south, although its roots can be traced to the famous dramatic school known as the 'Pear Garden', founded by the Tang Emperor Ming Huan in the 8th century.

The subject matter was familiar material from myth and history. As always, the performance was paramount, and the company developed a remarkable amalgam of music and songs, dancing, mime and recitation. Many of these features were characteristic of the Kunqu, but the Peking Opera added lightning-fast acrobatics, including brilliantly staged duels.

All parts were played by men (mixed companies were rare until after 1949; even audiences were segregated by sex until the 1920s), and, in its early years, the Peking Opera was noted above all for its female impersonators, commemorated in surviving love letters from their patrons, who referred to them as 'flowers'. Later, actors in other specialized, male roles – warriors, villains, wise-counsellor types – gained greater prominence, but the most famous of Chinese actors, Mei Lanfang (1894–1961), was, like his father and grandfather, a dan (female impersonator). He restored that function to its leading position in the Peking Opera. There were five types of the role, and Mei Lanfang was apparently the first to combine all five. The only Chinese actor of international fame, he visited Europe and the U.S.A. in the 1920s and became friendly with Stanislavsky in Russia.

Conflict between *The Sun and Moon*, a print of 1843 based on a painting by a European, George Newenham Wright. At about this time, the so-called Peking Opera was taking over from the classical Kunqu as the chief form of popular theatre.

In spite of the powerful cultural influence of China on Japan, the best-known forms of Japanese theatre owe little to China, though Chinese legends sometimes supplied subject matter. Japanese society developed differently. The influences there included the native nature-religion of Shinto, the variety of Buddhism called Zen, and the social dominance of Zen-orientated military castes, shogun (ruler), daimyo (lord) and samurai (knight).

The interior of a Kabuki theatre c.1745, by Okumura Masanobu.

Japan

Noh drama

Although the original sources of the classical, ritualistic Noh drama lay in early religious ceremonies, and ritual dancing remained the prime ingredient, the style, which was later to have a marked influence on some Westerners (including W. B. Yeats), can be attributed to two individuals, Kanami and Zeami, father and son, whose lives spanned the era 1333–1443. Kanami developed the style from traditional song and dance and placed more emphasis on the central event and character. His son, a great actor, took the drama to the court of the Ashikaga shogun, as well as writing many of the plays in the existing Noh canon. Both are revered by actors, since they helped to improve the hitherto debased social status of actors.

Noh drama appealed to the elite. There are two actors and a chorus of singers. There is often little or no plot; conflict – the element crucial to Western drama – is absent, and there is no concession to realism. In a striking parallel with the satyr-play of ancient Greece, there are humorous interludes (kyogen), sometimes involving the same characters, now appraised comically, and in less courtly language. Actors wear stylized masks and the lead actors have splendid costumes, but otherwise the principles of Zen Buddhism, austerity and economy, are evident in the bare stage and minimal props. Although the plays are often based on historical events, such as the wars between the Genji and Heike clans, some plays are set in an indeterminate period, and the Aristotelian unities of time and place are ignored.

Kabuki

Under the Tokugawa shogunate in the 17th century, the growth in the cities of a well-to-do, hedonistic middle class, which was far from sharing the disciplined principles of the samurai, encouraged the development of a more obviously popular form of theatre known as Kabuki (ka·bu·ki = singing·danc·ing·acting). Although Japan's most famous playwright, Chikamatsu Monzaemon (1653–1724), originally wrote for the Kabuki theatre, no more than the Noh drama did it produce great works of literature. The subject mat·ter is usually historical events and love stories that tend to end not with con·summation but twin suicides. Themes that in a Western context might be described as 'Gothic' were also popular. A highly eclectic form by comparison with the Noh drama, Kabuki also took material from the popular Bunraku pup·pet theatre, when a narrator would tell the story while the actors mimed it, and from the Noh drama itself.

There were more individual roles in Kabuki and masks were not worn. Actors were all male, at least after 1629 when actresses were banned, and when boy actors were also ruled out a generation later, all female roles were played by grown men. Since this type of performance had a special appeal for Edo (Tokyo) audiences, the star actors enjoyed great prestige, in spite of the dis·approval of the authorities, but for those who formed the troupes that toured the provinces, life was hard.

A Kabuki play can last all day, at one time for several days, and the audience would tend to concentrate its attention on the big set·pieces, reserving its eating, drinking and gossip for the less enthralling parts. Some might leave and come back later.

The stage

The Noh plays were performed on a raised thrust stage, with the audience on three sides and a roof, supported by pil·lars, similar to that on a temple. The audience was segregated by class. The common folk sat in front in the open, the better·off being housed in structures much like the boxes in a Western theatre. Besides the two main actors and the eight·man chorus, other occupants of the stage are four musicians, typically flute and drums, who occupy a semi·parti·tioned area towards the rear, and two stage·hands who are conventionally regarded as invisible. In the early Kabuki theatre, these assistants held lights to illuminate the actor's facial expressions. Another feature of the stage of particular interest is the raised walkway, the hashigakari, orhanamichi, 'flower way', in Kabuki, that projects from the stage and traverses the auditorium. Actors make their entrances and exits along it, and it is exploited in Kabuki for 'asides' and other episodes separate from the main performance. The Kabuki theatre, which employed a wider but shallower stage, was also fertile in stage machinery, introducing a revolving stage in 1760, many years before the device was copied in the West.

This scene, from a Japanese painted screen of about 1800, shows fashionable people at a Noh play.

puppet
theatre

Puppet theatre, a performance in which inanimate figures representing people or animals are given the appearance of life by human handlers, is a large and fascinating subject demanding a large book in itself. Its history may be as ancient as any theatre, and its many manifestations occur throughout the world. But the most fruitful areas have been the Far East and eastern Europe, where puppet theatre has figured in everything from primary education to sophisticated late-night entertainment. In the West it has more often been considered as children's entertainment, though theorists such as Gordon Craig have drawn attention to certain dramatic advantages of puppets over live actors.

Above: Performance of a Bunraku play, 1993. Although the puppeteers are in full view of the audience, the eye simply does not take them in.

The players

Puppets come in all shapes and sizes, but may be categorized in four main types. Probably the most common is the hand puppet, which fits the hand like a glove, so that its head and arms can be independently moved by the fingers and thumb. The rod puppet is an extension of this, in which the puppet is controlled from below, like the hand puppet, but with long, thin rods.

The most advanced type of doll-puppet is the marionette ('little Mary'), or string puppet. It is controlled from above by a number of thin threads, originally, in the West at least, probably by rods or fine wires. Though a simple wooden marionette with few joints can be operated with three strings, linked to head and arms, the usual number is nine. More elaborate versions can have many times that number. The strings are gathered on a wooden frame or 'crutch', which the operator holds with one hand while manipulating the appropriate individual string or strings with the other. Expert puppeteers display almost unbelievable dexterity.

A fourth, strangely enchanting form is the shadow puppet which, unlike the former types, is flat, and held against an illuminated screen on which its shadow appears, sometimes in different colours according to the light or the material of the puppet. It is characteristic of east and south-east Asia, and the relatively primitive type of shadow show occasionally seen in villages in the Balkans in recent times may ultimately derive from Indonesia.

In folk theatre throughout the world, there are countless varieties of puppet show. One type of rod-puppet theatre native to Vietnam takes place in a tank of water. The puppets, human or animal, are manipulated on rods by invisible operators and emerge suddenly from below the surface with startling effect. A politically orientated New York group in the 1960s made strikingly effective street theatre with giant puppets partly manipulated by ten-metre rods.

Bunraku

Joururi is the original name for the popular puppet theatre of Japan, which survives as a folk art in varying forms in some rural areas. The popular name, Bunraku, reflects the theatre specially designed for it in Osaka, where the form developed in the late 17th century. It was a popular entertainment of the towns and was off-limits to the samurai class. For some time, the popularity of Bunraku made it a serious challenger to Kabuki in the cities, and the most notable Japanese playwright, Chikamatsu Monzaemon, wrote for it. The puppets are marionettes about two-thirds life size. Each figure has three handlers since there are a great number of strings, allowing the movement of an eyelid or a single finger. The handlers remain in full view of the audience, yet their presence goes unnoticed. The text of the play is spoken or sung by one person, accompanied by music.

South-east Asia

The countries of south-east Asia have a rich tradition of popular theatre of many kinds, some influenced by India or China, many deriving from early efforts to communicate with the spirit world. They include many forms of puppet theatre, of which the most famous are probably the shadow puppets of Indonesia, especially Bali and Java. Performances usually take place at night, traditionally in connection with temple festivals. The performance is controlled by a master of ceremonies or puppeteer, who is also the narrator, backed by the gamelan orchestra (stringed and woodwind instruments with a variety of percussion – gongs, drums, chimes etc.), characteristic of other forms of south-east Asian theatre. His assistants manipulate the puppets, sometimes up to fifty of them. The two-dimensional puppets, cut from leather, pass between a translucent screen and a light source, traditionally candles, with the audience in front of the screen, so that what they see are shadows. The puppets are controlled by rods attached to the back and operated from below the screen.

Punch and Judy

The hand puppet still survives as popular entertainment in England as Punch and Judy. The whole show, including the narrow, vertical tent or booth with the 'stage' at the top, can be both operated and transported by one man, though he needs an assistant to collect money at performances – nowadays usually on the beach. Punch himself derives from the Italian commedia dell'arte, and was originally a marionette, although the hand puppet represents the older tradition in Europe. There are also obvious connections with the medieval mystery play.

Above: Schoolgirls watching Guignol, the French equivalent of Mr Punch, who gives us the term Grand Guignol, originally applied to short, sensational melodramas.

early European theatr

chap

Scenes from the Passion of Christ and the Last Judgement, by Fra Angelico (c.1387-1455)

early Christian theatre

Although drama was in decline under the Roman Empire, theatrical entertainment was booming, and many new theatres were built.

Roman theatres

The ruins of extraordinarily grand Roman theatres may still be seen all over southern Europe and north Africa. They were very different from Greek theatres, and they staged very different fare – crude farce and mime, acrobatic dancing with near-naked dancers, the stuff of low nightclubs rather than the art of the drama. Theatres were built on level ground, not on a slope, and the backdrop had become an impressive architectural 'scene building', similar to the elaborate public buildings of the time, two or even three storeys high and incorporating an array of sculpture and ornament. The performance took place on a raised stage, usually standing on columns and called the proscenium ('in front of the "scene"'), with a roof. The façade of the scene building consisted of open columns, so that there was a space between them and the wall behind, providing a kind of inner stage.

With the demise of the chorus, the orchestra was limited to a semicircle or abandoned completely. A curtain, which was not raised but lowered, fitting into a groove in the ground, was introduced. It offered opportunities for quick changes of costume and scenery, which were more abundant than in the 5th century B.C. The whole arrangement became more of an architectural whole, with orchestra, stage and auditorium enclosed by containing walls, and that, plus the enlargement of the scene building, blocked off the view of distant mountains and the sky which was a feature of early Greek theatres. In the Imperial period, awnings were sometimes erected across the auditorium (remarkably, the Romans sometimes managed this on their giant amphitheatres), completing the impression of a theatre that had moved indoors.

The Christian reaction

The early Christians were implacably opposed to the theatre and all forms of vulgar entertainment. About the end of the 2nd century, the Carthaginian Tertullian, a convert who became one of the early fathers of the Church, savagely attacked all dancers, mimes, singers, wrestlers and athletes as followers of a shameful way of life. Entertainers responded in kind, making crude mockery of Christianity, but, as the theatre became increasingly debased and Christianity grew in strength, the ferocity of the attacks increased. In view of the grotesque tortures which Christians underwent in the amphitheatres in the cause of entertainment, their hostility is not surprising. With the accession of Constantine (A.D. 312) and the acceptance of Christianity, these horrors ceased, but by then the Roman Empire in the West was in serious decline, and less than 100 years later Rome was sacked by Alaric and his 'barbarian' Visigoths. Soon, the theatres were silent, the barbarians having accomplished in a few years what the Christians had failed to do in over two centuries.

Byzantium

Theatre survived longer in the East Roman Empire. Theodora, the able partner and wife of the Emperor Justinian (reigned A.D. 527–65), was said to have been an actress and courtesan – two vocations with a long association. Justinian did close the theatres, but to little effect. In the 690s the Byzantine

Church was still declaiming against 'dancing and mysteries' and forbidding anyone to 'wear the masks of comedy, the satyr play or tragedy'. A Christian passion play, of undetermined date, survives. It was probably written to be performed in a church, and large parts of the text are appropriated from Euripides.

St Augustine

The early fathers of the Church were faced with a cultural dilemma. Christianity was naturally opposed to paganism, but their very civilization was essentially pagan, and no intelligent person could condemn the whole Classical heritage to perdition. The late Roman theatre contained little worth saving, and it was not necessary to be a Christian to think so. However, it is inconceivable that intelligent, educated Christians were hostile to serious drama. St Augustine (A.D. 354–430), the greatest of the early Christian fathers and second only to St Paul as founder of Christian theology, is a case in point.

By his own *Confessions*, Augustine was a rake in his youth, a frequent spectator at the amphitheatre which still stands at El Djem in Tunisia. He was converted to Christianity by Bishop Ambrose of Milan, where Augustine was teaching rhetoric – a discipline, incidentally, requiring sophisticated histrionic talents. The most powerful intellect of his age, Augustine was devoted to Classical learning, and attempted to form a synthesis of the Christian Gospel and the Idealism of Plato and his successors. It is absurd to imagine that such a man would have been hostile to the poetic drama of Classical Greece.

It is worth remembering, too, that if drama disappeared for 500 years, it was the Church itself that brought it back to life.

Dark ages?

Theatres may have been closed and the performers silenced, but they did not simply disappear. They took to the road. Direct evidence is so scarce as to be almost non-existent, but if all forms of theatre disappeared in Europe in the 5th century, why did Christian councils and bishops continue to rail against 'games', 'mysteries' and 'spectacles'?

Above: Peasants take part in a ritual dance at a rural festival in southern Germany, from a print of about 1530.

Below: Angels defend the Tower of Faith from devils, from a 15th-century manuscript. The Tower of Faith became an important device in the elaborate popular dramas, especially of southern Europe, towards the end of the Middle Ages.

The history of European drama during the Middle Ages is hard to track. An obvious difficulty is the lack of records, especially from the 5th to 11th centuries. Another difficulty is the absence of cultural centres like Athens or Rome – or Babylon for that matter. Similar things were going on in different countries, but there was no central theme, no continuing tradition, no point of reference. For five or six centuries, no permanent theatres were built, and no true drama was written. Cultural life was dominated by the Church, which was hostile, but the Church could not suppress every kind of performance, nor could it banish the human urge to investigate the circumstance of life through art. In fact, it was largely the Church that was responsible for the revival of drama.

The drama of the Mass

The Mass, the main service of the Roman Catholic Church, celebrates the Eucharist, the rite instituted by Jesus at the Last Supper. Besides prayers and readings from the Bible, the rite is concerned with the preparation of the Eucharist, in which bread and wine are transformed into the body and blood of Christ, and the bread, though not the blood, is distributed to the worshippers. Now, this is surely a drama. In fact it was seen as such. Honorius, who wrote a religious encyclopedia about the end of the 11th century, compared the actions of 'those who recited tragedies in the theatres' with the actions of the priest in the Eucharist 'in the theatre of the Church'. (Incidentally, here is more evidence that Classical drama was by no means unknown to educated men.)

The Church and paganism

The difficulty faced by the early fathers of the Christian Church, as exemplified by St Augustine of Hippo, of reconciling Christianity with a pagan culture was not quickly overcome. It was to continue throughout the Middle Ages. Intelligent churchmen recognized that the beliefs and customs of untold centuries could not be obliterated by a policy of confrontation. They adopted the policy of the takeover. The instructions of Pope Gregory the Great to his missionaries in England in the 6th century were to destroy idols and purify the pagan temples, fill them with Christian relics and make them into Christian churches. Then people would come to worship at the customary place. Instead of sacrificing their cattle to pagan deities, Gregory added, let them come to church on the day of the saint to whom the church is dedicated and slay their animals, not as a sacrifice, but for a communal feast in honour of their saint.

The festivals in the Christian calendar were timed to coincide with pagan festivals. Easter was placed in the spring, so that the Resurrection, a time of

Right: A mid-12th century frieze depicting scenes from the Passion. The powerful imagery of Christ's story was an important vehicle in ingraining Christianity into a pagan culture. In the later Middle Ages Passion Plays became a common form of Christian celebration.

hope and celebration, was equated with seed time and the joyful expectation of summer. 'Easter' itself is the name of a pagan goddess who was associated with the spring equinox.

Liturgical drama

This cross-fertilization ultimately had two significant effects for the future of theatre. In the first place the Church became associated with activities which involved performance, such as masquerade and carnival. In the second, the Church adopted more or less dramatic means the better to convey its message to an ignorant and illiterate people.

The Resurrection provided an early example in the dramatization of the visit of the three Marys to the tomb of Jesus after the crucifixion. The four characters were represented by priests and acted out the events around the altar, representing the tomb. A short dialogue ensued, beginning with the question, 'Quem quaeritis...' (Whom do you seek...). From across Europe, no less than 400 versions, some with additional action, even comic by-play, of the Quem quaeritis have survived.

Christmas offered an even more dramatic story, the Nativity. It posed a problem, however, in the character of King Herod, a villain and non-Christian by any judgement, who ordered the massacre of infants. How could he be represented by a priest? One solution was to have him played by a layman.

Hroswitha

The problem of portraying evil in a Christian context was confronted by the 10th-century German nun Hroswitha, sometimes described as the first woman playwright. She had read, with enjoyment, the plays of Terence (more evidence of the survival of at least Roman drama), but was disturbed by some of the material, which 'often brought a blush to my cheek', and by their pagan influence. She wrote at least six plays, modelled on Terence but on Christian themes and celebrating in particular 'the laudable chastity of Christian virgins'. Though her Latin was not up to Terence's, the dialogue is lively and there are comic episodes. As there were no professional companies and no theatres, her plays were probably never performed. The first English production was by Gordon Craig in 1914.

Below left: The preparation of the Eucharist in the Catholic Church was compared to tragic theatre by the 11th-century religious writer Honorius.

mystery
plays

The liturgical drama was partly responsible for the development of the European community dramas known as miracle or mystery plays. They were religious plays, like the liturgical drama, but less didactic in purpose and less sacred in the performance, which took place not inside a church, but in the churchyard or market place, not in Latin, but in the vernacular.

Corpus Christi

The three main festivals of the Early Church commemorated the birth of Christ (Easter), the Crucifixion and Resurrection (Easter) and the visitation of the Holy Spirit to the Apostles (Pentecost or Whitsun). It occurred to St Juliana, abbess of Liège, that there should also be a great festival to mark the miracle of the Eucharist, distinct from the usual celebration on the day before Good Friday (the Crucifixion), a time of year when the Christian calendar was already rather full. Juliana had good connections, including the Archdeacon of Liège, who later became Pope Urban IV (1261). As pope he embraced the idea, partly because it gave him another weapon against the heretical theologian Berengar of Tours, whose denial of transubstantiation (the central doctrine of the Eucharist) was attracting worrying support.

The festival was placed on the Thursday after Trinity Sunday, crucially, in the summer, and it developed into a great popular celebration. There was a sense that at Corpus Christi, the human aspect of Jesus, not just his divinity, was being celebrated. All the leaders of the community were involved, the church dignitaries, the town guilds and corporations, who combined in a great procession through the town, carrying their banners, through crowds swollen with country-folk, and civil life came to a temporary halt. At some point, tableaux on carts, representing biblical scenes, and organized by the guilds (not the clergy), were included, then narratives in mime, finally *The Play of Corpus Christi*, possibly the first miracle play.

Mystery plays

Miracle plays, as they were originally called, were dramatizations of miraculous episodes from the lives of the Christian saints. Later they included stories from the Bible and were called mystery plays. 'Mystery' was a word for a craft or trade, and mystery plays were mounted on a movable stage, called a 'pageant', by local guilds. Each guild was responsible for a particular story, often one apposite to their occupation. Thus the shipwrights' guild might perform the story, a popular one, of Noah's ark. The plays included a good deal of humour, often the peculiarly macabre humour so characteristic of the Middle Ages, contemporary allusions, sometimes satirical, and even an irreverent attitude to holy writ. In the famous Noah play of Wakefield, Yorkshire, Noah and his wife, the pair whom God selected as the only couple fit to survive the destruction of the human race, are comic figures, with Noah an early version of the hen-pecked husband.

Mystery plays are first recorded in the 13th century. A later development was the 'morality play', in which the characters are personified virtues and vices (Beauty, Truth, Greed, etc.). The 15th-century Everyman, originally Dutch or Flemish, is the best known.

Left: A scene dramatically depicting *The Martyrdom of Ste Appoline*, from a famous miniature by Jean Fouquet, about 1460. This type of production was essentially a popular successor to liturgical drama, performed in the vernacular on a 'pageant' in the open, often with elaborate effects. The figure consulting a book is usually taken to be the director.

Mystery plays, or something very like them, were common throughout Europe. The equivalent in France was the *mystère*, in Germany the *Mysterienspiel*, in Spain the *auto sacramental*, in Italy the *sacra rappresentazione*. There is evidence that similar performances in Scandinavia and eastern Europe took various forms. In France, for example, it seems to have been the custom to arrange the stages in a curved line, each one with a scene for one significant episode and the total ranging across the whole Christian experience from the Creation to the Last Judgement, the Garden of Eden to the Mouth of Hell. A 16th-century painting records such a series on a single stage for the Valenciennes Passion Play in 1547, the performance of which lasted for days.

Enormous trouble was taken over these productions and some remarkable special effects were employed. The Mouth of Hell belched forth flames and smoke when required. At Mons, the flight of the dove from Noah's ark was brilliantly managed. In the Bible, the dove is set loose to look for land, but returns to the ark. The second time it returns with a sprig of olive. The third time it flies off and does not come back. In the play, a live dove was released then retrieved by a string. For its second flight it was released with no tether, and a model dove then lowered on a wire from 'Heaven' (behind a cut-out cloud) with the tell-tale sprig in its beak. For the third flight another live dove was released.

Complete cycles of mystery plays in England have survived from Chester, Wakefield, York and a fourth, unknown town, but many other towns had them. Some have remarkable literary as well as dramatic merit. They have been revived in the 20th century and the Passion Play of Oberammergau, Bavaria, which dates only from 1633, is still produced.

The Oberammergau Passion Play, the production of 1890. It is produced and performed, at longish intervals, entirely by the residents of this Bavarian village.

secular traditions

Since there were no purpose-built theatres and no written drama in Europe for many centuries after the collapse of Roman civilization, the question may be asked: Where did all the talent evidently deployed in the mystery plays – by actors, writers, stage technicians and others – come from? There were in fact many sources, besides the liturgical drama of the Church. Theatres and plays, in a modern sense, may have been absent, but performers were not.

Jongleurs and minstrels

The medieval jongleurs were itinerant entertainers of various sorts and both sexes who travelled throughout Europe from town to town. They included jugglers and acrobats, singers and comics. Some worked in groups, often family groups, others on their own. They were widely regarded with suspicion by authority, and, in spite of the fact that they were often patronized by the monasteries, the Church was hostile. 'They are ministers of Satan; they laugh in this world [but] God shall laugh at them in the last day', declared the theologian Honorius, an attitude that outlasted the Middle Ages.

Although there is little evidence of them before the 10th century, the tradition was undoubtedly older. Their origins probably lay in the scattering of performers when the theatres closed in the ruins of the Roman Empire. The wandering goliards often associated with the jongleurs – men of some education, lapsed clerics and the like – manifested knowledge of Latin literature and even dressed in a 'Roman' style. Such people depended on their own resources and must have often lived dangerously close to the margin of existence, but others, the original 'minstrels', were in the employment of feudal lords, and their position was generally more comfortable. Some minstrels, or troubadours, especially the trouvères of, mainly, northern France, were of much higher social status, nobles and, in the case of Thibault IV of Navarre, even kings. There are many stories and legends about troubadours such as Blondel, who was said to have discovered where his friend and patron, King Richard Lionheart, was imprisoned by playing a song under the walls of every likely castle until he heard the King joining in from the dungeon within. Many other individuals are recorded and, although their music is lost, much of their poetry has survived, notably in the Chansons de Geste. This tradition of aristo-cratic poet-musicians reached its peak in Germany in the 13th–14th centuries with the Minnesingers, such as Wagner's hero Tannhaüser, forerunners of the Meistersingers in the 15th century.

Fairs, festivals and the Feast of Fools

For itinerant entertainers of every sort, the great fairs of medieval Europe pro-vided potentially rewarding audiences. The largest annual fairs were truly international, attended by merchants from all over Europe, as well as enter-tainers of all sorts.

Besides these professional entertainers, ordinary people had many opportu-nities to indulge their enjoyment of 'play' (the chroniclers use the Latin word *ludus* to mean both kinds of play, theatrical and recreational). The ancient practice of mumming was associated with the giving of gifts to some feudal magnate, sometimes the king himself. The mummers wore disguises to visit the lord's abode where they performed a silent dance among themselves before presenting their gifts and taking their leave, still 'keeping mum'.

The Feast of Fools took place in December. Although there is no evidence of it before about A.D. 1100, its roots may have lain in the Roman festival of Saturnalia. The normal social conventions were abandoned for a week, and ultimately it became notorious for 'riot and debauchery'. The essence of it was that relationships were reversed, the servant becoming the master and vice versa. A common medieval example was the custom of the 'Boy Bishop' (or abbot), when a choirboy was installed in a mockery of that office for one day. Such a custom was described in Sir Walter Scott's novel, *The Abbot*. It too became an excuse for bad behaviour and was condemned by the Church from the 15th century. An official complaint originating in the University of Paris described how 'priests and clerks may be seen wearing masks and monstrous visages at the hours of service... They sing wanton songs. They eat black pud-dings at the altar itself, while the celebrant is saying Mass.' Such customs no doubt provided the background for the rough and sometimes irreverent humour of the mystery plays.

Folk theatre

As we have seen, Latin comedy was never forgotten (Hroswitha cannot have been the only exponent) and, by the 15th century, folk theatre was common everywhere. An example in England was the Robin Hood plays, probably based on ballads (fragments of one script have survived), which also incorpo-rated an element of role reversal. Edinburgh burghers were chosen for such roles as King of May, Abbot of No-Rent and Lord of Inobedience, as well as Robin Hood, and King Henry VIII of England once took part in a Robin Hood play, though they were later suppressed as dangerously subversive. There were many social occasions where some kind of folk theatre might take place at village festivals or tournaments, which involved many less aristocratic activ-ities than armoured knights jousting (and, latterly, even the jousting became largely a 'show').

Gonella, the jester at the d'Este court in Ferrara, detail from a panel painting of about 1445 attributed to Jean Fouquet, which captures the mix of humour and melancholy that characterizes that precarious profession.

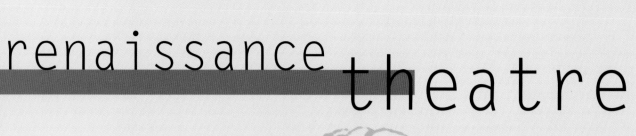

renaissance theatre

chap

'The two Pantaloons' (a character from Commedia dell'arte), c. 1622.

er4

In the Middle Ages, theatre, especially written plays, remained a fringe activity. In the Renaissance, it re-entered the cultural mainstream. Written drama, not surprisingly, emerged most strongly in countries with the liveliest tradition of folk plays and religious drama, and most of the broad patterns of Renaissance theatre, as of other arts, were established in the country where the Renaissance began and where the Classical heritage was strongest: in Italy.

renaissance
Italy

Above: Ludovico Ariosto, whose epic poem *Orlando Furioso* was adapted for the stage, also wrote satires and comedies including *I Suppositi* (1509), which influenced the plot of Shakespeare's *The Taming of the Shrew*.

The late Middle Ages

Two characteristically Italian developments were the laudi and, later, the *sacre rappresentazioni*. The former consisted at first of devotional songs based on the Gospels, from which narrative and dialogue developed in the 13th–14th centuries. They were performed by groups of penitents, like the Flagellants (so called because of the extreme methods they employed to punish their own sinfulness). The writers are unknown, and although some cycles of laudi ('praises') survive, they are of later date. *Sacre rappresentazioni* bore some relation to the mystery plays of England and France, but were performed in the 15th century, sometimes in the open, by young people connected with religious or educational institutions. They are associated particularly with Florence, though the form spread widely. They were religious dramas but with plenty of music and spectacle and including realistic, often comic, characters as well as contemporary, sometimes satirical comment. No less a figure than Lorenzo de'Medici, Il Magnifico (1449–92), wrote at least one *sacra rappresentazione* and the form had a marked influence on 16th-century playwrights.

Tragedy

Serious drama was imitative of Seneca and guided by the study of Aristotle and Horace, but there were also more recent influences, notably the tales of Boccaccio's *Decameron*. Though Classical literature was now being rapidly translated, they were written in Latin. They were moral in purpose, but themes from recent history appeared alongside Classical subjects. In the hands of playwrights like Giambattista Giraldi (1504–73), who wrote for the court of Ferrara, they contained plenty of gore and a high body count. Although Seneca was Giraldi's model, his successors were more likely to choose near-contemporary plots and were prepared to abandon the restrictions of Aristotle's dramatic unities.

Right: Lorenzo de'Medici by Giovanni da San Giovanni (1590–1636). Lorenzo 'the magnificent', himself a poet, was a great patron of the arts in 15th-century Florence.

Pastoral

The pastoral evolved from poetry – shepherds and shepherdesses, nymphs and satyrs, leisurely rustic contemplation of the ways of love, etc. – and represented a new development, much less indebted to the ancients. The first true pastoral is usually said to be *L'Aminta* (1573) of Torquato Tasso. Although very popular for a time at princely courts, pastoral, like tragedy, did not command a wide audience and it was less popular in other countries, although its influence is easily observed in France and England, where Fletcher wrote his pastoral *The Faithful Shepherdess* in 1608.

Comedy

Comedy was the most promising form of drama and presented the most successful combination of Classical and contemporary. Early comedies were often written in Latin and carried a firm didactic message, but generally a more liberal attitude towards the Classical 'rules' (or to what contemporaries assumed the Classical rules to be) prevailed. A play written by Cardinal Bibbiena, which was directed at the court of Urbino by Baldassare Castiglione (some years before he wrote his influential dialogue *The Courtier*) in 1513, rather wittily proclaimed itself to be 'not in verse, not ancient, [and] not in Latin', and denied – tongue in cheek, since in part it clearly was – that it was 'stolen from Plautus'. Boccaccio's influence is also evident, however, and although the characters are largely based on Classical prototypes, they also include some new stock figures, such as the pedantic humanist scholar. The play, which did approximately obey the Classical unities, was in five acts with intermezzi of song and dance (see page 64). It was performed again the next year in Rome, before Pope Leo X, a Medici, and a keen patron of the theatre.

One of the earliest – and best – writers of comedies was Ludovico Ariosto (1474–1533), best known for his great romantic epic in praise of his d'Este patrons at Ferrara, *Orlando Furioso*, itself adapted for the stage in 1969. His plays, with scenery designed by Raphael, are in structure thoroughly classical, but are set in contemporary city life and were originally written in prose. Among other Renaissance comedies, the best and most original is *La Mandragola*, written about 1513 by the Florentine Niccolo Machiavelli, another writer who is best known for his work in another field and above all for that famous political manual, *The Prince*.

Even comedies were written for an elitist audience: the form was called commedia erudita, or 'learned comedy'. There was, of course, another form of comedy, for which no plays were written because the dialogue was largely improvised, and it was this, the commedia dell'arte, that was to make the greatest impact on Western theatre.

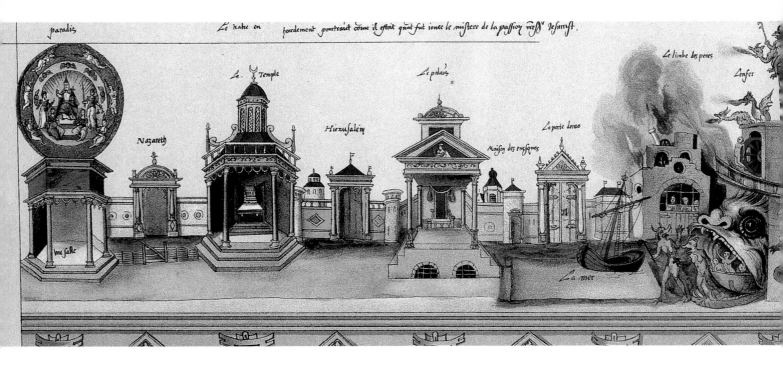

paradis · Le maire on · hourdement pourtraict come il estoit quat fut iouee le mistere de la passion nře Sesignrst.

Le Temple · Le palais · Le limbe des peres · Lenfer

Nazareth · Hierusalem · Maison des euesques · La porte doree

Vne salle · La mer

renaissance
France

In France, theatrical traditions were strong but disparate. It is possible to detect several themes, the most important being the tradition of mystery and morality plays, and the religious drama of the Church. The development of a coherent, central, national drama took longer than in Spain or England mainly because of the troubled state of the country. The endless dynastic and religious civil wars, which only ended in 1589 with the accession of Henri IV, were inimical to cultural life generally, especially in Paris.

Beginnings of secular drama

By the 13th century, religious drama had ceased to be the exclusive product of the Church, but had passed into the market places and streets. One result was the increasing use of the vernacular, since Latin was understood by few people outside the ranks of the clergy. Equally significant was the intrusion of 'folk' elements, much as happened in England, especially the comic. It often took the form of comic characters introduced into familiar stories from the Bible, with a growing tendency towards coarseness and farce. At about the same time, strictly secular plays made their appearance. They often developed from the ballads of the minstrels, several of whom, escaping the general anonymity that cloaks medieval drama, are known individually as playwrights. Another development was the rise of professional entertainers other than the minstrels (themselves 'professionals') which, typically, originated in groups of amateur performers like the students in universities, or the craft guilds. At times of festival, there was probably extensive mingling of these different associations.

The 15th century

By the 15th century, it is possible to see at least the outline of a national drama based on the vernacular, rather than the 'international' literary language of Latin. At the centre was the Confraternity of the Passion, a semi-religious guild who were essentially amateurs, although they were paid a fee for their performances. They enjoyed an acting monopoly in the capital, and no doubt similar groups existed in other regions. The Brothers performed primarily the mystery and morality plays, but also topical satirical pieces called sotie, often as a curtain-raiser to the more substantial drama to come, in which the actors wore the traditional costume of jesters and fools (sot = fool). It seems that there were specialist companies for these plays, and their repertoire also included pure farce. There is here an obvious affinity with the Italian commedia dell'arte.

'Secular, honest and decent'

Two developments in the mid-16th century changed the course of French national drama. The old mystery plays had encountered increasing hostility, largely because the rough comic element seemed to be verging on blasphemy. In 1548, the Paris parlement decreed that such plays should cease, and production confined to plays that were 'secular, honest and decent'. This marked the end of religious drama in the capital – and also deprived the Confraternity of the bulk of their material. About the same time, Joachim du Bellay published a cultural programme which, so far as theatre was concerned, demanded the propagation of the French language, an end to 'decadent' drama, and devotion to the higher, antique forms, tragedy and comedy. Du Bellay was a leading member of the influential group of poets known as La Pléiade, who were inspired by the literature of antiquity and the early Italian Renaissance. His manifesto signifies the cultural 'takeover' of French drama by Renaissance classicism.

Tragedy and comedy

The Confraternity of the Passion was based in the Hôtel de Bourgogne, but by the 1570s they were leasing it out to various, more or less professional provincial companies, which, though they performed predominantly neo-classical drama in Paris, were also, no doubt, still playing the traditional mystery plays in the provinces. Otherwise, French drama followed du Bellay's prescription. Tragedy was well developed by 1600. It was Classical in structure and its subject matter was predominantly drawn from mythology or ancient history, although more contemporary subjects, such as that great favourite of European playwrights, Mary Queen of Scots, also figured. The ground plan for the golden age of French classical drama is apparent, although the plays themselves hardly measured up either to their antecedents, such as Seneca, or their successors, such as Corneille. The writers were humanist scholars first, playwrights second, and their plays were usually slow-moving and wordy, 'consisting all too often of elegiac lamentation about an event that has already taken place'.

In comedy too, the ancients and the Italians provided the models, and there were no more soties and farces, although there was a certain amount of knockabout fun and the comedies were certainly livelier than the tragedies. But this was no less an elitist drama for audiences who were rich and well educated. There is no certainty whether the plays (like Seneca's) were actually performed. Nevertheless, drama began to take a clearer form in the late 16th century, thanks partly to the building of public theatres and to Italian infusions, in particular the commedia dell'arte.

Opposite: The remarkable setting for the *Mystère de la Passion* at Valenciennes in the 16th century, ranging from Paradise (left), through Nazareth, the Temple, Jerusalem, etc., including the Sea, and culminating in the monstrous gate of Hell, with belching flames.

Below: Louis XIV, aged 14, in his costume as the Sun in *La Ballet de la Nuit*, 1653, which earned him his soubriquet, the Sun King.

commedia dell'arte

The name, one of many contemporary names, that has survived for this popular form of comedy, is usually translated as 'comedy of the profession', i.e. of professional performers, distinguishing it from the commedia erudita, which was amateur. Another fundamental respect in which it differed was in the absence of a script. There was an agreed framework or scenario, and even some memorized speeches that could be adapted according to the way the performance developed, but the dialogue, and much of the action, was improvised.

Origins

The origins of this popular form of comedy, which flourished from the mid-16th to the early 18th century, is uncertain. It was clearly based on folk tradition, though it appealed to princely courts as well as to market-day crowds, and it has an obvious correspondence with ancient Roman comedy, though that may mean only that it is one manifestation of a universal delight in clowning and satirical farce, appealing to all ages. Antecedents may equally be found in the medieval drama. Many different locations in Italy have been suggested as a source, without great conviction. Padua is one, since this was the home of Angelo Beolco, known as Ruzante, who with a few friends in the early 16th century put on plays exploiting different dialects during the Carnival season and devised for himself a comical, masked, talkative-rustic role. But Ruzante's plays were scripted and he appears to have been a solitary, literary talent rather than the originator of a great tradition. Some of the stock characters of commedia dell'arte are also linked to specific cities, such as Venice and Bologna, but that does not prove they originated there. The fact that the learned-pedant character is usually a Bolognese lawyer no doubt reflects Bologna's position as the seat of Europe's oldest university.

Production

Productions could range from pure farce to, in later years, melodrama. The performance was adapted to changing circumstances and the perceived mood of the audience. A high degree of professionalism was required and, no doubt, lengthy study and rehearsal. There were a number of well-known companies, usually named after the leading actor, an early impresario, who was often a member of a family on which the group of a dozen or so was centred. The nature of the performance demanded close affinity among the actors. Touring companies carried their own scenery, usually no more than a couple of wings, if that, and also their own collapsible stage, unless sufficiently prosperous to hire a building or to attract princely patrons like the Gonzaga of Mantua. Patrons could have a disruptive effect, since they would sometimes try to attract star performers from different companies, and there were many intrigues and rivalries.

Characters

The actors, of both sexes, specialized in a single part, playing no other, although a young Arlecchino, a part demanding great athleticism, might gravitate with age to an older, less physically active character. They required many skills, besides the ability to improvize. They had to be acrobats, singers, dancers and, sometimes, musicians too. Most male roles were masked. The characters can be divided into three main groups: two young lovers (unmasked) around whom the plot revolves; an assortment of obtuse and obstructive elders representing satirical versions of well-known types such as the boastful soldier, and a crowd of servants led by Arlecchino, whose activities, like the crafty slave in Classical comedy, exploit the foolishness of their social superiors. They provide the true spirit of the commedia dell'arte. The best-known characters include Arlecchino (Harlequin in the English derivative known as the harlequinade, forerunner of pantomime), who wears patchwork clothes and a black mask, Columbina (Columbine, who in the harlequinade is Arlecchino's lover), Pedrolino (Pierrot), in loose white clown's costume, and Pulcinella, from whom derived the English Mr Punch and the German sausage-wielding Hanswurst. French equivalents include Crispin, from Scaramouche, originally the bragging soldier (a satirical portrait of a mercenary captain, a common figure in 16th-century Italy), who developed into a scheming valet.

Influence

The commedia dell'arte reached Spain before 1570 and France in 1571, eventually becoming established at the Hôtel de Bourgogne in the 17th century as the Comédie-Italienne. A member of the Martinelli family, one of whom is reputed to have been the original Arlecchino, was in London in 1577, and an Italian company appeared at the court of James I in 1602. Although the commedia dell'arte faded away in the 18th century, its traditions lingered on, not only in the Comédie-Italiennne, by then performing in French, and in England's Punch and Judy, but in a more subtle fashion, more broadly. There are strong links to the commedia dell'arte, for instance, in some recent experimental theatre, which employs a certain amount of improvization.

Left: Arlecchino (Harlequin), a comic character whose suit was originally made of scraps of cloth patched together, and Pierrot, originally Pedrolino, whose character was developed by an Italian actor in the Comédie-Italienne in Paris about 1665; from a painting by Philippe Mercier (1689–1760).

Below: A dispute between Arlequin (Harlequin) and Scaramouche, a character introduced at the Comédie-Italienne but deriving from the original Scarramuccia, 'Little Skirmisher'; from an 18th-century painting.

Spain

Having been practically excluded from Christian Europe throughout the Middle Ages, Spain was projected to the centre of the European stage by the events of the late 15th–early 16th centuries. In 1479 the major Christian kingdoms were united by the marriage of Ferdinand of Aragon to Isabella of Castile. In 1492 the last Moorish (Muslim) state was conquered, and Columbus reached the Americas, opening up immense and profitable Spanish enterprises overseas. In 1519 the young Habsburg king was elected Holy Roman Emperor as Charles V, commanding a bigger empire than Charlemagne's. All this power and wealth, plus a sense of national fulfilment, stimulated enterprise, not least in the arts and drama.

The Church

Broadly, the two main themes of late medieval drama, the religious and the secular, were similar in Christian Spain to the rest of Europe, but with significant, exclusively Spanish, differences. In secular drama there was the unique addition of Moorish and Jewish cultural influence, which had an effect on the importance and style of dance. Spain was the most loyally Catholic country in Europe – the Reformation made little headway there – and religious drama survived much longer. Moreover, the Church, augmented after 1543 by the productions of the Jesuit foundations, was largely responsible for the development of secular, professional theatre. In about 1500–20 the playwrights Juan del Encina, who wrote for the court of the Duke of Alba, and Gil Vincente, whose patron was a Castilian queen at the Portuguese court, wrote both religious and secular plays. By 1500, plays in the vernacular were being performed in the churches and, although their purpose was still didactic or devotional, they included more dialogue, more spectacle, and more comedy. As a result religious drama flourished in Spain well into the 17th century; the Church was largely responsible for the development of secular drama and professional theatre, including, though largely by chance, the actual buildings.

Professional theatre

Italian influence reached Spain about the same time as the young Habsburg king, and the commedia erudita, in both Italian and native examples, was established at court by the 1520s. A professional Italian company appeared in 1538.

Full-time professional companies arguably existed in Spain even earlier than in Italy, and certainly earlier than anywhere else. This development is not easily explained although, in general terms, the rise in economic activity and consequent growth of urban population – stimulated by imperial expansion in the Americas – provided the actors with a potential audience that had hardly existed previously.

Seville, the chief port for the New World, was perhaps significantly also the base of Spain's first great impresario, Lope de Rueda (c.1505–65), who is regarded as the individual chiefly responsible for establishing theatre as a full-time, professional occupation. He formed and toured with his own company, for which he wrote the plays and often played the leading part, typically a loveable rogue or crafty 'fool'. Rueda wrote relatively naturalistic comedies with a keen sense for the comic and some acute contemporary satire, as well as

17th-century theatre

chap

A performance in the gardens of Versailles of Molière's *Le Malade Imaginaire*.

Plays

The chronology of the plays is sketchy so the following dates refer to first publication

1590 *Tamburlaine Parts 1 and 2*
1594 *The Tragedy of Dido, Queene of Carthage*
1594 *Edward II*
c.1594 *The Massacre at Paris*
1604 *The Tragical History of Doctor Faustus*
1633 *The Jew of Malta*

Poems

1599 *Hero and Leander* (completed by George Chapman)
1599 *The Passionate Pilgrim*

Translations

1597 Ovid's *Amores*
1600 Lucan's *Pharsalia*

comedies and very informative on social customs, as was his *The Gull's Handbook*. Most of his plays were written in collaboration with others, including John Marston (c.1575–1634) and Thomas Middleton (1580–1627). More than half are lost, the majority of the remainder perishing among the manuscripts used to light the kitchen stove by a servant of the 18th-century collector, John Warburton. The romantic comedies of Robert Greene (c.1560–92) are similar in atmosphere to Shakespeare's, and Greene, another reprobate in personal life, felt he had been plagiarized. The most famous of partnerships was that of Francis Beaumont and John Fletcher, though both also co-operated with others, possibly including, in Fletcher's case, Shakespeare (in *Henry VIII*). Scholars now believe that their most famous comedy, *The Knight of the Burning Pestle* (1607), was actually written by Beaumont alone.

Ben Jonson

Ben (short for Benjamin) Jonson (1572–1637), eleven years younger than Shakespeare and a good but not uncritical friend, wrote at least twenty known plays and was, with the possible exception of Marlowe, the finest playwright of the age, though his late works and tragedies have never aroused much enthusiasm. His first notable play, in which Shakespeare acted, was *Every Man in his Humour*, produced in 1598. *Every Man out of his Humour* was one of the first productions at the Globe in 1599. *Volpone* (1606) is a brilliant satire on greed set in Venice, in which the names of the characters reflect their natures. *The Alchemist* (1610) mocks human gullibility and impales types of whom Jonson disapproved, such as fanatical Puritans. *Bartholomew Fair* (1614) is a lively pageant, without much plot, of London life at the great annual fair held at Smithfield. Jonson lacked the Shakespearian gift for character but was a more learned man than Shakespeare (who, he tells us, had 'small Latin and less Greek'). Both men aroused the scorn of the so-called University Wits – men like Marlowe, Peele and Greene – because they had not been to Oxford or Cambridge, but Jonson, who never minced his words and once spent a spell in prison for criticizing the government, got his own back in the fairly savage *The Poetaster* (1601). Jonson upheld the Classical unities of place and time, and in this as in other ways he stands somewhat apart from his contemporaries.

Quotes

Let Pluto's bells ring out my fatal knell,
And hags howl for my death at Charon's shore;
For friends hath Edward none but these and these,
And these must die under a tyrant's sword.
Edward II, Act V, Scene I

Instead of music I will hear him speak;
His looks shall be my only library;
And thou Æneas, Dido's treasury,
Dido, Queen of Carthage, Act III, Scene I

But tell me Faustus, shall I have thy soul?
And I will be thy slave and wait on thee,
And give thee more than thou hast wit to ask.
Doctor Faustus, Act I, Scene V

Genius is seldom found in isolation: not many good generals emerge in peacetime. Renaissance Florence seems to have been awash with fine painters, whilst Shakespeare lived in a uniquely propitious time for the drama in England. He was in contact with many other playwrights, a few of them not far beneath him in talent.

Shakespeare's contemporaries

Above: 'Dr Faustus in his Study', from a drawing attributed to Rembrandt. Marlowe's protagonist was drawn from *The History of Dr Johann Faustus*, an anonymous compilation, published about 1580, of legends attached to the name of a German 'magician' of the early 16th century.

Marlowe

Shakespeare may have arrived in London in time to see the first performance of *Tamburlaine* (probably in 1587) by Edward Alleyne and the Admiral's Men. The first tragedy of Christopher Marlowe (1564–93), Shakespeare's exact contemporary, it is a landmark in English drama. Marlowe's thundering language showed what could be done with blank verse by a poet of great power and vision. Marlowe was young, and his language sometimes verged on the bombastic (Shakespeare indulged in some amiable mockery of *Tamburlaine* in *Henry IV* Part II). He had a better subject in *Dr Faustus*, based on the German legend of the astrologer who sells his soul to the Devil, and showed increasing depth of characterization in *Edward II*. That play resembles *Richard II* by Shakespeare whose *The Merchant of Venice* must have been influenced by Marlowe's *The Jew of Malta*. Marlowe's temperament was troublesome – it is hard to imagine him quietly pursuing a professional career for twenty years as Shakespeare did – and he died in a brawl, possibly arising from some dirty work by or for the Elizabethan secret service.

Had *Tamburlaine* had been his only surviving play, Marlowe would still be considered a notable figure, but would seem a cruder talent than he later proved to be. His friend, Thomas Kyd (1558–94), is posthumously less fortunate, as he is represented only by *The Spanish Tragedy*, which may have predated *Tamburlaine* by a year or two. The prototype of what became a very popular genre, the 'revenge tragedy', it was frequently performed into Restoration times.

Comedy

John Lyly (1554–1606) wrote for the boys' companies. He demonstrated that it was possible in comedy to blend wit and romance, and purged the old English comedy of its coarseness. His plays seem to take place in a kind of fairyland, and his influence on Shakespeare appears in *Love's Labour's Lost*. He was a friend of Thomas Nashe (1567–1601), who co-operated with Marlowe on *Dido, Queene of Carthage* but whose plays, except for one decorative comedy, are lost. Lyly's faint air of fantasy is also characteristic of George Peele (died c.1597), but Thomas Dekker (c.1572–c.1632) is more robust, especially in *The Shoemaker's Holiday* (1599), one of the best of Elizabethan

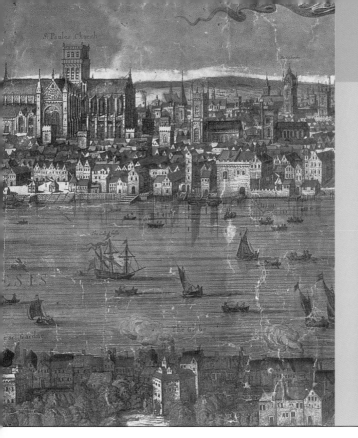

Plays *in approximate order of writing*

Before 1590
Henry VI, Parts I, II and III
Richard III
1590-1600
Titus Andronicus
The Two Gentlemen of Verona
The Taming of the Shrew
The Comedy of Errors
Love's Labour's Lost
King John
Richard II
Romeo and Juliet
A Midsummer Night's Dream
The Merchant of Venice
The Merry Wives of Windsor
Much Ado About Nothing
As You Like It
Henry IV, Parts I and II
Henry V
Julius Caesar

1600–1611
Hamlet
Troilus and Cressida
All's Well That Ends Well
Othello
Measure for Measure
King Lear
Timon of Athens
Macbeth
Antony and Cleopatra
Coriolanus
Cymbeline
The Winter's Tale
The Tempest
Henry VIII

Poetry

Venus and Adonis (published 1593)
The Rape of Lucrece (published 1594)
Sonnets (written c.1595)

been an actor of great range, and it can hardly be doubted that Shakespeare, as a member of a close-knit company, created his characters with specific actors in mind. It is generally said that the female parts were played by boys, since there were no women on the stage. A boy would probably have played Juliet (just as many great actresses since have essayed the role of Romeo, or indeed other male characters, such as Richard II), but it seems more likely that older women in comedy, and very probably Lady Macbeth (hard to imagine played by a prepubescent boy), were played by men. From Hamlet's interesting instructions to the First Player (see right), it seems likely that Shakespeare favoured greater naturalism in acting. The prevailing style was probably loud and grandiloquent, if only to overcome interruptions from the groundlings and comments from the fashionable young gentlemen who occupied seats on the stage itself – though audiences were probably less rowdy than in the 18th century.

The plays

Shakespeare wrote his plays to be performed – the idea that they are better read than seen still occasionally crops up, but seems very misguided – and he took no interest in their publication. Most of them would have been lost had it not been for the devotion of a few people after his death who, collecting former prompt copies, put together the collection in the First Folio of 1623. One of the ways in which he is unique is in his extraordinary diversity. He applied his intellectual power and imagination not to academic humanist studies, but to human psychology, probing universal feelings in an unlimited variety of characters and putting them into unforgettable poetry. Tragedy has always, since Classical Greece, held a higher place than comedy, so it is probably Shakespeare's great tragedies – *Hamlet* (above all), *Othello*, *King Lear* and *Macbeth* – that are considered his supreme achievement. He was, however, equally capable of comedy, and in the hard-to-categorize late plays (neither tragedy nor comedy, nor tragi-comedy either), such as *The Winter's Tale* or *The Tempest*, he tapped a spirit that is uniquely moving and uniquely his own.

Quotes

O for a Muse of Fire, that would ascend
The brightest heaven of invention,
A kingdom for a stage, princes to act
And monarchs to behold the swelling scene!
Then should the warlike Harry, like himself,
Assume the port of Mars . . .

But pardon, gentles all,
The flat unraised spirits that have dared
On this unworthy scaffold to bring forth
So great an object: can this cockpit hold
The vasty fields of France? or may we cram
Within this wooden O the very casques
That did affright the air at Agincourt?
Henry V, Prologue

Hamlet: Speak the speech, I pray you, as I pronounced it to you, trippingly on the tongue: but if you mouth it, as many of your players do, I had as lief the town-crier spoke my lines. Nor do not saw the air too much with your hand, thus, but use all gently; for in the very torrent, tempest and, as I may say, the whirlwind of passion, you must acquire and beget a temperance that may give it smoothness . . .

suit the action to the word, the word to the action; with this special observance, that you o'erstep not the modesty of nature: for any thing so overdone is from the purpose of playing, whose end, both at the first and now, was and is, to hold, as 'twere, the mirror up to nature . . .
Hamlet, Act III, Scene ii

William Shakespeare

Shakespeare's protean genius was acknowledged in his own lifetime. In the words of his younger contemporary, Ben Jonson, he 'was not for an age, but for all time', and his plays are performed today in dozens of different languages throughout the world (one of their great assets, from a theatrical point of view, being that they are infinitely adaptable). He was out of fashion in the century after his death, epic poetry being little to the taste of the Augustan age, and it took longer to establish his international reputation, unique in any comparable field, of being almost universally acknowledged as the greatest master who ever lived.

Above: A view of London from south of the river in the early 17th century, showing the theatres of Southwark, including the original Globe, on the South Bank.

Below: There is no contemporary portrait of Shakespeare. This, no doubt reasonably authentic, is from the First Folio of 1623.

From Stratford to London

We know very little about the man. He was born in Stratford-upon-Avon, son of a tradesman. At least four brothers and one sister survived childhood. He probably attended the local grammar school, and in 1582 he married Anne Hathaway, eight years his senior and pregnant with a daughter. Twins were born in 1585, but in his will Shakespeare famously, if enigmatically, left his wife his 'second-best bed'. He may have taught at a local school at some stage, but by 1592, when he was attacked as an 'upstart crow' by a rival, Robert Greene, he was associated, as writer and actor, with Burbage's company. He may have started as an apprentice under James Burbage. Along with other leading members of the company, such as the comedian William Kempe (famous for dancing his way to Norwich), he owned a share of the Globe and became a fairly rich man. He was granted a coat of arms, making him officially a gentleman, bought a large house, New Place, in Stratford, and seems to have retired in 1612. He died on St George's Day in 1616, and was buried in Holy Trinity, Stratford.

Man of the theatre

Shakespeare was originally an actor, though it is generally assumed that he was not a particularly good one. He is associated with the role of the Ghost in *Hamlet*, but most of his leading characters were first played by James Burbage who, with Edward Alleyne, leading actor of the rival Admiral's Men, is regarded as the first great English actor. Burbage must certainly have and in France, was condemned by educated critics like Sir Philip Sidney because it infringed the Classical model, i.e. as exemplified by Seneca, though in fact it was less heretical in this regard than Sidney and his friends supposed.

The work of these early playmakers (the word 'drama' was first used by Ben Jonson, the name 'dramatist' even later in the 17th century), though not without some popular appeal and vivid language, was rather crude stuff. As one modern critic observes, there is an air of amateur theatricals about it. The revolution in English drama occurred, with startling suddenness, in the 1580s, and was led by Thomas Kyd (1558–94), whose hugely popular *The Spanish Tragedy* is the only surviving play that can be definitely attributed to him, and Christopher Marlowe (see page 60).

Blank verse

English was still a young and lively language in the 16th century. It had acquired a national identity only from about the time of Chaucer and, in a sense, it was still being invented. A sensuous (a word invented by Milton!) delight in words, combined with vigorous, colloquial speech and a large, still-growing vocabulary, enlivens even the rudimentary dramas of the pre-1580 period. But form was a problem. Like Chaucer, John Heywood wrote his comedies in rhyming couplets (e.g. Seven cities warr'd for Homer, being dead,/Who, living, had no roof to shroud his head – one of his best in fact). The end-stopped rhyming couplet is not a very suitable form for drama, if only because it is hell for actors. Blank verse – non-rhyming verse of ten-syllable lines (iambic pentameter) – was first used by the poet Henry Howard, Earl of Surrey (died 1547), also the inventor of the English form of the sonnet. Extremely versatile, and capable of grand rhetorical effect without sacrificing faithfulness to the rhythm of natural speech, blank verse proved to be the perfect vehicle for poetic drama.

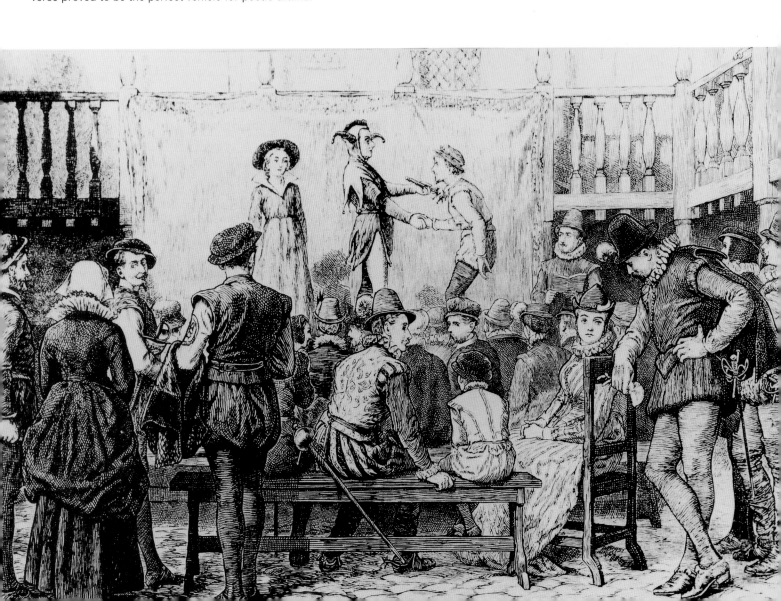

In the late 16th–early 17th centuries theatre was probably more popular in England than at any time before or since. Towards the end of Elizabeth I's reign, out of a total population of about 160,000 in London, someone has estimated that theatregoers numbered about 20,000 per week. Under Elizabeth, London had both the actors and, by the end of the century, the theatres. It also had at least a dozen playwrights whose works are still performed to this day (although rarely, in some cases), and many more whose works are not, sometimes because they have not survived. Where did these plays and playwrights come from?

drama before Shakespeare

Traditions

The strength of English drama towards the end of the Middle Ages, especially in the hands of the guilds, has already been noted. Though superseded by the commercial theatre during the 16th century, the old forms did not die with the Reformation, but continued in some towns until quite late in the century, and then only succumbed to pressure from the government. In Coventry, Chester and other places, the old mystery cycles were being performed well after the middle of the century, while new allegorical 'moralities' were still being written. Another contemporary form was the 'interlude', already encountered in Italy and Spain, an instructive and/or entertaining piece originally designed to fill in a vacant half hour or so. It was a speciality of John Heywood, sometimes called the first writer of English comedy, who wrote naturalistic dialogue, though without much dramatic content, in the 1520s. These works were written for the court, a more sophisticated audience than that of a provincial town, though they may have been performed there too.

Precursors

Not many of the early plays were ever printed, and few have survived to the present. One exception is *Ralph Roister Doister*, which was probably written in the 1530s. Its author, Nicholas Udall, was head master of Eton and the play was probably intended for boys, as many plays were. Not only did boys play female roles in the 16th century, they also had their own companies. (The Children of the Chapel, i.e. the royal chapel at Windsor, who alternated with the King's Men at Blackfriars Theatre, were serious rivals to the adult companies in around 1600.) *Ralph Roister Doister* shows traces of classical influence (Udall also translated Terence), and a later comedy, performed in 1566, was based on a play by Ariosto which in turn was based on Plautus. On the other hand, another famous survivor, *Gammer Gurton's Needle* (about 1560), is entirely English.

The first known English tragedy, in five acts, *Gorboduc*, was performed at court in 1562. A worthy but uninspiring exercise after Seneca, it may well have induced some restlessness in the young Queen. More popular was *Cambyses*, which was memorably described by its producers as a 'lamentable tragedie, mixed full of pleasant mirth'. This form, the so-called tragi-comedy, which was to have some future both in England

The Earl of Leicester entertains Queen Elizabeth I at Kenilworth Castle, a famous party, the cost of which exceeded national revenue for the equivalent period. Leicester's Men, founded 1559, formed the earliest organized company of actors, and often performed at court.

The first theatres

In spite of opposition, several companies were active in London, usually taking over the courtyards of inns. One of these, the Red Lion in Mile End (then a village outside the City), may have been converted totally into a theatre in 1567, but it seems to have mounted only one production and so must be regarded as a false start. The first permanent public theatre was founded in Shoreditch, also outside the City, in 1576 by James Burbage, leading actor in Leicester's company, and was named simply The Theatre. It was soon joined by a neighbour, The Curtain, which, however, did not last long, and several others appeared elsewhere within the next few years. In 1598, The Theatre was pulled down after a row over the lease. By that time, both Leicester and James Burbage were dead, but Burbage's sons, leading what was now the Lord Chamberlain's, later the King's, men and with Shakespeare as one of the shareholders, used the timbers to build a new theatre. To avoid the restrictions imposed by the City, they chose a site on the other side of the river in Southwark, which was already the centre of the kind of entertainments of which the City fathers disapproved and was easily accessible across London Bridge. This theatre, which was soon one of four, was called the Globe.

Elizabethan theatres

For many years scholars wondered exactly what Elizabethan theatres looked like. Almost the only solid contemporary evidence, besides cityscapes showing exteriors at some distance, was a rough sketch by a Dutchman of the Swan in about 1596. In recent years, great advances have been made, largely through the excavation of the Rose whose remains were discovered during building works, and London now has a new Globe Theatre (opened 1997) which, while not a copy of 'Shakespeare's' Globe, is probably very close to what a typical Elizabethan theatre looked like. Like its successor, the Globe of 1599 was more or less round in plan (actually octagonal), built of wood and largely open to the sky, but with three-tier galleries, containing the expensive seats, and acting area, thrust stage with balcony above, under a thatched roof. Although this seems to have been the general plan, of course no two theatres were the same. The Rose, for instance, was probably much smaller than the Globe. Theatre historians have often expressed wonder at the originality of what Shakespeare called the 'wooden O'. Certainly, inn courtyards were rectangular, not round, but there were other precedents including, of course, the Classical, although that probably did not figure with the Burbages. A possible consideration is that a circular plan made it easier to convert a theatre into an animal-baiting arena, as happened with the Hope.

Drawing of a temporary stage set up in an inn yard. In contrast to developments in Spain, the earliest purpose-built theatres in England adopted a different plan from their immediate, makeshift forerunners.

actors and theatres
in England

The rise of the professional theatre in the 16th century produced especially remarkable effects in England. The tradition of medieval drama was strong there, a relatively stable government under the Tudors created congenial conditions, and the rise of mercantile London provided an audience, but there is no conclusive reason to explain the vigour and quality of the English drama. Historians tend to resort to comparisons with the 'miraculous' rise of Classical drama in Greece.

Actors and patrons

King Henry VII (reigned 1485–1509) employed a permanent group of actors, four men and a boy who, since 'pure' drama was as yet unknown, were closely related to the other entertainers – musicians, jesters, acrobats – forming part of the flamboyant pageantry that surrounded royal courts. And not only royal courts: the same was true of lesser lords and major officials who were important enough to maintain a grand household (though too much display was dangerous with a monarchy seeking greater power and security). They might retain their own permanent company of actors, or hire one of the travelling companies, otherwise seen at markets and fairs. These companies, like those of the commedia dell'arte, often travelled widely (a company of English actors appeared at Elsinore in Denmark 20 years before Shakespeare employed such an episode in Hamlet), but London was increasingly, though not exclusively, the centre to which actors gravitated.

A powerful patron, like the Earl of Leicester, Queen Elizabeth's favourite, was desirable for reasons of security. The reformed Church was hardly more tolerant of the profession (in spite of some late morality plays mocking the Pope and Catholic doctrine) than the Church of Rome, but the main threat came from civic authorities. The government was naturally frightened of large and potentially unruly crowds, and there were instances of performances provoking riots. The actors in a topical satire, *A Sack Full of News*, at the Boar's Head in Aldgate in 1557 were arrested and their company subjected to censorship of future productions. An act of 1572 classed travelling actors with rogues and vagabonds and prescribed severe penalties, culminating in death for a third offence.

theatres of a long and narrow auditorium, though this was also a characteristic of the Hôtel de Bourgogne.

Spain

Among the buildings that acting companies found most useful in Spain from the mid-16th century were the courtyards of the charity hospitals run by religious orders, who were quick to perceive a lucrative source of income. When the first theatres were built they followed a similar plan. Such was the popularity of the drama that by 1600 almost every Spanish town of any size, plus a few in the Americas, had one. In Madrid there were two. Today, one or two of these early theatres, such as that at Almagro, have been restored and returned to their original use. They generally took the form of a rectangle, slightly longer than wide, surrounded by buildings but otherwise open to the sky except for an awning against the fierce Spanish sun. The platform stage occupied one of the narrower ends, with galleries and an attic containing stage machinery above. The audience sat in benches along the sides or in 'boxes' in the two galleried floors above, with special quarters for clerical dignitaries and apparently for women, rather surprisingly in view of the presence of women on the stage. There are obvious similarities, though also marked differences, with the contemporary English theatres, including the unruly behaviour of the groundlings, who as in England paid lower admission and stood in the 'pit'. In Spain they were called 'musketeers', from their habit of launching missiles at the performers.

The Teatro Olimpico, Vicenza, designed by the great proponent of Classicism, Andrea Palladio, and completed by his pupil, Vincenzo Scamozzi, in 1585.

er5

Although the 16th century witnessed an unprecedented flowering of 'public' theatre, the court continued to be a vital patron of the drama, and in the 17th century increasingly so. Although some of Shakespeare's plays, for example, were performed before the Queen, the court was also the origin of dramatic performances of different types from the tragedies and comedies of the public stage.

courtly
entertainments

Intermezzi

Mention has already been made of the Italian intermezzi and similar forms in other countries, such as the 'interlude' in England and the entremet in France. They appear to have originated in the 15th century as short entertainments to keep the guests amused between the courses of a banquet, which could take a long time to serve, and later to provide light relief between the acts of a drama. The subject was usually Classical, the setting pastoral, and the tone might be moral or purely comic. According to Isabella d'Este, the intermezzi at the court of Ferrara were sometimes more enjoyable than the play. Costumes and scenery were spectacular, and the ingredients included dance and music, which was increasingly popular in court festivals and led to the development of opera. Intermezzi offered a welcome challenge to writers to provide material that would support lavish visual effects, with goddesses arriving on clouds, cities going up in flames, and other extraordinary spectacles calculated to inspire awe and admiration for the regime that could display – and pay for – such wonders. The designs of many of the machines invented to produce the spectacles are known from Nicola Sabbattini's *Design and Construction of Stage Machinery* (1638) and other sources. They would have done credit to Leonardo but, unlike most of his mechanical flights of fancy, they worked!

Entremés

The Spanish word entremé is derived from the French entremet, and was first applied to the short dramatic episodes that were part of the Corpus Christi processions in Catalonia and to other festivals in the northern Christian kingdoms of medieval Spain. Later, as elsewhere in Europe, the name passed to entertainments punctuating a feast and the light-hearted episodes, in which dance figured prominently, between the acts of a drama, for which the floats or 'pageants' of the religious festivals were often appropriated. The Spanish form, however, had a longer and more productive life, and was occasionally even revived in the 20th century.

Court theatre in general, where cost was not a major consideration, contributed most to the development of scenery and stage machinery. But the royal court in Spain also called upon the same writers and performers as contemporary religious drama, subsidized by the Church, and secular drama, financed by its audience. However, neither Charles V nor the equally serious-minded Philip II – still less Philip's psychopathic heir Don Carlos, whose idea of entertainment might have shocked the Roman emperors – had any interest in the theatre, so the court style languished until the accession of Philip IV in 1598. Under Italian influence, new buildings and gardens were created for court entertainments. These were sometimes the work of courtiers, and sometimes the plays of the professional companies, including works by the dramatists of Spain's Golden Age such as Lope de Vega, who also wrote specifically for the court. After 1621, spectacular production reached its peak under Philip IV. His palace of Buen Retiro included a theatre designed for every conceivable scenic effect by the Italian designer, Cosimo Lotti. He was a specialist in spectacular scene changes, hidden lighting, etc, and one of his productions, staged on an island in the lake before the permanent theatre was completed, included an earthquake, real ships, a joust, cloud machines – and live fish.

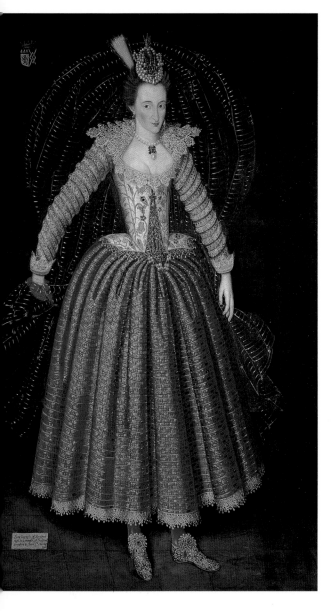

The masque

The distinctive English form of court drama was the masque (originally 'mask'), which derived from ancient folk traditions, including the 'disguising' play, a celebration of gift-giving by guests wearing masks. Under the early Stuart kings (1601–49), it gained distinction through the productions of a partnership of geniuses, the court poet, Ben Jonson, and the brilliant, Italian-influenced designer, Inigo Jones, often called England's first architect (the Banqueting House in Whitehall is his).

The rustic form of the masque is mocked by Shakespeare in *Love's Labour's Lost*. At court, it included, besides music and dancing, lavish costumes and stunning scenery. Courtiers, even royalty, sometimes took part. The theme was usually pastoral – monarchs always enjoy pretending to be country folk – and the language was highly poetic and allegorical. The proscenium arch made its first appearance in England for masques that were staged in a ballroom. Following a suggestion of James I's Queen Anne, Jonson also originated the 'anti-masque', or 'ante-masque', so called because it often preceded the main entertainment of the evening and provided a deliberate contrast. Jonson and Jones frequently disagreed, and Jonson withdrew in 1634, when the literary content of the form was already in retreat. In 1642, the Civil War finished off the masque, along with English theatre in general. The theatre would be revived, but not the masque.

the Jacobean
age

It is terminologically inconvenient that the renaissance of English drama spanned the Elizabethan and Jacobean ages: one frustrated critic even proposed the term 'Jacobethan'. We may think of Shakespeare as an Elizabethan dramatist, but many of his plays were written after the accession of James I (1603). Other playwrights who are often vaguely classed as Elizabethan, such as Fletcher (1579–1625), Ford (1586–1639) or Middleton (1580–1627), belong entirely to the 17th century. However, there are marked differences between Elizabethan and Jacobean drama in both the character of the theatre itself and the nature of the drama, especially tragedy.

Jacobean theatre

There were already signs that the brief, splendid period of a truly popular theatre was drawing to an end. Open-air theatres were generally abandoned (though one was built as late as 1613). Burbage's Company moved from the Globe to Blackfriars, where the theatre was covered. No doubt the vagaries of the English weather made such a move inevitable, but at Blackfriars, tickets were more expensive, out of reach of many of the audience at the Globe. Significantly, covered theatres were known as 'private' theatres. The broadly middle class people of London were becoming alienated, partly because of the growing influence of Puritanism.

Puritans and the court

Puritan hostility is sometimes exaggerated. Most Puritans – an extremely disparate group – were not totally opposed to theatre in general, but there was much about it to which they did object, not least (naturally) satires against themselves. The targets of the Puritan pamphleteer William Prynne, who produced his *Histriomastix: the Players Scourge* in 1632, were Roman Catholic influence at court and the court masques rather than the commercial theatres. The fear of Roman Catholicism was widespread and genuine, hence the popular celebrations when the proposed marriage of the royal heir to a Spanish princess failed. This project prompted Middleton's *A Game at Chess* (1624), a political satire which savagely mocked the Spanish ambassador, Count Gondomar, the moving force behind the marriage project, and some royal favourites. It ran for nine days, a very long run in those days, probably because the King was out of London, before the Privy Council stopped it, imposing a ten-day ban on the Company and issuing a warrant for Middleton's arrest. The play is of no great dramatic interest today: the prolific Middleton is chiefly remembered for one or two comedies, especially (thanks partly to a successful recent revival) *A Mad World, My Masters* (1607).

Jacobean tragedy

The court masque presented a picture of blissful social harmony under a beloved and divinely appointed monarch. Jacobean dramatists saw things differently. Their main aim, demanded by audience taste (or so they insisted against critics), was horror. Jacobean tragedy abounds with frightful atrocities, morbid desires and cruel cynicism. Though they often work very well on the stage, a description of the plot of a typical Jacobean tragedy makes it sound like absurd melodrama. John Ford's most famous play, *'Tis Pity She's a Whore* (1633), like many of these plays, is set in Italy, regarded by the English as a nest of Catholic plots and poisonings and 'Macchiavellian' (i.e. wickedly cynical) schemers. In one scene, a brother enters bearing the heart of his sister (whom, having first seduced, he has just murdered), impaled on a dagger. In Webster's *The Duchess of Malfi* the heroine marries her steward for love and thus offends her aristocratic brothers who, with the aid of their villainous agent Bosola, subject her to grotesque physical and psychological torments before strangling her and her young children.

Webster

It is sometimes suggested that the horrors of Jacobean tragedy represent some sort of anticipation of the coming Civil War. Others see them as a symptom of contemporary decadence, the deliberate rejection and perversion of Renaissance ideals of love, beauty and honour. However, they are far from negligible as drama, and in John Webster (c.1580–1634) they produced an acknowledged genius.

Webster is the most Shakespearian of the Jacobeans, but his personal life is a mystery. An actor named John Webster appeared in an English company in Germany in 1596, but we cannot be certain that actor and playwright are the same man. He wrote a number of plays in collaboration with Dekker and others, and he may have had a hand in *The Revenger's Tragedy* (1606), sometimes thought to be Middleton's, but traditionally credited to Cyril Tourneur (1575-1626), another playwright of whom little is known. Webster's reputation rests on just two plays, *The White Devil* (1612) and *The Duchess of Malfi* (1614). Both are set in aristocratic Renaissance Italy and packed with fashionable horrors. The difference is that they are written in superb poetry, comparable with Shakespeare's and unequalled by any later writer. Webster's plays also contain some marvellous parts for actors, which has helped to keep them popular.

Above: Helen Mirren in a famous performance as the Duchess of Malfi in Webster's tour-de-force of Jacobean horror, at the Royal Exchange Theatre, Manchester, 1980.

Opposite: The prolific Thomas Middleton, like other playwrights, often worked in co-operation with contemporaries. His own plays confirm striking poetic gifts, a fine sense of drama and an unusually perceptive view of female emotions.

A performance of Lope de Vega's *La Dama Boba* in the famous, restored Corral de comedias of Almagro, one of the earliest public theatres whose design was based on the *corrales* or courtyards of large houses.

the golden age of
Spain

The professional theatre in Spain in the 16th century existed on a national scale unparalleled in other countries, but the actual plays produced by the corrales (professional companies that first performed in a corral, or courtyard) were at first unimpressive. That changed with the appearance of some outstanding playwrights just before the gleam of the Golden Age began to fade.

Professional drama

Even then, there were no towering classics. Lope de Vega, Spain's greatest playwright and an undisputed theatrical genius, tends to be remembered more for sheer quantity than for any particular masterpieces. His rate of production was not untypical, as drama proliferated at a rate that must be unique. A list of dramatists in Castile, compiled in 1632, lists 77 names, and the total number of plays written in 17th-century Spain has been estimated at about 10,000. Most of the playwrights left little impression, and it is unfortunate that the international pre-eminence of Lope de Vega has obscured a number of highly talented contemporaries, such as Guillén de Castro, whose play about the Spanish hero El Cid was the basis for Corneille's more famous work; Tirso de Molina, notable for his creation of female characters of wit and intelligence; and the polished, Mexican-born Juan Ruiz de Alarcón.

As in England, the average run of a new play was extremely short. A play that ran for three weeks in 1631 was acclaimed as a record. Audiences demanded a constant stream of new works, and the professional playwrights supplied them. In 1625, Calderón completed a play about the siege of Breda within five months of news of the event reaching Spain. In the same year Lope's play about the recapture of Brazil from the Dutch was produced at court on 6 November, although news of the victory was only heard in Madrid the previous July.

Lope de Vega

Over 400 plays by Lope de Vega Carpio (1562–1635) have survived. Lope himself reckoned he had written about 1,500, and even if his estimate were halved, he would still have written at an average rate of more than one full-length play per month for about half a century! The majority of his plays are classed as comedies: he is regarded as the major influence on the Spanish comedia, i.e. a non-religious play. But his work does not fit easily into traditional categories, and some of his most famous plays are histories or 'romances'. He wrote in beautiful and economical lyrical verse, and believed that plays should consist of three acts and obey the Classical unity of action, although he interpreted that rather broadly. The society he portrays is idealized: things are simpler than they are in real life, which he justified by remarking, more or less, that the playwright should give the public what it wants, since the audience is paying. Important themes are honour and virtue, and though, in common with his contemporaries, Lope is not particularly interested in profound characterization, these themes are treated with subtlety. He was above all a great, seemingly instinctive craftsman, in total command of his medium.

Calderón

Lope and Calderón de la Barca (1600–81), nearly forty years his junior, together span the whole age of the Spanish popular drama. Calderón was less prodigious, known as the author of a mere 200 or so plays. His plays are even better organized than Lope's – every detail of a Calderón play is significant and the subplot is always productively linked with the main plot. Calderón was possibly an even stronger influence outside Spain, notably on English Restoration dramatists. Like other Golden Age playwrights, he wrote with equal facility for the three main strands of the drama, religious, secular and courtly. Equally typically, his outlook was basically conservative. He became a priest in 1651 (Lope had also taken holy orders in his fifties) and thereafter abjured the comedia, writing mainly *autos*: religious plays, as well as scripts for the spectacular productions at Buen Retiro. Calderón also wrote the first *zarzuela*, named after another royal residence. It was a type of musical play and was the main innovation in Spanish drama in the later 17th century, revived in the 18th century as light opera, but with contemporary rather than mythological subject matter.

Decline

Wars, rebellion and the deteriorating economy caused a hiatus in Spanish drama in the 1640s. The royal spectaculars went into temporary retreat and for several years all commercial production, which, as elsewhere in Europe, always faced hostile criticism, ceased altogether. The professional theatre never fully recovered, and the growing preponderance of court theatre, in which spectacular effects took precedence over text, contributed to a decline in dramatic creativity. The death of Calderón conveniently marked the end of the Golden Age. Spanish drama ceased to make any impact on the wider development of theatre until the revival of the 1890s.

Below: Title page of an early edition of Calderón's *autos sacramentales*, religious plays associated with the feast of Corpus Christi. They were presented on three waggons, the central one having a flat playing space, the others tower-like structures containing complex machinery.

Above: Lope de Vega, whose perhaps unequalled rate of production and frank admission of writing to popular taste do not deny him his place as the supreme exponent of the *comedia* in the Golden Age of Spanish drama.

Molière, actor, playwright, producer, is possibly the greatest writer of comedies in the history of the theatre, equally at home with verse and prose, and author of at least a dozen plays that are still frequently performed worldwide. Although he is not always easy to understand in English (some translators, such as Miles Malleson in the 1920s, opted for a very free translation), much of his penetrating social satire is as relevant today as when it was first written. His influence, as playwright, critic and all-round man of the theatre, was immense, not only in France but also throughout Europe, most notably on English Restoration comedy.

Below left: Molière, the supreme comic playwright, who had the insight and ability to combine the comical with the intellectual and showed that comedy could deal with profoundly serious issues.

Royal approval

Son of a Paris furniture maker and qualified as a lawyer, the young Jean Baptiste Poquelin rejected both professions. He joined the Béjart family (he was in love with their daughter Madeleine) to found a troupe of actors, the Illustre Théâtre in 1643. It flopped in Paris and for several years Molière (his adopted stage name) and his company toured the provinces. Returning in 1658, the company performed a Corneille tragedy before the young Louis XIV at the Louvre, and flopped again. Molière then asked if he could perform a farce of his own, *Le Docteur amoreux*. It was a great success and his company was granted a share of the theatre of the Petit Bourbon with the Italian comedy. *Les Précieux ridicules* established their reputation with the public.

From then until his death, Molière dominated the French theatre to such an extent that for a time tragedies were in danger of disappearing from the repertory, though Molière himself produced many. Success made him enemies and his satirical wit was easily misinterpreted. Both *Don Juan* and *Tartuffe* ran into intense hostility from moral bigots and the Church. But the King was on his side. When he married Madeleine's younger sister, Armande, in 1662, it was said by a jealous rival, Montfleury (a hugely fat actor, very successful in tragic roles in spite of what Molière regarded as gross overacting), that the girl, who was twenty years younger than Molière, was actually his daughter. Louis indicated his support by acting as godfather to their first child, and Molière's reply to Montfleury, as to other opponents, was to portray him as an idiot in his next play.

Chief plays *dates of first performance*
* = Court plays

1658 *Le Docteur amoreux*
1658 *Les Précieux ridicules*
1660 *Sganarelle*
1661 *Les Fâcheux**
1661 *L'École des maris*
1662 *L'École des femmes*
1663 *L'Impromptu de Versailles**
1664 *Le Mariage forcée**
1665 *L'Amour médecin*
1665 *Don Juan*
1666 *Le Misanthrope*

1666 *Le Médecin malgré lui*
1667 *Tartuffe* (written 1664)
1667 *Le Sicilien, ou l'amour peintre**
1668 *Amphitryon*
1668 *L'Avare*
1668 *Georges Dandin, ou le mari confondu**
1670 *Les Amants magnifiques**
1671 *Le Bourgeois Gentilhomme**
1671 *Les Fourberies de Scapin*
1672 *Les Femmes savantes*
1673 *Le Malade imaginaire*

Left: A scene from *Tartuffe*.

Molière's comedy

Problems with one or two plays did not diminish Molière's popularity. Plays such as *Le Misanthrope*, *Le Médecin malgré lui* ('The Reluctant Doctor' – even Molière's titles are hard to translate), Les Fourberies de Scapin ('The Trickery of Scabin'), *Les Femmes savantes* ('The Wise Women'), *L'Avare* ('The Miser') and *Le Malade imaginaire* ('The Imaginary Invalid') were immensely popular when first produced and have remained so. Molière's strongest influence, freely acknowledged, was the Italian comedy, but Molière refined its themes and techniques, set it in a French context, and raised the art of comedy to heights it had never attained before, or perhaps since, so that it stood on the same exalted level as the neo-classical tragedy of Corneille and Racine. He adopted the rhymed hexameter from tragedy, but adapted it to naturalistic dialogue. Like Shakespeare, he created many characters that have passed into popular myth as representations of a human type: Tartuffe, the hypocrite; Jourdain, the aspirant snob; Don Juan, the romantic rebel; Scapin, the trickster, and many more.

The House of Molière

From 1661 Molière's company was established at the Palais-Royal, originally Cardinal Richelieu's private theatre, but he also wrote many entertainments for the court. Comedy-ballets is one description of these spectaculars, with music by Lully, in which the King and courtiers often took part. They were also played, without the elaborate staging, at the Palais-Royal, and one of them, *Le Bourgeois Gentilhomme*, became one of Molière's most popular plays.

From the late 1660s Molière suffered from a lung disease, but he did not reduce his immense workload and overwork no doubt contributed to his collapse during a performance of his last play, *Le Malade imaginaire*. He died, aged 51, the same evening. As a result of ecclesiastical hostility (the Church had never forgiven him for *Tartuffe*, although it is not by intent an anti-clerical play), he was buried in a pauper's grave. In his honour the Comédie-Française, founded after his death, became known as La Maison de Molière, 'the House of Molière'.

Quotes

Géronte: It seems to me you are putting them in the wrong place. The heart is on the left and the liver is on the right.
Sganarelle: Yes, in the old days that was the case, but we have changed all that, and we now practise medicine on a completely new system.
Sganarelle, Scene iv

M. Jourdain: What? When I say, 'Nicole, bring me my slippers and give me my nightcap,' is that prose?
Philosophy professor: Yes, sir.
M. Jourdain: Good heavens! For more than forty years, I have been speaking prose without knowing it!
Le Bourgeois Gentilhomme, Act II, Scene iv

It is public scandal that causes offence,
A sin in private is not a sin at all.
Tartuffe, Act III, Scene iii

French

The great age of drama in 17th-century France arose partly from the love of Classical order, visible in contemporary architecture and formal gardens, and the protective defence of the nobility of the French language, which caused the Paris parlement in 1542 to attack a production by the Confrérie de la Passion for 'uncouth speech . . . lacking in vocabulary and faulty in pronunciation'. In the early 17th century, the company at the Hôtel de Bourgogne was called the Comédiens du Roi (the King's Men), but they also went on tour and at times their premises were used by a rival, junior company, the Comédiens du Prince d'Orange, who later acquired their own theatre in a former tennis court in the Marais district. The long, narrow auditorium and relatively small acting area helped to end the old tradition, a hangover from the open-air mystery plays, of a series of 'compartments' on stage, each representing a different location or scene, which in turn took over the stage as required, an inconvenient convention. The abandonment of this tradition was chiefly due to the writer whose work was also responsible for the company's popularity, Pierre Corneille, a young lawyer from Rouen.

Corneille

The first plays of Pierre Corneille (1606–84) were mostly comedies, set in contemporary Paris, and appealed to the fashionable world. His first tragedy, *Médée* ('Medea'), came in 1633 and was well received. Corneille was a devoted family man and a long-serving member of the Rouen parlement. He spent a year or two at home, from where he read Castro's play about the legendary Spanish hero, *El Cid*. His own version, *Le Cid*, opened in January 1637, the date that marks the beginning of the great age of French drama. It made a terrific impact; some would say it is Corneille's greatest play. It investigates the conflict between love (personal feelings) and duty (responsibility to society), a variant of Corneille's dominant theme – the need to make fundamental choices and the moral demands that this makes upon the hero – and the central role, like Hamlet in England, is still the great test for French actors, as Racine's Phèdre is for actresses. An English translation appeared in London before the end of the year. The play's popularity exacerbated the rivalry within the Comédiens du Roi, which sometimes took quite vicious forms. This gave rise to a long literary war between Corneille's supporters and opponents, though the public, and the all-powerful Cardinal Richelieu, took the side of Corneille.

Triumph and decline

A succession of fine plays followed, of which *Horace* (1640), *Cinna* (1641), *Polyceute* (1642), all at the Théâtre du Marais, are perhaps his greatest plays, along with *Le Cid*. His best comedy, *Le Menteur* (1643), a great favourite with the public, was also based on a Spanish play (by Alarcón), although the reputation of his remaining plays (he wrote 24 altogether) has varied. Some were

once thought to be dull, if not total failures, but more recent criticism has inclined to take his work as a coherent whole. *Nicomède* (1651), in which Molière chose to make his Paris comeback, is classed as a tragedy, but really belongs to another genre, the 'heroic comedy'. Molière also collaborated with Corneille on *Pulcherie*. In his later years Corneille preferred to reject criticism and resented his loss of popularity to his younger rival, Racine.

Racine

Jean Racine (1639–99) was a more 'popular' playwright than Corneille and has maintained a slight, though not unchallenged, ascendancy to this day. As a young poet of promise in the 1660s, he met Molière, who produced his first play, *La Thébaïde* (1664), and his second, *Alexandre le Grand* (1665). Racine then allowed himself and his mistress, Molière's best actress, to be 'poached' by the Hôtel de Bourgogne; Molière never spoke to him again. Racine later tried indirectly to downgrade Molière to a mere comedian.

Triumph and retreat

Racine was more in tune with the times than the ageing Corneille. His work is distinguished by greater passion and psychological realism, quite different in tone from the heroic drama of Corneille. Favoured by king and court, and revelling in his fame, Racine produced seven more plays, notably: *Andromaque* (1667); *Les Plaideurs* ('The Litigants', 1668), an immensely successful comedy, which is often revived; *Bérénice* (1670), which coincided with a less popular play by Corneille on exactly the same subject (possibly a deliberate ploy by Racine, who could be devious and lacked Corneille's moral stature); *Iphigénie* (1674); and finally his great masterpiece, perhaps the greatest play in the French repertory, *Phèdre* (1677).

After the *Phèdre*, either because his strict upbringing by the Jansenists (who regarded the theatre as devil's work) finally prevailed, or because he accepted a royal appointment incompatible with work in the theatre, or simply because he knew that in *Phèdre* he had reached an unsurpassable peak, he abandoned the theatre for ever.

Above: An 18th-century painting of Monsieur Bellemore as Pierre Corneille's character Matamore.

Left: A design from the frontispiece of one of Corneille's classical tragedies. For nearly 40 years, with one interval, Corneille kept the French court and the Parisian bourgeoisie entertained with his distinguished dramas, and in doing so virtually created a new art form.

Phèdre marked the end of the tradition of great French Classical drama, but it was quickly followed by the beginning of another great tradition: the foundation of the Comédie-Française. France's premier national theatre is still going strong over 300 years later.

Below: An early photograph (hand-tinted) of a 19th-century production of *Othello* by the Comédie-Française.

Théâtre-Français

After the death of Molière, three rival French companies existed in Paris: the Hôtel de Bourgogne, the Théâtre du Marais, which had produced the early works of Corneille, and Molière's company in Cardinal Richelieu's old theatre of the Palais Royal. The latter, now led by the actor and former close friend of Molière, La Grange, faced difficult times. It lost performers and writers to the Hôtel de Bourgogne and finally its own theatre, when it was displaced by Lully and the opera. The answer was an amalgamation with the Théâtre du Marais. Together they took over the theatre in the Rue Guénégaud. In 1680, the resident company of the Hôtel de Bourgogne confronted a similar problem when King Louis XIV made over their theatre exclusively to the Italian comedy, which had played there often in the past on an irregular basis. The Hôtel de Bourgogne company thereupon joined forces with the other two. The three French companies had become one.

The national theatre

It was first called the Théâtre-Français, or the Maison de Molière, but became known as the Comédie-Française (the Italian comedy became the Comédie-Italienne), and was soon established in a new theatre, another former tennis court, in St Germain-des-Prés. In 1781 it moved to a theatre on the site of the present Théâtre National de l'Odéon, France's junior national company which, for most of its history, has been under the control of the Comédie-Française. It split up and disintegrated in the turmoil of the Revolutionary period, but reformed in 1803.

The new company was in a strong position. It held a monopoly on the production of French plays in Paris, whose dominance of French theatre was now firmly established, and it had the right to sign up promising performers from the provincial companies. As organized by Louis XIV, it took the form of a cooperative, rather like its predecessor, the Confrérie de la Passion, with senior members taking a share of the profits and entitlement to a pension, normally after at least twenty years' service. Admission was by merit, though influence could sometimes be helpful, and a pleasant tradition arose that debutants could choose their own role for their first performance.

The weight of tradition

The Comédie-Française was to have enormous influence on French theatre. Such an institution has obvious virtues and equally obvious drawbacks; not everyone would agree that the former far outweigh the latter. The advantages included stability, the preservation of tradition and the cherishing of a rich national dramatic heritage. Among the concomitant disadvantages were the oppressive influence that a powerful tradition can exert, and a conservative

tendency that preserved some dramatic monuments of little worth and dis-
couraged new talent. On the other hand, the inertia of the Comédie-Française
has often provoked innovative reactions on the theatrical fringe which, in the
end, have had a reinvigorating effect on itself.

Decline of the drama

The period of the reorganization of the theatre coincided with a decline in the
quality of the drama. To some extent this was natural and inevitable: golden
ages are by nature short, and it would be absurd to expect a constant supply
of new dramatists of the stature of Corneille, Racine and Molière.
Nevertheless, the decline during the later years of Louis XIV was sharp. Of
course, new playwrights cropped up constantly, to be hopefully but unjustifi-
ably acclaimed as 'the new Racine' or 'the new Molière'. One example was the
remarkable prodigy La Grange-Chancel, who wrote his first play at thirteen
and had four tragedies in the repertory in his mid-twenties, but offended the
authorities and disappeared into exile.

Among reasons for the general deterioration of the Comédie-Française historians cite its conservatism and the dead, increasingly heavy hand of censorship. In 1697 the Comédie-Italienne, which by now performed many works
entirely in French, was expelled because the King considered they had
insulted his ultra-respectable mistress, Mme de Maintenon. They returned in
1716 after his death. Increasingly French, the traditions of the commedia
dell'arte abandoned, the Comédie-Italienne attracted new works from French
writers – and aroused strong opposition from the Comédie-Française.

The death of the Sun King, with all his faults a great patron of the theatre,
was also the end of an era. For over fifty years Louis XIV had been 'the greatest actor on the noblest stage with the most enthusiastic audience'. For sheer
theatricality, court life at Versailles, where the ordinary public queued and
paid admission to watch the King eat his dinner, matched anything to be
found at the Hôtel de Bourgogne.

Above: The Comédie-Française
in 1808. This theatre originally
opened in 1790. After
alterations, including
enlargement of the stage after
the disintegration of the
Revolution, it became the
Théâtre-Français (opened
1799). It was burned down
in 1900.

the English
restoration

In 1660 the English monarchy was restored in the person of Charles II, whose father had been executed as a traitor eleven years earlier. It was the beginning of a new age – pleasure-loving, cynical, the antithesis of the sober Puritanism of the Interregnum. (The term 'Restoration' covers an indefinite period, extending beyond Charles II's reign.) The public theatres, closed since the Civil War, were soon reopened. This was not quite such an innovation as it seems, since the Protectorate of Cromwell was not particularly hostile to the drama, and some public performances had taken place, usually disguised with greater or lesser transparency as something else, without interference from the government. Nor was the appearance of women on the public stage for the first time quite so revolutionary as it seems. Women had, after all, taken part in masques, and not only at court, while the King and his close associates had become familiar with professional actresses during their enforced exile in France.

Restoration theatres

The times were more relaxed, but all the same the government was aware of the subversive potential of the theatre and kept it under supervision. Only two theatres were licensed in London, and they were answerable to the government. The old theatre buildings, if they had survived, were deemed unsuitable, not least because they could not accommodate the royal court. Sir William Davenant, who had succeeded Ben Jonson as poet laureate and had staged what he called 'music and instruction' (*The Siege of Rhodes*, sometimes called the first English opera) during the Interregnum, held one licence. His company moved into the Duke's House, a former tennis court, in Lincoln's Inn. The other licensee, Thomas Killigrew, operated from 1663 in the purpose-built Theatre Royal. At first in Bridges Street, it later moved to Drury Lane, while the eventual descendant of Davenant's theatre was Covent Garden (1732). The new theatres, following the French and Italian models, had a proscenium arch (and probably scenery), new to the English theatre but, again, familiar from court masques. Although they accommodated the rising middle class of London, the audience spanned a much narrower band of society. Shakespeare's groundlings, had they wished, could not have afforded the price of admission, though servants of the fashionable audience were accommodated in the upper gallery. The boxes included a royal box, which was frequently occupied.

Actresses

The royal licence specified that women's parts should be played by women, and it is impossible to imagine the female roles in Restoration comedy being played by boys. The first actress to appear on the public stage is said to have been Margaret Hughes in 1660. The role was Desdemona: although Shakespeare was out of fashion, too 'heroic' and too 'poetic' for Restoration gallants, women often found their best roles in Shakespeare. Not, however, the most famous Restoration actress, Nell Gwyn, who started as an orange-seller (and prostitute) and ended as the King's mistress. She was something of a Marilyn Monroe figure, hugely popular, excellent in comedy, but otherwise probably no great actress.

It was generally assumed that all actresses were courtesans, but there were exceptions, including two of the greatest of the era, Elizabeth Barry, Otway's muse, and Anne Bracegirdle, loved by Congreve, many of whose heroines she first played. As popular and as beautiful as Nell, she skilfully exploited her reputation for virtue and, like Peg Woffington later, was not averse to playing men's parts which showed off her legs. Audiences became rather too obsessed by actresses as sex objects, and it has been suggested that this was a factor in the ascendancy of actor over writer that led to the decline of drama after Congreve.

Left: Nell Gwyn, one of Sir Peter Lely's revealing portraits, which did nothing to raise the moral repute of 17th-century actresses.

Above: A scene from *Le Bourgeois Gentilhomme*. The influence of Molière on English Restoration comedy was enormous, and his plays were freely plundered.

It turned out that not only could women act, they could also write. The best-known of women playwrights is the formidable Aphra Behn (1640–89), who was also a government spy on the Continent. Her most successful play, *The Rover* (1677), is a fairly representative comedy of marital intrigue.

'Prodigious artistry'

Actresses, having featured in the commedia dell'arte from the beginning, were no novelty on the Continent. Among the most notable in Spain was Maria Riquelme, who played in Lope de Vega and was reputed to have the remarkable ability to change her complexion to suit the moment, visibly turning pale when supposed to be frightened. Another, unnamed, Spanish actress in a moment of passion, tore her silk handkerchief to shreds. The gesture had such an impact that she repeated it in subsequent performances although, we are told, the handkerchiefs cost twice as much as she earned.

Among the finest French actresses of the 17th century were Mlle de Brie (d.1706), who played many of Molière's female roles and was a founding member of the Comédie-Française; Mlle du Parc (1633–38), Racine's mistress and the first Andromache; and Mme Beauval (d.1709), whose habit of getting the giggles was exploited by Molière in the part of Nicole in *Le Bourgeois Gentilhomme*.

the comedy of
manners

When the theatres reopened in 1660 there was unsurprisingly an initial shortage of contemporary plays. But that quickly changed. This was a talented age: Milton, Locke, Newton and Purcell were all active. Many of the new playwrights emerged from the courtiers and gentlemen down to the prospering merchants and squires who formed the theatre's audience – the people for whom and about whom many of the plays were written. They prided themselves on their wit, sophistication and progressive views. These, especially wit, were certainly present, but other prominent characteristics were extreme cynicism and an eye for the main chance.

Tragedy

Not all Restoration drama is witty, urbane comedy concerned with illicit sex and the acquisition of a fortune. John Dryden (1631–1700), poet laureate from 1668 and perhaps the greatest writer of the age, though not primarily a dramatist, wrote thirty plays, generally heroic dramas in rhyming couplets. His best play, *All For Love*, is a tragedy in blank verse concerning Antony and Cleopatra. Dryden genuinely thought his play was an improvement on Shakespeare's version, and it was probably more often performed throughout the 18th century.

The finest tragedian was Thomas Otway (1652–85), who died at 33, after writing his two best plays, *The Orphan* (1680) and *Venice Preserv'd* (1682). The chief roles were first performed by Elizabeth Barry, adored by Otway, briefly an actor himself, and Thomas Betterton (c.1635–1710), the greatest actor of the age.

The comedy of manners

The new comedy owed a great deal to Molière, by 1660 widely translated. The plot, usually associated with one or more often confusing subplots, was broadly concerned with sex and money, the schemes engineered by gentlemen in their efforts to acquire a rich wife or conduct an adulterous liaison. Characters had names like Sir Fopling Flutter, Pinchwife and Loveless. The victor was usually the greatest wit, and the repartee was slick, steely, amoral. The dialogue was often licentious and would have been regarded as obscene in most later ages, though the imagery, to a 20th-century audience, is frequently obscure.

Initially, the outstanding dramatists (the word was now coming into use) in the first phase were George Etherege (1634–91), William Wycherley (1640–1715), followed by John Vanbrugh (1664–1726), and George Farquhar (1678–1707). Etherege's first play was a tragi-comedy in verse, but his reputation rests on two sparkling comedies, *She Would if She Could* (1668) and, especially, *The Man of Mode* (1676), containing a satirical portrait of the poet Rochester. Wycherley, who was educated in France and thus knew Molière's work in French, is the most interesting, as well as the sharpest. His mockery of contemporary mores is so fierce that his superficial amorality probably concealed a secret moralist though, paradoxically, complications over marriage and money beset his own private life. Two of his plays are fairly often revived, and his masterpiece, *The Country Wife* (1675) is studied in schools. However, after *The Plain-Dealer* (1676), he wrote no more for the stage. Vanbrugh, a prodigious character, also the architect of Castle Howard and Blenheim

Above: Wycherley's *The Country Wife* which, like Congreve's *The Way of the World*, turned out to be one of the last plays of a writer apparently in his prime.

Palace, was yet another playwright who spied for the government, serving a term in a French prison as a result. His best-known plays are his first, *The Relapse* (1696), hugely successful on first performance, and *The Provok'd Wife* (1697), in which the debauched husband is named Sir John Brute. Vanbrugh's social satire is more genial than Wycherley's. Farquhar who, more unusually, was Irish and a former actor, is also easygoing, though his satire sometimes packs a considerable punch. His last two plays, still often revived, were *The Recruiting Officer* (1706), adopted by Brecht in the 1950s, and *The Beaux' Stratagem* (1707).

Congreve

The greatest writer of the Restoration was William Congreve (1670–1729), who became famous at 23 with his first comedy, *The Old Bachelor* (1693), with Betterton and Bracegirdle. As witty as any of his contemporaries, Congreve was more subtle in his dramatization of the effects of social pressures on matters of the heart. His early reputation was confirmed by *The Double Dealer* (1693), *Love for Love* (1695) and above all *The Way of the World* (1700). All three are regularly produced today.

One reason why Congreve gave up writing plays after 1700 was that Restoration comedy was coming under increasing attack from moralists. A sign of the times was that in *Love's Last Shift* (1696) by Colley Cibber (1671–1757), the rakish hero is reformed at the end. When Jeremy Collier (1650–1726) published his *Short View of the Immorality and Profaneness of the English Stage* in 1698, Congreve was stung. He published a refutation of Collier, and *The Way of the World* came down on the side of morality. However, it was not well received and Congreve, well-off and well-liked, thereafter opted for a more tranquil existence.

Opposite: Joan Plowright (left) and Maggie Smith in *The Way of the World*, Congreve's last play. It is the most refined of his comedies, in which the traditional battle of wit against foolishness is transformed into a battle between good and evil.

18th-century theatre

chap

The Theatre Royal, Drury Lane, London as it appears from the stage after being decorated in 1775.

As the earliest forms of theatre included dancing and singing, probably before speech, ballet and opera might claim antecedents as old or older than drama itself. In Renaissance Italy, however, opera evolved as a separate performance art. As it demanded many of the same skills, and as there was inevitably much interaction, as well as rivalry, between them, opera cannot be divorced entirely from drama.

Italian
opera

The Italian renaissance

Opera originated in the elaborate, 'multi-media' shows of the Italian princely courts in the 16th century, spreading quickly to France and reaching England in the form of the masque. It was strongly influenced by the academic desire of the humanists to return to pure Classical values, so far as they were understood. However, the Italian scholars had no more notion than we do of what ancient Greek or Roman music sounded like. The credible form that they developed consisted of a solo vocal line rather like speech (recitative), with simple accompaniment, in contrast to the type of popular song (madrigal) in which the words were more or less lost by many voice parts in harmony.

Sometimes called the first opera, *Dafne* (1594) was based on a pastoral play, had words by the poet Rinuccini and music by the brothers Corsi, members of the group of poets and musicians in Florence known as the Camerata. Only fragments remain, but the same team's *Euridice* (1600) has been preserved entire. Besides the recitative, it includes some songs in regular metre that anticipate the aria. A great step forward was taken by Monteverdi, whose earliest surviving opera is *Orfeo* (1607), a true musical drama, i.e. a work in which the music is integral. It draws on the madrigal and on Venetian church music, combines the monodic melody with songs, and demands a relatively large orchestra.

Theatres and singers

Monteverdi's early works were written for the Duke of Mantua at Cremona, the composer's birthplace. All early opera depended on rich patrons, notably the Barberini family in Rome, and a landmark was established in 1637 when the first public opera house, San Cassiano, opened in Venice. Monteverdi's last operas, of which only two, *Il ritorno d'Ulisse* and, perhaps his best, *L'incoronazione di Poppea* (1642), survive, were written for San Cassiano. The form was developed further by Scarlatti, who wrote over 100 operas between 1679 and 1725, including some early comic operas (opera buffa).

In the late 17th century attempts were made to create national opera elsewhere: Reinhard Keiser in Germany, Henry Purcell (with *Dido and Aeneas*) in

Left: Alessandro Scarlatti (1660–1725), the founder of Neapolitan opera and composer of over 100 operas. He raised the popularity of opera to such a level that it triumphed over the objections of the Church.

Right: The King's Theatre – originally named the Queen's, after Queen Anne, and renamed on the accession of George I in 1714 – in the Haymarket. It was London's first opera house. It was rebuilt after a fire in 1789 and later became Her Majesty's, the name of the present theatre on the site.

England and, most notably, Lully in France, though Italian influence was omnipresent. Indeed, opera is essentially an Italian form and was largely Italian-led, at least until the days of Wagner, a fact signified by the Italian terminology still universally used. Thanks to the innovations of Lully, the first great operatic composer in France (though ironically he was Italian by birth), the Paris Opéra was also to have strong international influence. He co-operated with (and later, some would say, double-crossed) Molière, gained the favour of Louis XIV and was appointed court musician. On Molière's death in 1673, Lully was granted a monopoly of operatic productions in Paris with, tenancy of the Palais-Royal Theatre. Lully, who had a remarkable talent for manipulation and intrigue as well as music, also established a higher social status for his performers. The royal decree that founded the Paris Opéra in 1671 explicitly stated that 'the new establishment is to enjoy quite a different standing from the non-musical theatres' and that 'ladies and gentlemen' should be able to perform without jeopardizing their aristocratic status. The singers who came to dominate the opera were the castrati, de-sexed males who commanded the 'heroic' roles, followed by the leading sopranos – though the recent desire for 'authentic' performance of baroque music has resulted in the revival of the custom by counter-tenors.

Opera seria

The dominant opera form was the formal, increasingly complex opera seria ('serious opera'), which was immensely popular in London, thanks to the presence there of its outstanding practitioner, the German-born Georg Frederick Handel, who had played violin under Keiser at the Hamburg opera. Although Mozart wrote opera seria (notably *Idomeneo*, 1781), the form was already losing popularity before the mid-18th century: Handel gave it up in 1741 and turned to oratorios. Its decline was partly due to rivalry from opera buffa, which had originated in Naples, and from other forms of comic opera such as the Parisian Opéra-Comique, but chiefly because of an intrinsic dramatic drawback. The great da capo arias (in which the first part is repeated), though the greatest glory of the form, inevitably brought the action to a grinding halt.

France and Italy

The 18th century is often dismissed as an uninteresting period for the drama, at least by comparison with the 17th and the 19th. In France, as in England, the capital dominated the theatre. Paris had only one theatre, where revivals of the Classical tragedies of Corneille and Racine and the comedy of character of Molière alternated with imitative contemporary works that tended towards melodrama and the superficial comedy of manners.

The Comédie-Française and its rivals

The finest writer and most promising dramatist of the early 18th century was Alain René Le Sage (1668–1747). His best play was *Turcaret* (1710), a fierce satire on the financial exploitation and corrupt taxation system that gave the last years of Louis XIV's reign a nasty flavour. He then quarrelled with the Comédie-Française and wrote no more serious plays. Though more famous as a novelist, particularly of the immortal *Gil Blas*, he did not give up the theatre entirely. He wrote farces for the semi-permanent booths in the market places, which represented the only rival to the Comédie-Française in Paris. Though unlicensed, and frequently the object of hostile legislation, they ingeniously circumvented the laws and attracted enthusiastic audiences.

Although he wrote 50 plays, the most notable tragedian of the century is also better known for other work. Voltaire (1694–1778) maintained the Classical tradition, in fact terminated it, since the new middle-class audience was more interested in contemporary settings and preferred the new genre known as comédie larmoyante ('tearful comedy'). Voltaire was also influenced by Shakespeare, employing crowd scenes for example, which resulted in the overdue banishment of members of the audience from the stage. His fellow philosopher, Diderot (1713–84), wrote a few plays, mostly domestic dramas of what he himself named the drame bourgeois ('middle-class drama'), but his most interesting contribution was his dialogue on acting, *Observations sur Garrick* (published 1830).

Marivaux

In 1716, the Comédie-Italienne returned to Paris, now almost entirely French and attracting French performers and writers. Among them was Pierre de Marivaux (1688–1763), who preferred its freer spirit to the overweening Comédie-Française. His subject was mainly the affairs of the heart, and he was particularly sympathetic to young women, naming his characters after the actresses who played them. But Marivaux was a one-off. The subtle form of his dialogue, which made his plays untranslatable, gave rise to the term marivaudage. At first it was a term of derision, since Marivaux's psychological sensitivity was not much to 18th-century taste, and his true worth was not appreciated until Madeleine Renaud's revivals in around 1950.

Beaumarchais

From the 'welter of tears, piety, blood, sentimentality and sheer dullness' of French drama in the late 18th century emerged the sparkling genius of Pierre-Augustin Caron de Beaumarchais (1732–99). Though he wrote many plays, he is remembered now for two, *Le Barbier de Séville* (1772) and the harder-hitting *Le Mariage de Figaro* (1784), which shocked Louis XVI by its attack on the aristocracy: he is said to have protested that for such a play to be produced, 'the Bastille would have to be torn down first'. Both plays invoked such opposition that they were not performed until three years after the Comédie-Française accepted them, and it was allegedly the adroit charm and wit of the dramatist – for Beaumarchais was something of a Figaro himself – that won over Louis

Above: Carlo Goldoni, who transformed Italian comedy in the 18th century, which had been dominated by commedia dell'arte.

XVI. Nevertheless they were hugely popular, and aristocrats (though not the King) went to *Figaro*, the first production to be lit by oil lamps. Later playwrights were indebted to Beaumarchais for standing up to the Comédie-Française and insisting that he should be paid proper royalties.

Goldoni

The commedia dell'arte tradition was moribund, and several Italian playwrights, including Carlo Gozzi (1720–1806) and his greater rival, Carlo Goldoni (1709–93), had plans, though quite different ones, for a new comedy. Gozzi kept much of the tradition and allowed for considerable improvisation, but his plays were based on fable and fantasy, sometimes suggesting a foretaste of Pirandello. Goldoni's solution was a realistic comedy of character, more in the manner of the later drame bourgeois in France. In contrast to Gozzi's cultured Tuscan, the dialogue employs Italian dialects. It is fully written, not improvised, although his early plays, including *Il servitore di due padrone* ('The Servant of Two Masters', 1743) did allow for some improvisation. That play and several others are still often revived. The best of them, perhaps, is *La locandiera* ('The Landlady', 1751), which became a fabulous international success, especially when Mirandolina, the seductive landlady, was played by Eleonora Duse 150 years later. Shortly after this, Goldoni left the Teatro Sant'Angelo in Venice, and both his plays and his popularity suffered. He eventually went to Paris (1761) and wrote, in French and Italian, for the Comédie-Italienne. Like many others he was ruined in the Revolution and died poor at the age of 84.

Below: The Théâtre de la foire St Laurent, one of the hard-pressed subsidiary French theatres founded in the 18th century.

Garrick

Although the 18th century produced few great playwrights and witnessed no great technological advances in the theatre, it was by no means a stagnant period. The most fundamental change was in the nature of its audience. Theatre ceased to be stylized court entertainment or knockabout peasant fun and became more concerned with the lives of its new, middle-class audience. It was more politically aware, and more realistic.

New theatres

In the 18th century, the population of London was growing and the theatre audiences were growing even faster. Until 1720, there were still only two licensed theatres, Drury Lane and Lincoln's Inn Fields. In that year The Little Theatre in the Haymarket opened but, being unlicensed, could not stage 'legitimate' plays. About 1728 John Rich, emboldened by the success of *The Beggar's Opera*, commissioned a new, larger theatre in Covent Garden, which opened in 1732. The two-theatre monopoly, however, had already been broken by Thomas Odell's theatre in Goodman's Fields, Whitechapel, far from West End theatres. In spite of opposition from the City authorities, it kept going for many years, showing mainly what would later be called variety shows, although Henry Fielding's first play opened there. Permanent theatres were also being built outside London: in Bristol (1729), forerunner of the famous Theatre Royal/Bristol Old Vic, in York (1734) and in Ipswich (1736), where Garrick first appeared on stage.

The Lord Chamberlain

The Licensing Act was passed in 1737. Like most such legislation, it represented an attempt by government to control the theatre for its own interests. Ostensibly intended to curb 'licentiousness' it was really motivated by fear of political satire. It formally established the powers of the Lord Chamberlain not only over theatres, by licensing, but also over plays, by censorship. Its immediate cause was a lost play, *The Golden Rump*, in which the King, having bowels of gold, requires the Queen's assistance for his enemas. There was a suspicion that the play was a plant, and the government itself the *agent provocateur*, but the act was supported by the licensed theatres, which feared competition. Various ways were found to circumvent it, for instance by allowing free admission to the play while making an equivalent charge for refreshments.

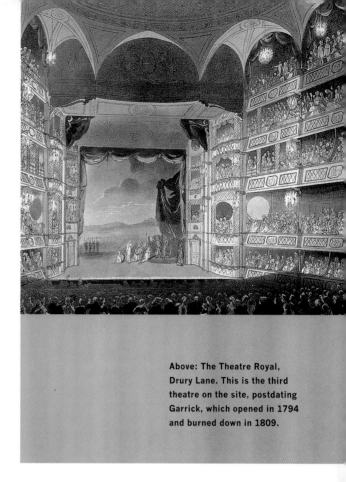

Above: The Theatre Royal,
Drury Lane. This is the third
theatre on the site, postdating
Garrick, which opened in 1794
and burned down in 1809.

Actors

The status of actors had changed enormously. Once social outcasts, they
were now accepted members of society. Actresses still attracted gossip, but
many were perfectly respectable; those who were not were high-class courtesans, rather than common prostitutes. In England, Garrick, who moved freely
in high society, contributed to this enhanced status, but his influence was
more important in the changing style of acting. The rhetorical style of the
past, in which speeches tended to be declaimed rather than spoken, was
abandoned in favour of the intense realism of Garrick's performances, on
which many contemporaries commented in tones of wonder, as if he were a
magician. Garrick was not alone, nor the first innovator in this area. Charles
Macklin astounded audiences by playing Shylock in *The Merchant of Venice* as
a formidable man, rather than a figure of anti-Semitic fun, and later produced
the first 'tartan' Macbeth.

The star

But David Garrick (1717–79) was a star – indeed, the first actor to be so
described – the greatest man of the theatre since Shakespeare. There is a profound mutual debt, and although Shakespeare was obviously the better playwright (Garrick's plays being unpretentious seat-fillers), Garrick was surely the
better actor. He was born in Lichfield and came to London with his friend and
former teacher Samuel Johnson. He went into the wine trade but was more
interested in acting and, after a few small parts, he enjoyed overnight success
as Richard III in 1741. Hired by the Drury Lane Theatre, he became its manager from 1746 until 1776. He was a comparatively small man and his voice,
though clear, was not especially powerful, but all who saw him noted the
expressiveness of his features and the conviction of his performance. He took
his business seriously, demanding intensive rehearsals by his company, and
went to great trouble over details. As Hamlet, thanks to a special wig, his hair
stood on end when the Ghost appeared. Possessing great range, he was successful in tragedy and comedy, though not all tragic roles suited him. His
greatest contribution as a producer was to make the performance a coherent
whole, with innovations in lighting and scenery and authentic costumes, all in
the cause of naturalism.

Garrick lived near London in a splendid villa in Hampton, mixed with
Johnson's cultured circle and was treated as a great celebrity in Paris, where
he influenced Diderot, among others. Besides acting, writing, managing and
producing, he is especially remembered for reviving, indeed rescuing,
Shakespeare. His 'editing' of Shakespeare (e.g. *King Lear* without the Fool) is
understandable in view of the travesties of earlier productions and the need to
please an ignorant audience.

Richard Brinsley Sheridan

The 18th century was not a great age for tragedy, and although Classical tragedy in the French manner maintained a certain popularity, there were no tragedians that measured up even to Otway, though some notable writers essayed the genre, including Samuel Johnson. *Douglas* (1756), by the Scottish minister, John Home, a great success in Edinburgh, is remembered for the enthusiastic outburst of a spectator at Covent Garden, 'Whaur's your Wullie Shakespeare noo?' Comedy was less derelict overall, but in the early 18th century, although audiences flocked to the theatre, they flocked more enthusiastically to the Italian opera at the Haymarket, despite paying up to a guinea for a seat.

Right: Sheridan, dissolute Anglo-Irish genius, whose extraordinary career included two duels fought over a woman he had married out of gallantry and, during the trial of Warren Hastings before the Commons, a speech that lasted for four days.

Below left: Laurence Olivier and Vivien Leigh as Sir Peter and Lady Teazle in what is generally agreed to be Sheridan's greatest comedy, *The School for Scandal*.

The Beggar's Opera

John Gay's *The Beggar's Opera* (1728) introduced a new genre, the ballad opera in which contemporary, satirical lyrics were set to popular tunes. It was turned down by Colley Cibber at Drury Lane, but accepted by John Rich at Lincoln's Inn Fields. It was a triumphant success, and, as the saying went, it made 'Gay rich and Rich gay'. Indeed, Gay told a friend it had made him £600. Partly a take-off of the Italian opera, it was not only the first but also one of the best of its kind, and was adapted by Brecht in the 1920s as *The Threepenny Opera*. A sequel, *Polly*, was kept off the stage by political censorship until long after Gay's death in 1732.

Comedy

Otherwise fashion, as in France, favoured the tearful or 'sentimental' comedy, a rather dismal genre, though it produced morally worthy plays such as *The West Indian* (1771) and *The Jew* (1794), by Richard Cumberland (1732–1811), which challenged popular prejudice by treating their central characters sympathetically. Genuine comedy, as Oliver Goldsmith (1730–74) complained, was neglected, though it was shortly revived by Sheridan, and Goldsmith himself struck a blow at sentimental comedy with the ever-popular *She Stoops to Conquer* (1773).

Plays

1771 *Jubilee* (farce, unperformed)
1775 *The Rivals*
1775 *St Patrick's Day* (farce)
1775 *The Duenna* (comic opera)
1777 *A Trip to Scarborough* (based on
    Vanbrugh's *The Relapse*)
1777 *The School for Scandal*
1779 *The Critic*
1781 *Robinson Crusoe* (pantomime)
1799 *Pizarro* (adaptation)

Sheridan

Like Goldsmith, Sheridan was an Irishman, whose father was a well-known
theatre manager and mother Frances a successful writer (her comedy *The
Discovery* was staged by Garrick in 1763). He was educated at Harrow, which
he loathed, and had a somewhat chequered start in life, fighting two duels
over a girl, whom he married illicitly (but later legally). Rather than pursue a
career in the law, he decided, after his sketch on fashionable Bath had
aroused some admiration, to try writing a play. *The Rivals*, produced at Drury
Lane in 1775, brilliantly restored the comedy of manners, with all its wit and
snap, but none of its coarseness. The character Mrs Malaprop, who constantly
picks the wrong word ('reprehend' when she means 'comprehend', 'deranged'
for 'arranged', etc.), gave the language a new word, 'malapropism'.

    The play made Sheridan something of a second Garrick, whose share in the
Drury Lane theatre he bought in 1776, later becoming sole proprietor. *The
Rivals* is frequently revived, as are the even better *The School for Scandal*, produced with Garrick's co-operation, which made a £15,000 profit, and *The
Critic*, also a huge contemporary success. But Sheridan did not like the theatre, and though it had provided him with much of what he did want, namely
status and money, he used to say he never saw a play unless he was forced to.
In 1780 he entered Parliament, where he was a brilliant speaker, but never
achieved high office and sank into horrendous debt. He raised money to build
a new Drury Lane Theatre (1792), but it burned down in 1809, perhaps the
final straw (accosted watching the fire from the street with a glass in his hand,
he remarked, 'A man may surely be allowed to take a glass of wine by his own
fireside'). He was arrested for debt in 1813, when his house was discovered to
be empty of furnishings and thick with dirt. He received a grand funeral, but
the theatre claimed him at the last, for he was buried, not next to his old
political ally, Fox, as he wanted, but next to Garrick where, like it or not, he
surely belonged.

Quotes

Yes, sir, puffing is of various sorts; the principal
are, the puff direct, the puff preliminary, the puff
collateral, the puff collusive, and the puff oblique,
or puff by implication.
The Critic, Act I, Scene ii

I open with a clock striking, to beget an awful attention in the audience: it also marks the time, which
is four o'clock in the morning, and saves a description of the rising sun, and a great deal about gilding
the eastern hemisphere.
The Critic, Act II, Scene ii

He is the very pineapple of politeness!
The Rivals, Act III, Scene iii

Mrs Candour: I'll swear her colour is natural: I have
seen it come and go.
Lady Teazle: I dare swear you have ma'am; it goes
off at night, and comes again in the morning.
The School for Scandal, Act II, Scene ii

the rise of
German theatre

Unlike the Latin nations and England, with their national theatres, Germany had none, largely because Germany was divided into about 350 separate and not always friendly states. An associated problem was language. France was still the centre of European culture, and French was widely spoken by educated people. Frederick the Great of Prussia is said to have remarked that German was a language only to be used when addressing one's horse.

Vienna

Vienna, the Habsburg capital, was the greatest cultural centre after Paris. However, Vienna's theatrical achievements have famously been dominated by music and opera, while, as elsewhere, the weakness of spoken drama was exacerbated by the lack of outstanding dramatists before the Romantic period. Vienna's great Burgtheater, built in 1741 inside the imperial palace, at first staged mainly productions by foreign companies. From 1776, however, when it became officially the Austrian National Theatre, its repertory steadily expanded under two famous directors, Josef von Sonnenfels and Josef Schreyvogel, to include modern German drama. The tradition of knockabout comedy, deriving from the commedia dell'arte tradition, was popular enough to find a place occasionally in respectable theatre until it was banned (1776) in an endeavour to raise the cultural tone and support the Burgtheater. However, its popularity meant that it survived on the Vienna fringe. Otherwise, the chief form of theatre from the late 16th to the mid-18th century was the Jesuit drama. (See below.)

Germany

About 1700 travelling companies in Germany still performed in places such as tavern yards in addition to court engagements. In spite of the primitive conditions and the need to attract the kind of spectators who were entranced by the coarse clown-figure of Hanswurst, contemporary prints show that the actors sometimes had splendid costumes and quite elaborate sets.

The other source of popular theatrical tradition was the Jesuit drama. This was originally a product of the Counter-Reformation, didactic in purpose and performed – in Latin – by students in Jesuit colleges to practise their rhetoric. At first it was strictly controlled. Not only were women forbidden to appear on stage, they were banned from the audience too, but such restrictions were gradually relaxed and by the 18th century the Jesuit drama had developed from a kind of studious school play into something much more polished, varied and ambitious. In south Germany it frequently included songs and music, and sometimes orders were issued to control what was seen as unseemly and costly extravagance. In general, though, the form was conservative and its influence on the development of the drama comparatively small. The whole tradition came to an end when the Jesuit Order was banned in 1773.

Left: Lessing in 1771. He was perhaps the finest critic of his time, who liberated German drama from the constricting influence of French Classicism.

Right: Gottsched, together with Carolina Neuber, laid the foundations for the revolution in German drama led by Lessing.

Lessing

Early attempts to create a national, literary drama were spearheaded in Saxony by the critic Johann Christoph Gottsched (1700–66) with a company headed by the lively actress-manager Carolina Neuber (1697–1760). However, it largely relied on French Classical drama and, although a few German plays were included, they were of indifferent quality. The scene changed dramatically with the arrival of Gotthold Lessing (1729–81), who advocated the broader tradition of Shakespeare as a guide and preferable to the French classicists – the beginning of the powerful Shakespearian tradition in Germany. Lessing's own early plays, mostly light-hearted comedies in verse, were not particularly Shakespearian, nor was his one tragedy, but he improved when he forsook verse for prose in his fine comedy, *Minna von Barnhelm* (1767). Perhaps his best work was his last, *Nathan der Weise* ('Nathan the Wise'), the first German play in blank verse, a condemnation of the blinkered intolerance against which he had himself struggled for years. It was not produced until 1778, after his death, and was more or less ignored until Goethe revived it at Weimar in 1801. However, Lessing's importance lies not so much in his plays as in his critical writing and his influence on the movement for a national drama.

The Hamburg Enterprise

The importance of this project was widely recognized. The drama provided a focus of cultural identity not to be found in politics, law or in any institution. In 1767 a group of civic leaders in Hamburg led by Konrad Ackermann (1712–71) established what they hoped would be a national theatre. They hired Lessing as resident writer and staged *Minna von Barnhelm*, with variety turns in the intervals between the acts in hope of attracting the vulgar. In spite of these expedients, the Hamburg Enterprise foundered after two years. Without doubt there was a growing audience among the public, but it appeared that the drama would have to rely on the traditional centres – the courts of German rulers. The National Theatre of Mannheim, founded in 1777 and directed by Baron von Dalberg, attracted a number of talented people including August Wilhelm Iffland (1759–1814). Among them was a promising young poet, appointed writer-in-residence. This was Friedrich von Schiller. He was to provide the vital missing ingredient for German drama – plays of outstanding quality.

Schiller and Goethe

The late 18th century was a period of great literary excitement in Germany, which culminated, as far as drama is concerned, with the brief but glorious period of partnership between Schiller and Goethe at Weimar. The literary excitement sprang largely from the early Romantic movement called Sturm und Drang ('Storm and Stress').

Sturm und Drang

Like all such movements, it was essentially a revolt against established conventions. In poetry and drama, it called for strong feelings, greater realism, and the kind of creative genius that Shakespeare represented. It derived its name from a play by a now unregarded German playwright (Klinger), but the first real dramatic sensation of Sturm und Drang was Johann Wolfgang von Goethe's *Götz von Berlichingen* (1772). Based on a famous, or notorious, medieval robber baron, it was written in the Shakespearian tradition with many changes of scene and a large cast of extras. It gave rise to a specific sub-school known as Ritterdrama ('Knight plays'), offering, if nothing more, extended use of expensive medieval costumes.

Schiller

The first play of the 22-year-old Friedrich von Schiller (1759-1805), *Die Räuber* ('The Robbers') was a characteristic Sturm und Drang piece, influenced by *Götz von Berlichingen*. The plot concerns an evil brother and a good – or sympathetic – brother, whose father is alienated and career blighted by the machinations of his evil sibling: there is an obvious debt to Shakespeare's *King Lear*. Produced at Dalberg's National Theatre of Mannheim in 1782, it was an immediate success. An English translation appeared at Drury Lane before the end of the century, though in general Schiller has been strangely neglected by the English-speaking world.

Schiller was in many ways representative of the popular image of the Romantic poet, young, handsome and oversensitive, harassed by misfortune and poor health into an early grave. The son of an army doctor, he followed his father's profession, got into trouble through absenting himself at the theatre and through debt. He lived under an assumed name, sheltered by a kindly patron, in Mannheim, where he wrote several later plays for Dalberg, although the tragedy *Don Carlos* (1787) was written at Dresden. A transitional work, it marked Schiller's movement away from the over-emotional Sturm und Drang to the more thoughtful, beautifully written and constructed plays of his later period, which began after a gap of twelve years with his move to Weimar. These plays, the peak of German poetic drama, included: *Wallenstein* (1799), about the imperial general in the Thirty Years' War (a subject on which Schiller was an expert); *Maria Stuart* (1800), about Mary Queen of Scots, which took some liberties with historical fact; the operatic *Die Jungfrau von Orléans* ('The Maid of Orléans', 1801); *Die Braut von Messina* ('The Bride of Messina', 1803) and *Wilhelm Tell* (1804), a drama about the Swiss national hero, and a masterpiece of stagecraft and dramatic verse.

Weimar

Originally, the court theatre at Weimar mounted amateur productions performed by courtiers for ceremonial occasions, but in 1784 a new theatre opened with a resident, professional company. Besides his staggering literary activities and membership of the government, Goethe, Germany's greatest literary giant, both directed the court theatre and, besides producing works by Lessing, Shakespeare, Calderón and Voltaire, wrote plays for it. Famous actors also appeared, like Friedrich Schröder, a notable Shakespearian and leader, with his mother Sophia, of a famous Hamburg company. Schröder was noted for his realism and psychological penetration, and some of Weimar's critics held him superior to the more formal, Classical style espoused by Goethe, now long past his Sturm und Drang days. Weimar became the most famous theatre in Germany, not only for Schiller's tragedies and foreign classics, but also more popular works by playwrights such as August Wilhelm Iffland, a Mannheim virtuoso who wrote sentimental domestic dramas, and August Friedrich von Kotzebue, prolific author of melodramas who, in his day, was more popular than Schiller, much to Goethe's disgust.

Goethe

As a playwright, Johann Wolfgang von Goethe (1749–1832) offered no great innovations, and seems to have been rather reluctant to stage his own plays. After his early Sturm und Drang melodramas, he turned towards Classical tragedies in the French manner. His greatest work, the lengthy *Faust*, based on the German legend exploited earlier by Marlowe, occupied him from 1774 until his death. It tends to confirm the impression, apparently shared by the author, that his plays were better read than performed. In the theatre, he is more significant as a producer, moulding his tight-knit, well-paid company into a superb ensemble. The actors were associated closely with every aspect of the production, and for important new works such as Schiller's tragedies, weeks of discussion preceded even longer rehearsals – this at a time when many plays were mounted with virtually no rehearsals and with actors having only the vaguest idea of their lines. Goethe made Weimar a beacon in the highly confused, quarrelsome and feud-riven German theatre of the period.

Top: Goethe as a young, Romantic poet; from a painting by Georg Melchior.

Above: A scene from *Faust*, Goethe's great work which occupied him for most of his life. Whereas the first part is dramatically viable, the intellectually demanding second part defies theatrical production.

During the 18th century the theatre finally resumed the place it had occupied in Classical Greece as an important institution in society influencing current ideas and politics. It was no longer merely a stylized entertainment for princely courts, nor a knockabout amusement for the streets. Its new role reflected a new audience, the middle classes, whose rising influence was paralleled by the relative decline of the traditional aristocracy. It became, in spite of censorship and other government restrictions, a forum for political debate mirroring, sometimes provocatively, the lives and concerns of its audience in a realistic, if sometimes sentimental, style.

Northern Europe

These changes are evident in the growth of 'bourgeois' theatre not only in Germany, but also in other northern, especially Protestant, countries where, unlike the established theatrical nations (Italy, Spain, England, France), there was no tradition of public or national theatre. In the Netherlands, for example, there had never been a court theatre and, since throwing off foreign rule, the Dutch were the most progressively urban, commercial nation in Europe, it is not surprising that a national theatre, the famous Schouwburg in Amsterdam, was founded as early as 1638. It opened with a patriotic historical tragedy by Joos van der Vendel (1587–1679), which thereafter remained the traditional season opener. Generally, native Dutch drama languished somewhat under the influence of French Classical drama and later, the 'sentimental' drama, until the appearance of Herman Heyermans in the late 19th century. The Schouwburg burned down in 1772, when an attempt to reduce the lighting for a gloom-ridden scene resulted in the screens around the candles catching fire. It was rebuilt the next year, when the first theatre in Rotterdam also opened.

Scandinavia

The establishment of a national theatre in Denmark dates from the founding of the Grønnegarde, later the Royal Theatre, in Copenhagen in 1722. Though it opened with a Molière translation, it was soon staging the plays of Ludvig Holberg (1684–1754) who, though Norwegian by birth, was the first playwright to write in Danish. His influence prevented Danish drama from being overwhelmed by the powerful influence of Germany or France, and at the end of the century Denmark experienced a literary golden age, when the most influential, and nationalistic, of the dramatists was Adam Oehlenschlaeger (1779–1850).

French enterprise lay behind the Grønnegarde, and another Frenchman founded the first national theatre in Sweden, in 1737. It collapsed after some years, but was revived by King Gustavus (or Gustaf) III, a keen thespian who acted in many plays and also wrote some. During his reign (1771–92), no fewer than four theatres with permanent, resident companies existed in Stockholm. However, Sweden produced no Holberg and, lacking dramatists of great stature, the theatres mostly produced musical plays and translations.

Eastern Europe

In Bohemia, German culture prevailed. The old passion plays were of course in Czech, but they disappeared in the 14th-century Hussite era. However, by the 1780s, Czech plays, about Czech affairs, were to be seen in Prague, though there was no resident company of Czech-speaking actors until the mid-19th century,

under the actor-playwright Josef Tyl (1808–50). His dramas about national heroes such as Jan Hus and the silver miners of Kutná Hora are still popular. The tradition of popular, native theatre was perhaps stronger in Poland, where the National Theatre was founded under royal patronage in 1706 as part of a deliberate plan to popularize Enlightenment ideas. No Polish playwright of the first rank emerged, however, and by the 1790s the country itself had disappeared in the partitions of its greedy neighbours.

Russia

In 1648 Tsar Alexis banned all forms of public entertainment, and even the strolling players disappeared for a time. The Tsar's attitude subsequently changed and the beginning of professional theatre can be traced to his reign. His son Peter the Great saw a didactic and political role for the drama and had a theatre built opposite the Kremlin in Moscow. But Russia lacked a powerful bourgeoisie, and the aristocracy were not very interested. Since attendance was compulsory for the court, the theatre was full when the Tsar attended, but otherwise nearly empty. A more determined effort was made by the Empress Elizabeth, who in 1756 founded a professional theatre with a resident company in St Petersburg. It included the first internationally famous Russian actor, Ivan Dmitrevsky, 'the Russian Garrick'. The Imperial Theatre School was founded under Catherine the Great in 1779. In general, there was little sign of the greatness that Russian drama would achieve in the 19th century, but among several dramatists of quality, Alexei Sumarokov (1718–77), in his nationalistic history plays, tried to 'Russify' the drama and subdue the powerful French influence. As in later times, censorship was an extremely inhibiting factor.

Of particular interest are the 'serf theatres' founded by nobles on their provincial estates where, unlike in St Petersburg or Moscow, foreign influence was insignificant. The purpose was to provide entertainment for guests, and serfs were hired as performers. The quality was variable, but some fine private theatres were built and a few of the performers eventually moved into the professional ranks, though in general their status was not improved by their unusual duties.

Below: The Schouwburg Theatre in Amsterdam, with a permanent architectural set in the Classical manner (left, the view towards the stage; right, part of the auditorium). Built by Jacob van Campen in 1637, it was the first permanent, purpose-built theatre in the Netherlands.

private theatres

During the 18th century private theatricals became increasingly popular, reaching a peak by 1800 and continuing well into the 19th century. As a result, many private theatres were built, i.e. not generally open to the public and not charging admission. One recent authority claims that such theatres existed in 'every house and city'. They may have been less common than that, but they were certainly more numerous than might be expected from the small number that have survived. Some were simply 18th-century equivalents of the court or princely theatres of an earlier age, but they were generally purpose-built and staged different forms of music and drama. Performers included both amateurs and professionals.

Celle

One of the earliest surviving private theatres in Europe was built in the ducal palace of Celle, northern Germany. It dates from the 1670s although altered more than once since. Baroque in style, it had a U-shaped auditorium seating 330. Italian opera was staged there, and the Elector of Hanover used it for a few years, but it was more or less abandoned when he became King of England in 1714. It was briefly revived in the 1770s by a sister of George III, Caroline Matilde, who spent her last years in Celle, and the great actor Schröder appeared there. There seem to have been few productions thereafter until the theatre was restored in the 1920s.

Sweden

Drottningholm, on the island of Lovö, was the summer residence of the Swedish monarchs, a fine Baroque palace built in the 1660s. Its most famous feature today is its theatre and museum. The original theatre was burned in 1762 but its replacement, completed four years later, is still one of the oldest in Europe and is virtually unchanged today. Its most brilliant era was in the reign of Gustaf III. In the 19th century it was used as a storeroom, but it was fully restored in 1921. The original stage machinery is still operational, and many sets from Gustaf's time have survived, as well as some even older French ones, exhibited in the museum that occupies the former state apartments. The theatre holds about 450 and has always been used more for opera and ballet than drama, although in recent years the Swedish Royal Dramatic Theatre has sometimes performed there.

One of the smallest and most beautiful royal theatres was built in 1782 in one of the round towers of the castle of Gripsholm, built by Gustavus Vasa in the early 16th century. Restored in the 20th century and still occasionally used, it retains the original stage machinery and sets, one of which exactly reproduces the design of the semicircular auditorium. This has the effect of creating a perfect circle where the audience feels 'enclosed in a circular jewel box, glowing with colour'.

Cesky Krumlov

The theatre in the great Bohemian castle of Cesky Krumlov replaced an earlier wooden building. It was built in the same year as that at Drottningholm, for the Austrian Schwarzenburgs, when Prince Karl Philip, the future victor over Napoleon at Leipzig (1813), was a child. The small, U-shaped auditorium has a splendid Baroque proscenium arch. The 18th-century sets, great Baroque perspectives by the finest Italian scene painters of the day, can be seen in the

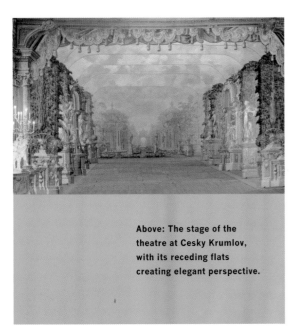

Above: The stage of the theatre at Cesky Krumlov, with its receding flats creating elegant perspective.

adjacent riding stables and, in spite of their priceless value and fragile condition, some have been used in recent productions.

England

A number of private theatres were built in England from the late 18th century.
A certain Sir Watkin Williams Wynn built one from a converted kitchen, and
the Duke of Marlborough had one of the conservatories at Blenheim Palace
rebuilt as a theatre in the 1780s. The Duke of Richmond had a theatre in
his London house, made from two rooms and capable of seating up to 150
people, and there was a particularly ornate theatre at Wargrave in Berkshire.
The earliest survivor, however, is the theatre built at Chatsworth in Derbyshire
by the 6th Duke of Devonshire in the 1820s.

Theatre architecture

Early public theatres had a rectangular auditorium that was often, following
the tennis-court tradition, long and narrow, so that spectators in the boxes
along the sides must have had a rather poor view of the stage. Before the end
of the 18th century the form had changed to a curved shape, often more or
less U-shaped, partly an effect of the Baroque style, but also more suitable in
terms of seeing and hearing, especially from the boxes: the opera house in
Munich in 1657 was an early example. Such a plan represented a return to
something closer to the form of ancient Greece. There was little provision for
space between the auditorium and the front of the theatre. Some German
opera houses had grand and spacious ceremonial halls, but this sort of development was not widespread until the 19th century, when grand, ornate theatres were built on open sites rather than crammed in among other buildings.

**Above: A performance of a
play about Richard Lionheart,
to entertain Queen Victoria at
Versailles in 1853. The Queen
impressed Parisians by never
looking back to make sure the
chair was in position before
sitting down.**

19th-century theatre

chap

Sir Henry Irving as Mathias in *The Bells*.

ter 7

Romantic elements may be present in the literature and art of any period, but the term refers specifically to the intellectual movement that was a powerful influence on society and the arts from the late 18th to the mid-19th century. It was connected with the growing contemporary political forces of liberalism and nationalism, and was largely a reaction against the rational, cosmopolitan spirit of the Enlightenment. In contrast to the Enlightenment conception of the universal character of humanity, Romantics stressed the uniqueness of the individual and the importance of individual expression, of which the influence of national character was a component. Intensity of feelings and the power of the imagination drove the Romantic movement, which was marked by a mystical sense of the infinite, the 'sublime' and often by love of nature, particularly of nature in her wildest aspect – rugged mountains and thunderstorms. A powerful appeal was exercised by the strange and the exotic, the Celtic twilight, Gothic fantasies, or the myth of the Orient, as in Coleridge's poem about Kubla Khan (supposedly, though not actually, the product of an opium-induced dream).

the romantic movement

Production

The Romantic spirit had a marked effect on scenery, stagecraft and acting, most evident in melodrama but influencing drama in general. Scenic effects became increasingly spectacular, advancing the status of scene painters and the numbers of stage hands, which in some cases ran into hundreds. Storms, falling snow and Gothic moonlight demanded ingenious lighting, though the greatest innovations, resulting from the inventions of gas and electricity, came later in the century. Acting had to be emotional and intense. The lion-like Edmund Kean (1789–1833), who sprang to fame as Shylock in 1814, was the outstanding Romantic actor, a huge sensation who reduced audiences to near-hysterics, though a modern audience might find his style a little over the top. Unfortunately, he had the personal deficiencies that often accompany inspired actors, a frightful temper and an ultimately fatal drink problem. He died on stage at 44 while playing Iago to the Othello of his less brilliant son Charles (1811–68).

Germany

The Romantic movement generally affected literature earlier than the other arts, and it took different forms in different countries. An early manifestation was Sturm und Drang in Germany, and Goethe was the first Romantic literary hero, though his Romantic period was comparatively short. *Faust* was a thoroughly Romantic subject, but Goethe's two-part master work is as difficult to categorize as it is to stage. Otherwise, German Romanticism in the early 19th century produced some good writers, but no new Schiller. The plays of Ludwig Tieck (1773–1853) are rather pallid, and he was most influential as a proponent of Shakespeare. Heinrich von Kleist (1777–1811), later recognized as a near-genius, had no success in his lifetime and committed suicide not long

Below: The Romantic actor Edmund Kean in perhaps his most famous role, playing Shylock (in *The Merchant of Venice*) as a terrifying villain.

after his brilliant comedy, *Der zerbrochene Krug* ('The Broken Jug'), was produced by Goethe at Weimar.

The major figure of the period was the Austrian, Franz Grillparzer, whose plays,
often revived, included *Der Traum ein Leben* ('Life is a Dream', 1834), adapted
from Calderón. But, disappointed by the failure of his only comedy *Weh' dem, der
lügt* ('Thou Shalt Not Lie'), in 1838, Grillparzer gave up writing plays. The young
revolutionary Georg Büchner (1813–37) had a closer association with Sturm und
Drang. He wrote only a couple of complete plays in his brief lifetime and saw
none produced. He was rediscovered by Hauptmann in the 1890s and today his
reputation, though controversial, stands very high, particularly for his last, unfinished masterpiece, *Wozzeck*, a precursor of Expressionism.

Romanticism v Classicism

The contest between conservative and radical, Classical and Romantic, was
fought, literally, in France, where the Comédie-Française maintained its
Classical heritage in face of popular English melodramas produced in the new
theatres that sprang up in Paris after Napoleon relaxed the restrictions. French
Romantics, like German, were strongly influenced by Shakespeare, whom they
saw as a weapon against the dramatic establishment, increasingly heavy
handed after the imposition of stricter censorship in 1826. The scene of the battle was the Comédie-Française on the first night of *Hernani* (1830), by the leader
of French Romanticism, Victor Hugo (1802–85). Hugo's play, a melodrama –
but the work of one of France's greatest poets – of love and revenge, played fast
and loose with Classical conventions, ignoring the unities, showing violence on
stage, spicing tragedy with humour, using colloquial terms, etc. The performance ended in uproar, as fights broke out between Hugo's opponents and supporters. It is the riot that gives the event its special notoriety, for this was not the
first play to attack Classical conventions, but it represents an important turning
point in the theatre. It did not, however, herald a great age of Romantic drama.
For all his glowing dramatic verse, Hugo's last play, *Les Burgraves* (1843), was a
flop. Romanticism had passed its peak, realism and prose took over, and even
melodrama turned to contemporary domestic subjects.

early American theatre

In the North American colonies, theatre was generally frowned upon, especially in the north, where Puritan influence remained strong. In the 19th century, this situation changed, but there were few significant innovations in native American drama, and the theatre was largely dominated by English (or European) plays and actors.

Above: The accomplished Augustin Daly, author of perhaps 100 plays, mostly adaptations, but best known as a manager of successful companies and theatres in New York and London in the 1880s–90s.

The 18th century

The first American productions, which appeared in about 1700, were amateur or, as in Russia, were run by servants; there were no native professional companies until the middle of the century. Theatre for the next 50 years was dominated by the American Company, which was founded in 1752 as the London Company of Comedians, a sign of its English origins. It was responsible for founding the first permanent, public theatres, usually converted from other buildings. They included the Southwark in Philadelphia (1766), probably the first, and the following year the more famous John Street Theatre in New York. John Street saw the production of the first American play, *The Prince of Parthia* (1767), by Thomas Godfrey (1736–63), an heroic tragedy in blank verse. In 1787, on the heels of the Declaration of Independence, the company produced the second, more notable, American play, *The Contrast*, a comedy inspired by Sheridan, which mocked the foppish British, compared with the honest dignity of the Americans, and introduced the stage Yankee. Its author was Royall Tyler (1757–1826), a man of parts who later became Chief Justice of the Vermont Supreme Court. For years the American Company had no rivals, until its leading actor, Thomas Wignell, broke away and founded his own company, recruited in England, in 1793. It was based in Philadelphia, in the Chestnut Street Theatre, a large and elegant theatre modelled on the Theatre Royal in Bath. Seating up to 2,000 in the auditorium, it was unchallenged in Philadelphia until the Walnut Street Theatre, originally a circus, opened in 1816.

The Astor Place riot

While there was no native drama of great dramatic interest in the early 19th century, there were some fine American actors, notably Edwin Booth (1833–93), America's foremost tragedian and member of a famous theatrical family that included President Lincoln's assassin. Ira Aldridge (1804–67), discovered by Edmund Kean, pursued his career in Europe since, being black, he got nowhere in America. Another was the powerful and flamboyant tragedian Edwin Forrest (1806–72). He was partly responsible for an incident in 1849, which occurred in New York at the recently opened Astor Place Opera House, an event no less startling than that in Paris on the first night of *Hernani*. In London two years earlier he had had a poor reception (though he had been a success on a previous appearance), which he blamed on his rival, the outstanding English actor Charles Macready (1793–1873), whom Forrest had publicly hissed in *Hamlet*. Their dislike was mutual and ferocious, but the incident that took place on Macready's next American tour sprang not so much from history as from class hostility, plus resentment at what the poet Walt Whitman called the 'usurpers of our stage', the British. On the second night, after the performance had been interrupted by Forrest, an anti-British crowd led by Bowery toughs attacked the theatre. Macready left by a rear entrance, the militia was called in, and 31 people were killed.

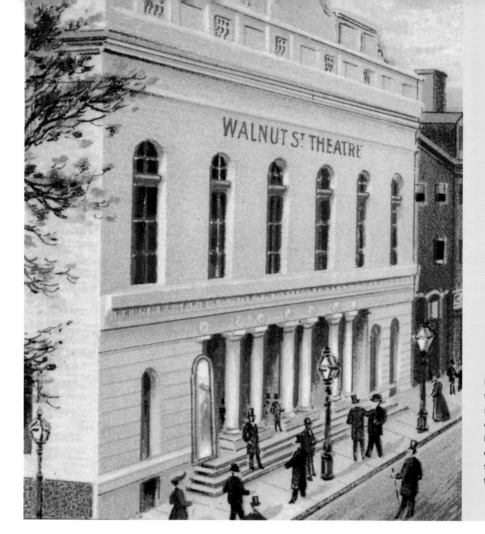

Left: The Walnut Street theatre is
the oldest theatre still in existence
in America. Originally opened as a
circus by two French acrobats,
Pepin and Breschard, in 1809, but
changed to a theatre in 1816. Many
famous actors made their debut
there including Edwin Forrest.

Metropolis and frontier

As the pioneers moved West, actors followed them, and their experiences provide a fund of anecdotes, some more credible than others. One touring-com-
pany manager recalled playing in a hastily converted log cabin in the 1820s
where the audience failed to fill the three wooden benches provided. Another
company lost its leading lady overnight, but found her next morning stuck up
a tree, besieged by wolves.

The theatres of the East in the later 19th century were largely dominated by
the classics, especially Shakespeare (surprisingly popular in mining towns);
melodrama, including the astonishingly successful dramatization of Harriet
Beecher Stowe's anti-slavery tear-jerker, *Uncle Tom's Cabin*; musical comedy,
vaudeville and minstrel shows with white singers impersonating blacks.

Perhaps the outstanding figure was the phenomenal Dion (short for
Dionysus) Boucicault (1820–90), an Irishman of Huguenot descent. Though
more famous in his own time as an actor-manager, he wrote about 250 plays,
including the first serious treatment of American blacks, *Life in Louisiana*
(1859), and the first play set in the American Civil War, *Lamar* (1872). He was
equally successful in London, and several of his plays have been revived with
great success. He was also largely responsible for the payment of royalties to
authors. There were a few at least competent American playwrights, such as
Bronson Howard (1843–1908), the first fully professional dramatist, and the
versatile Clyde Fitch (1865–1909), at root a serious and socially perceptive
writer, seduced by melodrama. Among the many famous actors and managers was Augustin Daly (1839–99), author of numerous melodramas, one of
which included the first use of a person tied to a railway line. There was a
Daly's Theatre in London as well as New York.

lighting

Of the many technological advances in the 19th century, perhaps the most significant in the theatre was the development in artificial lighting. Victorian melodramas would certainly have been rather ineffective without them.

Early artificial lighting

From the open-air theatres of Classical times up to the 17th century, light was provided by the sun. Torches might be required for the later scenes as the light faded, and in ancient Greece the moon seems to have been exploited occasionally for special effect. In Elizabethan England, a Shakespeare play beginning at 2 or 3 p.m. would certainly require lights before the end. The indoor theatres of the Renaissance had large windows, showing that they also relied on daylight, which was no doubt preferred, being cost-free. But artificial light must have been necessary more often than not. It was provided by candles in the ordinary way, a theatre being lit just like any other room.

The potential of artificial light in creating special effects was recognized in Italy early on. Sebastiano Serlio (1475–1554) described how coloured light was produced by placing lamps behind glass vessels containing coloured liquids and advocated barber's basins as reflectors.

The 17th Century

By the 17th century, special effects, such as dimming or extinguishing the lights at a tragic moment, were practised to great effect. Devices such as cylinders suspended over lights by wires from a frame, allowed lights to be extinguished simultaneously. Early period stage designers advocated extinguishing or dimming the lights in the auditorium, but it was a long time before their advice was followed. Audience resistance may have been a factor: fashionable people came to show off and observe each other as well as the play.

Footlights with polished reflectors were also introduced in the 17th century, as were concealed lights at the rear of the stage, though oil lamps at ground level were unpleasantly smoky and smelly. But the main light still came from ceiling-mounted chandeliers, dazzling the audience and obscuring the view from the galleries. In England, Garrick is credited with great improvements in lighting, although they seem to have amounted chiefly to more intelligent use of existing equipment.

Gas

Gas lighting, the first real revolution in lighting, was introduced in London in 1817. Its chief advantages were that it was brighter and – eventually – could be dimmed or raised instantly from a central control. Effects such as moonlight or dawn were more effective. The main drawback was the fire hazard. Gas lights proved to be even more dangerous than candles or oil lamps: figures for theatre fires show a marked increase after the adoption of gas. Like most changes, gaslight was not universally welcomed. People complained that the stage became a featureless glare, with shadows and subtlety obliterated. The great exponent of gas lighting in England was Sir Henry Irving (1838–1905) at the Lyceum, who at last achieved the aim of 16th-century stage designers that the auditorium should be dark. One important result of the revolution gas lighting brought was that the actors were able to retreat well beyond the proscenium arch, which facilitated the spectacular pictorial settings beloved of 19th-century audiences.

Limelight, producing a brilliant, lens-focused light from a calcium flare, was introduced soon after gas. It was used chiefly like a spotlight, to illuminate the main actor – putting him 'in the limelight'. Electric arc lamps, first used in Paris in 1846, had a similar effect, but they tended to flicker. Full electric lighting awaited the invention of the incandescent lamp (1880).

Electricity

The first building in London lit entirely by electricity was D'Oyly Carte's Savoy Theatre in 1881, although it was preceded by a theatre in San Francisco and electric light had been used somewhat earlier for the public parts of a theatre. That it took over so rapidly was partly due to pressure from the insurance companies, since it was much safer. It also provided light that was not only stronger, but also more adaptable. It had a profound effect on stage design – for example, it encouraged the replacement of perspective-painted scenery by three-dimensional sets – and it led to a huge variety of techniques, beginning with the impressive, though rather impractical, 'sky-dome' of Mariano Fortuny (1871–1949). His aim was to achieve predominantly reflected light, by projecting it from a concealed source on to a silk canopy, the only direct light coming from spotlights. By masking the light in various ways, all kinds of effects could be achieved, such as looming shadows of off-stage buildings. Drifting leaves, snowstorms and other movements were made with slides. The centrally operated controls became simpler to use, while achieving ever more remarkable effects. By the 1970s most large theatres had computerized lighting, and certain shows exploited laser light.

Above: Moonlight at the Paris Opéra. The introduction of electric light represented a huge advance – not least in reducing fire-insurance costs – but it was not always or immediately welcomed, since gaslight had its own distinctive charm.

ballet

Dancing is an ancient element of performance art, long predating speech, but ballet, a stylized form of dancing, originated in the Renaissance. Disregarding the rustic jollities of medieval peasants, the more elegant – though sometimes surprisingly energetic – dancing of royal and noble courts developed greater sophistication, to the extent that it demanded professional dancing masters. Ballet, as a pre-planned performance to accompanying music, may be said to have originated, along with opera with which it retained strong links, in Italy, where the first manual of dance was written about 1460. However, it developed towards its modern form chiefly in France, hence the French terminology still employed.

Beginnings

The princely Italian courts, competitively engaged in producing more specialized entertainments, transformed the dance into a new art form, directed by professionals and forming a part of the performances, whether as an unconnected interlude or more closely integrated into the show. Action replaced dialogue, and the dancers conveyed by their actions a story or a mood. From Italy the balletto passed to the French court in the early 16th century – the first true ballet is traditionally said to have been the *Ballet comique de la reine*, seen in Paris in 1581. In the 17th century, Lully produced the music for the highly formal dancing performed by courtiers in full court dress, including wigs, and ballet formed an important part of his later operas, in which he introduced the first professional female dancers. Louis XIV was a keen dancer himself, having gained his nickname 'the Sun King' from his performance in such a role aged 14, and he founded the Académie Royale de Dance in 1661. His teacher, Pierre Beauchamps, who co-operated with Lully, invented many of the traditional positions.

The 18th century

A more vigorous style, including jumps, developed in the early 18th century, although dress was still cumbersome, with skirts well below the knee. But it remained a fringe entertainment until the development of the dramatic, or operatic, ballet in five acts, pioneered chiefly by Jean Georges Noverre (1727–1810) in collaboration with Mozart, among other composers. He is said to have created over 150 ballets. Ballet became more realistic, masks were at last abandoned and period costume introduced. Among other famous ballet masters was Gaetano Vestris (1729–1808), 'the God of the Dance', who preceded Noverre as chief choreographer of the Paris Opéra. He founded a dynasty of dancers and choreographers, culminating in his grandson Armand (1786–1825), who made his debut in Paris aged four and spent much of his career in London. Armand married, though briefly, Lucia Elisabetta Bartolozzi, the famous Mme Ventris (1797–1856), whose innovations as manager of the Olympic and later Covent Garden theatres included the three-walled box set with a ceiling, said to have been the first stage representation of a room.

The Romantic era

By about 1800, ballet was discarding its image as a courtly pastime and becoming a professional entertainment comparable with the opera. Dancing became more athletic, and more demanding of the dancers, especially with the introduction of dancing on pointe (tip-toe), which required specially made shoes. Hitherto ballet had generally consisted of a set of dances, but in the ballet d'action, spectacle was harnessed to narrative, expressed through dance and mime. The music had often been provided by hack composers, but now more gifted musicians were increasingly involved. With the Romantic era emerged the first ballets that still find a place in the repertory today, beginning with Jean Daubervalle's *La Fille Mal Gardée*, first produced at Bordeaux in 1789 and originally based on French songs with a few extracts from Italian opera. Another was *Les Sylphides* (1832), choreographed by a key figure in the development of Romantic opera and founder of another balletic dynasty, Filippo Taglioni (1777–1871). He created it for his daughter Marie (1804–84), the greatest dancer of the day. Taglioni was largely responsible for the combination of a delicate, ethereal quality with earthier, more folksy material, a persistent characteristic of ballet up to recent times, and he furthered development of greater continuity. Skirts became shorter, though still below the knee, and wires and pulleys gave the dancers the opportunity to 'fly'. The modern idea of the ballerina was further enhanced by Adolphe Adam's *Giselle* (1841) and by the ballets composed by Léo Delibes (1836–91), *Coppélia* (1870) and *Sylvia* (1876).

The rise of Russian ballet dates from Marius Petipa (1819–1910), a Frenchman who joined the Imperial Theatre in St Petersburg in 1847. He became chief choreographer of the Maryinski, later the Kirov Ballet, and, with his assistant Lev Ivanov, founded Russian classical ballet, dominating the scene for half a century. He was responsible for the great works of the period in which the music indisputably matched the dance, Tchaikovsky's *Swan Lake* (1877, *Petipa's version* 1895), *The Sleeping Beauty* (1890) and *The Nutcracker* (1892), all three still among the world's most popular ballets.

Above and left: The Italian dancer Carlotta Grisi (1819–99) was one of the greatest ballerinas of the Romantic period. She made her debut at La Scala in 1829 and created the role of Giselle (left) in Paris in 1841.

Among other roles of which she was the creator were La Péri (1843) and (above) La Esmeralda (1844), choreographed by her lover, Jules Perrot.

pantomime
and circus

Pantomime, which has ancient and varied theatrical antecedents, is one of the most popular forms of live entertainment today, requiring no subsidies and making a good profit. Circus is a rather different type of performing art, a world of its own whose performers tend to form closely related communities and work in a different environment. However, there are clear affinities with the theatre, never more so, perhaps, than in the present era, when the theatre is colonizing many other forms of entertainment and circus is undergoing radical changes in style, while the figure of the clown belongs to pantomime and circus equally.

Pantomime

In ancient Rome a pantomimus was an actor who mimed many different roles, with frequent changes of mask, and thus it came to be applied to the type of entertainment, involving dance and music without words, in which he appeared. In 18th-century Europe, the name was applied to several forms that could not be classified as 'comedy' or 'tragedy'. In England, it was given to the version of the Harlequinade, deriving from the commedia dell'arte tradition, put on by John Rich at Covent Garden. Rich himself played Harlequin, transformed into various manifestations such as an English highwayman. These pantomimes were first presented as an addition to the main bill, but were so popular they soon became full-length performances. Mime had nothing to do with them, and modern dumb-show performers call their art 'mime', rather than pantomime, to avoid confusion. In France the name was retained, until about 1900, for a type of play without words.

The Victorian pantomime

Pantomime became increasingly elaborate in the 19th century, when technological advances such as limelight, electricity and sophisticated stage machinery made possible that favourite ingredient, the 'transformation' scene. The big Victorian pantomimes were shown in the largest theatres at Christmas time, and were extraordinarily extravagant. A production of *Sinbad the Sailor* at Drury Lane in 1882 had a cast of 650, with costumes made from 300 different designs. There were so many turns that the term 'a pantomime' came to mean a state of inept confusion.

Today's pantomime follows the basic form of Victorian times. It is essentially a variety show, chiefly for children, shown in theatres around Christmas and loosely based on old folk tales or nursery rhymes such as *Aladdin*, *Cinderella*, *Mother Goose*, *Dick Whittington*, etc. It usually includes comic and acrobatic turns that have nothing to do with the plot, simple-minded satire and topical allusions, and by tradition it involves cross-dressing: the leading role or 'principal boy' is played by a young woman, and the comic 'Dame' by an older man. Unlike music hall, panto survived the coming of films in sound and colour, as well as the sinister lure of television, from which it now draws most of its stars – not to mention its bad jokes.

Circus

Although most of the elements of circus can be traced to ancient times, it began in the form we know it in 1769, when Philip Astley (1742–1814) moved his trick-riding acts from London's riverside into permanent, indoor quarters. The circular ring was already established, being the only practicable way to display horse-riding – the main ingredient of early circuses – to an audience. Astley eventually built 19 'amphitheatres' in England, Ireland and France. By 1800 the circus embraced many other acts, such as acrobats, rope-walkers, wild animals, strong men, etc. It sometimes included an attached stage, but the dramatic element soon died out. Touring circuses performing in large tents began about 1830, and reached their apogee with Barnum & Bailey in the U.S.A. and 'Lord' George Sanger in England. Barnum was a prince of showmen, whose elephant Jumbo and midget 'Tom Thumb' became internationally famous. He also originated the three-ring circus, which became the customary form in the U.S.A., though the single ring was preferred in Europe. More acts were introduced, notably trapeze. The traditional white-faced clown was joined by others and clowns became one of the principal attractions.

In the 20th century, circuses encountered increasing financial difficulties, and many small ones disappeared. Changing sensitivities made performing animals less popular, and although traditional circus thrived, aided by state subsidy, in Russia, in general it survived largely by drawing closer to theatrical performance. Barnum & Bailey, now merged with Ringling Bros, abandoned the big top for a permanent, roofed, air-conditioned arena, and new, sometimes controversial types of circus appeared. This cross-fertilization was not one-sided, nor new. The inventive and ambitious theatrical genius Max Reinhardt (1873–1943), craving huge spaces, mounted productions in circus buildings before the First World War. Jean-Louis Barrault (1910–94), the great French director, employed many aspects of circus and, himself a mime by training, memorably portrayed the traditional clown, Pierrot, in Marcel Carné's film, *Les Enfants du Paradis* (1944).

Opposite: Tinsel print depicting pantomime characters with 'Jim Crow' (see page 133) second from right. It is clear to see how the characters derived from the stock characters of commedia dell'arte.

Below: Poster for the Barnum & Bailey circus, which thrived on hype, proclaiming itself absurdly, but not entirely unjustly, 'the world's largest, grandest, best amusement institution'.

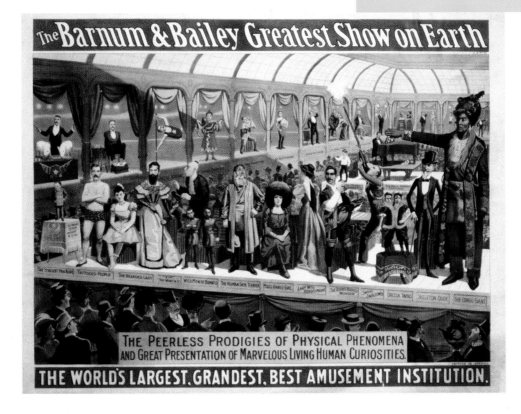

melodrama

[The increasing storm of lightning, thunder, hail, and rain, becomes terrible. Suitable music.
Enter ROMALDI from the rocks, disguised like a peasant, with terror, pursued, as it were, by the storm.]

Thus the stage directions from *A Tale of Mystery*, performed at Covent Garden in 1802. It was the first play to be described as a 'melodrama', by far the most popular theatrical entertainment in the 19th century, especially in English-speaking countries. Melodramatic elements are of course present in virtually all drama, from the Greek tragedy to the television soap, but the 19th-century melodrama is a distinctive form. Today it is either ignored or scorned, and Victorian melodramas, when occasionally revived, are played for laughs.

Gothic horrors

The word has changed its meaning. It originally meant 'melody + drama', and was applied to certain types of play with music, the mélodrame in France, melodramma in Italy. The early English melodramas, including *A Tale of Mystery*, were all accompanied by 'suitable music', which could be effectively used to heighten tension, as in a climactic scene from *The Shade* (1802):

> SHADE [i.e. a ghost]: –**There thy friend was foully murdered!** *(Music in a terrific chord)* **Blood for blood!** *(chord more terrific)* **Revenge!** *(chord)* **Revenge!** *(chord)* **Revenge!** *(chord – thunder)*.

The beginnings of melodrama were quite respectable, perhaps the earliest examples being Goethe's and Schiller's Sturm und Drang plays. Early English melodramas were often adapted from French originals, especially from Guilbert de Pixérécourt (*A Tale of Mystery* was one), though Pixérécourt in turn was influenced by 18th-century English Gothic novels as well, perhaps, as the genuine horrors of the French Revolution. The writers of melodrama seldom troubled to invent their own plots, and frequently adapted other writers' works, including novels, with little regard for copyright. Eventually, the predominantly Gothic settings faded out, like the musical element, and by about 1840, in response to the tastes of the growing middle-class audience, the plays more often had a domestic setting. There were always good plays, e.g. those of Dumas or Boucicault, which were written in melodramatic style without being too constricted by the form, and, later, subject matter was more varied. There were temperance dramas, nautical melodramas, even tragedies.

Plot and character

Plots were full of violent and terrible events – murders, suicides, fires, train crashes – and they moved at speed. The excitement of the plot was all, or almost all, for the characters were invariably two-dimensional stereotypes. There was a heroine, virtuous and usually poor, and a hero; there was a villain, often rich, or perhaps two villains, together with some comic relief and various minor characters. Typically, the heroine was placed in a ghastly predicament from which the hero, owing to dastardly machinations of some sort, was temporarily unable to rescue her. While enduring these frightening events, the audience could take comfort in the assurance that all would turn out well in the end. Virtue would triumph, villainy would be confounded.

Not used to our daily battery of electronic images, the Victorian audience derived great satisfaction from what seems to us crude and ridiculous. Whether their satisfaction can be equated with the catharsis identified by Aristotle as the key to Classical tragedy is a moot point. However, we should not forget the extraordinary effects that stage designers, benefiting from technological advances, could make, nor the power that an actor like Sir Henry Irving (a famous Shakespearian too) could bring to a role like that of the burgomaster in the well-crafted *The Bells*, by Leopold Lewis.

The audience

But the audience did not always watch transfixed with awe and terror. There seems to have been an element of the kind of actor-audience interaction that is familiar today in pantomime, or among students watching a hammy Hollywood costume drama. In the dramatization of Dickens's *Oliver Twist*, for instance, we hear that after dragging Nancy around the stage by her hair, the actor playing Bill Sykes would stop and glare at the gallery. Rewarded with a chorus of curses, he defiantly dragged her around once more, perhaps adding a kick, provoking an even greater roar of disapproval. One of the attractions of the melodrama was that audiences could have their moral cake and eat it. They would see conventional virtue rewarded, but on the way to that desirable result, they were entertained by less worthy events.

As time went on, melodrama became less simple. The straight Good v. Evil drama turned into something more complex. Towards the end of the century, extraordinarily spectacular melodramas were mounted at Drury Lane, which simulated gigantic natural disasters, massive shipwrecks and large-scale destruction in a manner that might have struck a chord with the young Cecil B. De Mille. But the melodrama was already dying, and the guns of August 1914 would extinguish its last, lingering breath.

Above: A scene from Augustin Daly's *Under the Gaslight*, which was the first play to use the device of a person tied to the railway tracks as the train thunders closer. The victim was a man, saved in the nick of time by a woman; later users of this device preferred to reverse the genders.

Below left: Sir Henry Irving in *The Bells*. In the 19th century, an actor like Irving, given a good part, could make an impact on the emotions of an audience such as today's inventors of costly cinematic special effects can only dream of.

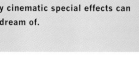

farce

Farce, one of the oldest types of drama, is a form of broad comedy which relies on fast-moving rough-and-tumble. It depends on universal human foibles and the inability of people to cope with unexpected problems or unusual situations – often of a kind that in real life would cause pain and stress – without getting themselves into a state of comical confusion or embarrassment. Elements of farce appear in other dramatic forms, including, for example, the drama of the Maya and other peoples of Meso-America. In general, however, it falls into two main groups: the knockabout comedy of clowns, mainly unscripted, of the kind that permeated folk entertainment for centuries and provided the basis for the clowns of the commedia dell'arte; or tightly plotted plays requiring actors of special gifts, particularly in timing. In such plays, although the characters must appear as reasonably credible individuals, there is virtually no characterization, as it would slow down the plot, in which the speed of events is crucial.

Ancient farce

Farce was an element in the Old Comedy of Classical Athens, and the short, informal entertainments known as Atellana of early Roman times. Performed at markets and similar gatherings, the Atellana featured stock characters such as the fat clown, the idiot, the glutton, etc. Transmitted orally, or extempore, farce characterized the folk theatre of the Middle Ages: a farce called *Babio* was specially written for the court of King Henry II of England in the 12th century. It featured a castration scene, from which it is reasonable to suppose that the actors wore the grotesque phalluses of Classical times.

France and England

Farce was especially popular in France, especially the provinces, from the later Middle Ages, and was an important part of the mystery plays after they escaped ecclesiastical control. It profoundly influenced the rise of Italian comedy and remained popular up to the time of Molière, who played in farces himself as a young touring actor and was strongly influenced by the form. It was the chief reason for the fame of actors such as Turlupin (Henri Legand, died 1637), who founded his own company to perform 'Turlupinades' at the Hôtel de Bourgogne, and ended up playing himself.

Since it depends primarily on action, farce translates more easily than other forms of drama. Traditional French farce was popular in England and influenced John Heywood (c.1497–1580), who wrote a number of short, comic pieces – the precursors of Elizabethan comedy – as 'interludes'. A few were printed, and some have been unearthed comparatively recently. In one of them, *The Playe called the foure Ps* , described as 'a newe and very mery enterlude of a palmer, a pardoner, a potycary, a pedlar', the four Ps compete to tell the most outrageous lies. (The palmer wins: he says he never knew a bad-tempered woman.)

In the 18th century, farce was usually a one-act play offering relief from a five-act tragedy. Though not regarded very highly as a genre, some farces, which often exploited the talents of a particular comedian, were very popular. They were one of the varied forms of entertainment offered by the enterprising John Rich. Garrick put on new farces at Drury Lane, and also wrote one or two himself. Farce was growing increasingly popular, perhaps more so than sentimental comedy. Writers were widening its potential – marital muddles becoming a frequent ingredient – but it generally remained part of a larger entertainment, not a full-length play.

Modern farce

Farce reached a new peak towards the end of the 19th century. Perhaps the most successful of all time was *Charley's Aunt* (1892), by the otherwise little-known Brandon Thomas (1856–1914), an English music-hall performer. Its original production in London ran for four years, and it is still frequently revived all over the world, having been performed in Chinese, Esperanto and Zulu, as well as other languages. Sir Arthur Wing Pinero (1855–1934) wrote several farces early in his career, including the still-popular *The Magistrate* (1885), perhaps the best of English farces (in 1969 it proved a perfect vehicle for Alastair Sim). Between the wars, the farces of Ben Travers kept audiences rocking at the Aldwych Theatre, and from the 1950s the tradition was continued by the actor-manager Brian Rix at the Whitehall. In North America and elsewhere, pure farce – with no trace of serious purpose – was less common.

The greatest exponent of farce was the enormously prolific Georges Feydeau (1862–1921), son of a successful French novelist, who wrote his first at the age of 24 and never stopped. His last, and approximately 70th, was published after his death. He was a master craftsman, demanding split-second timing and keeping his actors on their toes with rapid entries and exits. His *L'Hôtel du Libre Échange* was a huge success in London in 1956 performed as *Hotel Paradiso* with Alec Guinness, and a number of his other plays were adapted for English audiences by John Mortimer.

Below: Respectable gent flirts with pretty housemaid. Edwardian farce tended to revolve around certain basic situations, such as marital infidelity: hence the term 'Bedroom farce'.

Below: A scene from Walter Brandon Thomas's *Charley's Aunt*, probably the most successful farce ever written. It is said to have been running at one time in 48 different countries in 22 different languages.

'Romanticism' of various kinds persisted in the theatre after the Romantic movement had faded. 'Extravaganzas', spectacularly mounted entertainments similar to pantomime or burlesque, based on mythology or folklore and incorporating light-hearted songs and simple verse, were very popular in the mid-19th century. There was a vogue too for the 'fairy play', in which James Planché (1795–1880) and, later, W. S. Gilbert (before he teamed up with Sullivan) specialized. All these entertainments depended on production values, not literary merit, but Planché's popularity enhanced his influence on the tightening of the copyright law in 1860. Even the early works of an outstanding Romantic playwright, Alfred de Musset (1810–57), before he found his feet in the comédie-proverbe ('proverb play'), have an atmosphere of fantasy, although they have little in common with the lurid romantic tragedy of *Hernani*, the play that Hugo launched like a missile at classicism in 1830. *Hernani* gave rise to a brief period of romantic drama, if generally not as vigorous as Hugo's, whose exponents included Dumas and De Vigny (chiefly a poet), as well as a host of generally less talented European writers.

romantic theatre and
Wagnerian drama

Opera

Many romantic dramas, tragedies and melodramas made their greatest effect as the basis of operas. The theme of the heroine ensnared by the villain and subjected to fearful predicaments before she is rescued by the hero in the last act was a common one, in French opera especially. Beethoven's *Fidelio* might be cited as a more distinguished example. Opera audiences were growing fast, and their taste for romantic drama was a notable feature. History was ransacked by composers and librettists for suitable episodes, examples including Rossini's *William Tell* (1829), Bellini's *Norma* (1831) and Meyerbeer's *Les Huguenots* (1836). Verdi depended on literature for *Macbeth* (1847) and many others, not forgetting *Ernani* (1843).

Wagner

Romantic opera reached its peak with the German composer Richard Wagner (1813–83). His early work included a 'fairy' opera, *Die Feen*, but his fame rests chiefly on the great works of his maturity, from *Tannhaüser* (1845), through *Lohengrin* (1850), *Die Meistersinger* (1867) and the Ring cycle (1869–76), to *Parsifal* (1882). His earliest drama was a tragedy without music; Wagner subsequently decided he must become a musician, teaching himself composition and undergoing minimal formal training. His ambitions were as great as his gifts. He wanted to restore the drama, which in his time had come to consist of popular entertainment for the bourgeoisie, to the position it had once held as a place of profound social consciousness, political engagement and sublime poetry.

Wagner never called his works 'operas'. He wanted to create a whole new form, an artistic synthesis of music, drama and staging (Gesamtkunstwerk). His genius cannot be questioned, but he remains a controversial figure. He

sought his themes in Germanic folklore and legend, giving his work a strongly nationalistic emphasis which, combined with his own anti-Semitism, puts him in a dubious position in the context of subsequent German history, though his appeal to the Nazis does not make him one. Nor is there any doubting his success in achieving work of stunning theatricality, although, like all revolutionaries, his ideas were less wholly original than he and his supporters supposed. He was indebted first to Shakespeare and Goethe, no less to French romantic drama and even, in his command of structure, to such an 'unheroic' dramatist as the popular and prolific Eugène Scribe (1791–1861), chief exponent of 'the well-made play' – a kind of antidote to the passionate, romantic theatre that Wagner represented. Nor, of course, was Richard Wagner the first to seek themes of universal value in myth. In opera alone, he was preceded by Weber, among others.

Bayreuth

Such was Wagner's reputation that, with the support of Ludwig II of Bavaria, he was able to build his own theatre for his own works. He abandoned the customary arrangement of pit, boxes and gallery in favour of a simple, spare, curved auditorium, steeply raked. It opened in 1876 with a production of the four operas of the Ring cycle, Besides writing words and music, Wagner also controlled the staging, in fact every detail of the production, although on this occasion he did not conduct.

The Bayreuth theatre had some influence on theatre architects, not always for the best, into the 20th century. In other respects too, Wagner was an influential figure, though his ideas were not always understood any more than they were universally admired. In any case, he was wholly *sui generis* – of his own kind only. He had no disciples or followers, and his influence was dispersed and not easily earmarked. In *The Art Work of the Future* (1849), he wrote that one person should be in charge of all aspects of a performance, including staging and acting. By that time 'directors' did exist, and often bore that name, but they were not quite directors in the modern sense and the interpretation of a part remained the business of the actor.

Above left: Wagner's Festspielhaus or festival theatre, built on a hill above the town of Bayreuth. Wagner persuaded Ludwig II of Bavaria to subsidize the project in return for staging the world premières of the music dramas forming the Ring cycle in the Bavarian National Theatre in Munich. In fact, after the first two had appeared in Munich, Ludwig agreed to forgo this condition.

Above: The Flight of Sieglinde from *Die Walküre* ('The Valkyrie').

operetta

Musical drama takes many forms and there are no clear causal distinctions between comic opera, operetta and musical comedy. Musical comedy is commonly regarded as an American form, though it was not invented there and is not unique to the U.S.A., while operetta ('little opera') is the name generally given to the light opera of the late 19th century. It makes more demands on the singers than musical comedy and is distinguished from opera by its light-hearted plot and because it combines songs with spoken dialogue.

Antecedents

Among the progenitors of operetta were the English ballad opera, using popular songs, of which the first example was Allan Ramsay's *The Gentle Shepherd* (1725). The immense success of Gay's *The Beggar's Opera* (1728) started a vogue that lasted for 30 years. One of these ballad operas, *The Devil to Pay* (1731) by Charles Coffee, was translated into German and started the German equivalent of the form, known as Singspiel ('song-speech'), which influenced the development of grand opera in Germany. Mozart's *Die Entführung aus dem Serail* ('The Abduction from the Seraglio') and Beethoven's *Fidelio* are examples of operas that include ordinary speech.

Vienna

Vienna is often seen as the heart of operetta, thanks largely to the Strauss family, especially Johann Strauss the younger (1825–99), who frequently toured Europe and, besides his famous waltzes, composed 16 operettas, of which the most popular today is *Die Fledermaus* ('The Bat', 1874). His successor, the Hungarian Franz Lehár (1870–1948), who settled in Vienna after the success of his early operettas, hit gold with *Die lustige Witwe* ('The Merry Widow', 1905), not only in turn-of-the-century Vienna, but throughout the world then and since. He was followed by others, including Oscar Straus (1870–1954), Austrian-born but unrelated to the famous Strauss family. There are still theatres in Vienna and Budapest that specialize in operettas.

Offenbach

Perhaps the greatest composer of operettas was Jacques Offenbach (1819–80), a German Jew (son of a Cologne cantor) who settled in Paris and became, as Rossini said, 'the king of the Champs Elysées'. His command of humour and melody was unrivalled – even Wagner admired him – and in spite of topical satire that is now obscure (a persistent problem in operetta revivals), the finest of his 90-odd operettas are still performed, especially *Orpheus in the Underworld* (1858). Besides being the alleged source of the can-can, it is a brilliant satire of France during the Second Empire, the fall of which in the Franco-Prussian War also led to Offenbach's fall in popularity. His work declined in quality and his pre-eminence was challenged by Johann Strauss. He died a few months before the première of his greatest work and only grand opera, *The Tales of Hoffman* (1881).

Gilbert and Sullivan

In England, the dual monarchs of operetta were Gilbert and Sullivan (1842–1900). Gilbert was a well-known author of extravaganzas and burlesques when their collaboration began in 1871; Sullivan had made his name as a serious composer and had written two briefly successful operettas with another librettist. Both worked at various times with other partners, but with only passing success. The operettas they wrote together were shown, from *Patience* onwards, at the Savoy Theatre, opened in 1881 by Richard d'Oyly Carte specifically for their works. More than half have been performed steadily ever since, not only by the original D'Oyly Carte company, but also by

Above: Caricature of Jacques Offenbach, from the front page of *La Lune*, 4 November 1866.

Operettas

1871 *Thespis* (lost)
1875 *Trial by Jury* (one act)
1877 *The Sorcerer*
1878 *HMS Pinafore*
1879 *The Pirates of Penzance*
1880 *Patience*
1882 *Iolanthe*
1884 *Princess Ida*
1885 *The Mikado*
1887 *Ruddigore*
1888 *The Yeomen of the Guard*
1889 *The Gondoliers*
1893 *Utopia Limited*
1895 *The Grand Duke*

Plays by Gilbert

1886 *Dulcamara*
1870 *The Palace of Truth*
1871 *Pygmalion and Galatea*
1876 *Dan'l Druce, Blacksmith*
1877 *Engaged*
and several others

Verse

1869 *Bab Ballads*

Operettas by Sullivan with other librettists

1867 *Cox and Box* (Burnand)
1867 *Contrabandista* (Burnand)
1875 *The Zoo* (Stevenson)
1892 *Haddon Hall* (Grundy)
1895 *The Chieftain* (Burnand)
1898 *The Beauty Stone* (Pinero and Carr)
1899 *The Rose of Persia* (Hood)

Chief orchestral works

1862 *Music for The Tempest*
1864-66 *Symphony in E*
1866 *In Memoriam* (overture)
1866 *Cello concerto*
1871 *Overture di Ballo*
1890 *Ivanhoe* (opera)
1897 *Imperial March*
Also: oratorios and cantatas, incidental music,
anthems, hymns, ballads, songs

Quotes

When all night long a chap remains
On sentry-go, to chase monotony
He exercises of his brains,
That is, assuming that he's got any.
Though never nurtured in the lap
Of luxury, yet I admonish you,
I am an intellectual chap,
And think of things that would astonish you.
I often think it's comical
    How Nature always does contrive
That every boy and every gal,
    That's born into the world alive,
Is either a little Liberal,
    Or else a little Conservative!
Iolanthe

    My object all sublime
    I shall achieve in time–
To let the punishment fit the crime–
    The punishment fit the crime;
    And make each prisoner pent
    Unwillingly represent
A source of innocent merriment!
    Of innocent merriment.
The Mikado

When I was a lad I served a term
As office boy to an Attorney's firm.
I cleaned the windows and I swept the floor,
And I polished up the handle of the big front door.
    I polished up that handle so carefullee
    That now I am the Ruler of the Queen's Navee!
HMS Pinafore

Left: Poster for Gilbert and Sullivan's *The Yeomen of the Guard*, 1888.

amateur groups throughout the country. The most popular are: *HMS Pinafore*, *The Pirates of Penzance*, *Patience*, *Iolanthe*, *The Mikado*, *The Yeomen of the Guard* and *The Gondoliers*. Their association lasted 20 years, but it was a dream partnership only in terms of its products. Gilbert was a difficult, irascible man, and Sullivan placed far greater store on his 'serious' compositions. Some of Sullivan's other works are still occasionally performed today, though Gilbert is otherwise forgotten, except for the *Bab Ballads*. Later efforts to imitate or update them have served to demonstrate that the combination of Gilbert's sometimes cruel wit, intricate wordplay and command of verse rhythm with Sullivan's versatility, melodic facility and staggering gift for pastiche produced something unique.

actors and directors

By 1800, the theatre had become more self-conscious. Many books had been written about theatre history and about theatre as an art, many manuals published on theatre crafts, as well as more philosophical works on the nature of performance art. Perhaps the most significant change in the late 19th century was the continuing, accelerating trend towards stage realism. An older generation of famous actors had made some contribution. In England, Sir Henry Irving had challenged the old school of acting personified by Macready (though Irving was not a naturalistic actor, being famous for his unusual elocution). His American counterpart, the influential American tragedian Edwin Booth (1833–93), brother of President Lincoln's assassin, appeared at the Lyceum at Irving's invitation: they alternated the parts of Iago and Othello.

The Meininger Company

Notwithstanding the rise of public theatre, some companies still depended on private patrons. One of these was maintained by the Duke of Saxe-Meiningen (1826–1914), who was producer and designer, with his wife Ellen Franz (1839–1933), an actress. From 1866, the leading actor was Ludwig Chronegk (1837–91), who took charge of directing rehearsals and was partly responsible for the distinction of the company, which toured Europe from 1874 to 1890. It appeared at Drury Lane in London in the 1880s, playing Shakespeare in German, among other classics. The company was based on tight ensemble acting, and was particularly noted for handling large groups. Crowd scenes were carefully choreographed, with each member individually characterized as well as forming part of the larger 'character' – the crowd itself. Movement, space and grouping were subtly planned, and equal attention was given to authenticity of scenery and costume. Scenery was three-dimensional, employing the box set with an arrangement of 'flats' rather than the traditional, two-dimensional, painted set. The flow of the drama was maintained with versatile sets incorporating different levels, and the chief actors were expected to play minor parts as well as leading roles, anticipating Stanislavsky's dictum: 'Today Hamlet, tomorrow an extra . . .'. The Meininger Company appeared in Moscow in 1885 and 1890, when Stanislavsky saw it.

Stanislavsky

The Russian actor Konstantin Alexeyev (1863–1938), who took the stage name Stanislavsky, founded the Moscow Arts Theatre, together with Vladimir Nemirovich-Danchenko (1859–1943), in 1898. Though an amateur, Stanislavsky was fiercely committed to the art of theatre. In his day, in spite of the great flowering of realist drama in Russia, the style of acting was still rhetorical, with dialogue declaimed rather than spoken. Stanislavsky, dissatisfied with the style of both acting and production, worked out his own method as director of the drama productions of the recently founded Society of Art and Literature. He was also immensely stimulated by the Meininger Company in 1890. His famous meeting with the playwright Nemirovich-Danchenko took place in 1897. The latter was literary manager of the Moscow Imperial (Maly) Theatre, and also taught dramatic studies. He had an outstanding group of young actors in his class whom he was anxious to keep together. The meeting of minds with Stanislavsky produced a resolve to create a brand new kind of theatre, where the tired clichés of contemporary acting and production values would be banished.

The Moscow Arts Theatre

A theatre was acquired and the impending revolution was signalled at the very start of the first production when the curtain, instead of rising as was customary, parted from the middle. The opening production was a success, but the financial situation of the company remained fragile. The decisive breakthrough came with its fourth production, *The Seagull*, by Anton Chekhov. It was recommended by Nemirovich-Danchenko, though Stanislavsky was at first lukewarm. The play had been produced earlier in St Petersburg, where it was a complete flop – because the actors did not know how to handle

Chekhov's dialogue. As he studied the text, Stanislavsky perceived that Chekhov too was a revolutionary. He had created a new kind of drama perfectly attuned to Stanislavsky's ideas on production, a drama that depended as much on what is not said as on actual dialogue, where the characters, like real people, seldom speak openly about deep feelings. His production of *The Seagull* was a spectacular success (a seagull was adopted as the emblem of the Moscow Arts), and in due course was followed by Chekhov's subsequent masterpieces. But even Stanislavsky's actors had trouble with Tolstoy's peasant characters.

Antoine

Stanislavsky's insistence on 'inner truth', the emotional identification of the actor with the character, was to have great influence, especially in America, but he was not the only theatrical reformer of the late 19th century. André Antoine (1858–1943) founded the Théâtre Libre as a club in Paris in 1887, specifically for the new naturalistic drama of Ibsen and others. He demanded painstakingly accurate sets and a more natural performance. His influence was to be long-lasting. As the Théâtre Antoine, it was a centre of French existentialism after the Second World War. Many plays by contemporary British and American dramatists received their first French production there.

Below: Chekhov (wearing pince-nez, centre) reads *The Seagull* to the cast at the Moscow Arts Theatre in 1898. Stanislavsky is on his right, Nemirovich-Danchenko is standing at far left.

Right: Stanislavsky, one of the most influential of all directors. He was not at first keen on *The Seagull*, but changed his mind after more careful study. Though the association was the making of both Chekhov and the Moscow Arts Theatre, the playwright never much cared for Stanislavsky's productions.

stock companies
and repertory

The history of the theatre tends naturally to concentrate on great centres such as London and New York. They are not typical of theatre on a national level, where the long runs of modern Broadway and the West End were unknown.

Circuit companies

From the 18th century the main dramatic fare in England was provided by the circuit companies. They were centred on a major theatre in a provincial city, usually called the Theatre Royal and named after the two authorized theatres of Restoration London. Strictly speaking, any provincial Theatre Royal had no right to the name (since it was licensed not by royal authority, but by local magistrates), but through association the name had become a general term for a theatre. Besides its headquarters, the circuit included permanent theatres in neighbouring towns, sometimes one or two, sometimes a dozen or more. The system arose through general agreement after a number of embarrassing incidents when two touring companies arrived simultaneously in the same place, resulting, for example, in two productions of *The Beggar's Opera* opening in Newcastle on the same night. Some circuit companies were large enough to stage productions in two different towns at the same time. The company was run by a manager, such as Mrs Sarah Baker (died 1816), who inherited a company from her mother and ran the Kent circuit for about 50 years, building ten new theatres on her circuit.

Stock companies

The advent of railways made touring much easier, and led eventually to the disappearance of the circuits and of the stock companies. In Britain and America this term was generally used for a substantial, permanent company attached to one (or more) theatres and operating on the repertory system. Some circuit companies fell into this category, but it also included London theatres, one of the last stock companies being Irving's at the Lyceum. Although the name came into general use only in the early 19th century, there was of course nothing new about stock companies, since the Restoration theatres had operated on this principle, as do large subsidized companies today. In America the term 'summer stock' is applied to provincial theatres, often in resort areas, which provide a summer season and which are generally run on a semi-permanent basis, although the actors may change from year to year.

Stock companies, like the commedia dell'arte, were based on a group of actors who specialized in a certain kind of part – though they had to be

Left: The Mary Young Theater, named after its founder and director, on Cape Cod, Massachusetts, a 'summer stock' theatre, reliant on the annual retreat of the prosperous to their summer houses in attractive rural areas.

Right: A production of Noël Coward's *Hay Fever* at the Criterion Theater in the summer resort of Bar Harbor, Maine, in 1933.

prepared to take on others as the exigencies of the business dictated. The leader was the Tragedian, a senior actor who played the main dramatic roles. There was also a Juvenile Tragedian, who might play Macduff to his senior's Macbeth, an Old Man, Old Woman, Heavy Father (the villain in melodramas), Heavy Woman, Low Comedian, as well as various Utilities and Supernumeraries, or Supers, playing walk-on roles. The stock companies were a valuable training ground for actors, and most learned their business in this environment. Assuming they were paid – not all Supers were – they also gained a measure of security in a notoriously insecure profession.

Strolling players

In the 19th century, as in earlier times, not all theatre was performed in permanent buildings. The tradition of the strolling players, which dated back to Elizabethan times, was still going strong. Bands of performers travelled around the country, following fairs or any other events that attracted an audience, with their sets and costumes loaded on a cart, and appearing in taverns or barns. In America this was an adventurous business, and to reach the frontier settlements and mining towns companies had to contend with more menacing problems than the inadequacies of the venue. In England, such players were notoriously poor, some allegedly living on turnips snatched from the fields.

Repertory

Repertory, or repertoire, means a group of plays that are regularly produced, whether as to a whole national drama or the productions of a particular company in a single season. The long-running play, performed every night for weeks or months and subsequently perhaps going on tour, is a recent phenomenon associated primarily with big, multi-theatre cities such as London and New York. In earlier times all theatres had a large repertory, seldom performing the same play more than one night at a time. The system was also flexible: unsuccessful plays were quickly dropped, new ones introduced at short notice, and successful plays retained year after year. Most European theatre traditionally ran on a repertory system, but in England the name is particularly applied to the professional provincial theatres established in the 1930s–1950s, which normally ran the same play for a short, finite run and hence were not properly repertory theatres at all. More recently, of course, repertory theatre has increased, thanks largely to subsidies, in both Britain and America.

copyright

At one time the law of copyright did not exist; in fact the very idea of copyright was unknown. There was very little to stop someone producing a play for public performance without consideration for or consultation with its author, providing he could get hold of a script.

Above: Sir Robert Walpole, regarded as the first English prime minister, who dominated the government between about 1720 and 1740. He tried, not very successfully, to impose severe restrictions on theatres but did not prevent a series of copyright acts giving authors some property in their publications.

Printing

Before the invention of printing, however, it was hardly possible to obtain a script except by theft, an infringement of the law which provided considerable security. The fact that, once printed, a book did not belong to its author or publisher raised new questions, and eventually gave rise to the previously unknown idea of copyright. But the means by which an author's rights came to be protected were long delayed, bewildering in number and, for many years, unsatisfactory in their results.

From the early 16th century, the right to print books belonged with the Crown; printers had to apply for a royal licence. There were 22 master print-ers in London in 1591. They were required to be members of the Stationers' Company, which kept a record of every book published – now a useful resource for literary historians and then a safeguard against piracy by another printer. By the standards of the time, the Stationers' Company was strictly run. It had the right to destroy the presses of non-registered printers. Still, only about two-thirds of printed books were registered.

In the 16th–17th centuries, legislation was concerned with protecting liter-ary property only as an incidental, being mainly motivated by the desire of the government to exercise control over what was written or performed. Tightening of restrictions in the 17th century provoked the poet Milton's *Areopagitica* (1644), a defence (itself unlicensed and unregistered) of the free-dom of the press. A charter of 1684 reinforced the powers of the Stationers' Company, declaring that every member who 'shall be the proprietor of any book, shall have and enjoy such sole right, power, privilege and authority of printing such book . . .' The motive, however, was still state control.

The idea of copyright

Although the term had not yet been invented – it was first recorded in 1767 – the Act of Parliament 'for increase of learning' of 1709 implicitly acknowl-edged the notion of copyright, which in the book trade, at least, was already regarded as founded on legal principle, insofar as the author of a book, or the printer/publisher/bookseller to whom he had assigned the rights, was con-cerned. The motive for the act was largely agitation by booksellers, not authors, who had been suffering increasingly from piracy. The act gave authors exclusive rights (when they retained them) to publish their work for a period of 21 years. This of course applied to all literature, including plays. But the act, like most acts, created various new problems, the subject of much future legal and judicial action.

The Bulwer-Lytton Act

It is not, however, necessary to make a copy of a play in order to perform it. Dramatists therefore were less well protected, and although Common Law might have protected the author of an unpublished play from unauthorized performance, this seems never to have been tested in the courts. The anomaly was corrected in the Dramatic Copyright Act of 1833, known as the Bulwer-Lytton Act, after the popular and influential novelist and dramatist. It protected performing rights regardless of whether the play had been published and was thus licensed. Needless to say, the act contained the usual legal snags. A major fault was the failure to cover performances based on non-dramatic works, such as novels, and for some years, hack playwrights churned out melodramas by the dozen based on other people's work. Another snag was the presumption that if a play were published before it was performed, performing rights were lost. This gave rise to the custom of dramatists arranging a public reading of their play before publication.

The problems of copyright were no simpler in other countries. In the U.S.A., copyright law was as confused – and confusing – in the 19th century as it was in Britain. It was not properly overhauled until the Copyright Act of 1909.

Above: Edward Bulwer-Lytton was enormously popular in his day though now unread and unperformed. As an M.P., he played an important part in securing passage of the Dramatic Copyright Act of 1833, often called after him.

The Berne Convention

Originally agreed in 1896, and often amended subsequently, the Berne Convention established an International Copyright Union, which now includes about 80 states. An author from a signatory state is automatically assured of the same protection in a foreign state as a citizen of that state. Some large countries did not sign; foreign authors popular in the old Soviet Union, for example, used frequently to deplore this fact.

Copyright remains a fruitful field for lawyers, and the challenges grow on almost a daily basis as the rapid progress of information technology continues. The general trend has been in favour of authors' rights, for example by the extension of the copyright period and the creation of agencies that collect fees for library loans, photocopying, broadcasts, electronic reproduction, etc.

Left: Mrs Siddons as the Tragic Muse, after Reynolds. She was the eldest of twelve children in a notable theatrical dynasty, the Kembles.

Right: Eleonora Duse, Bernhardt's great rival, considered by some the finer actress. She was famous for her moments of stillness: the power to communicate while apparently doing nothing is often the sign of a great actor.

actresses

Although Noel Coward, a century later, might humorously advise, 'Don't put your daughter on the stage, Mrs Worthington', by the 19th century acting had ceased to be the dubious profession it once was. Successful actors could command admiration and respect – Garrick, for example, was buried in Westminster Abbey. It was an era of stars, whose popular stature was not equalled until the rise of Hollywood, but while glamour certainly featured, talent more than looks (or image) created the 19th-century star of the stage. Many of the great actresses came from theatre families. While that may suggest inherited talents, it also confirms that, though it was possible to achieve fame and respectability, the profession was not open to many young women without connections. However, few professions were.

The Kembles

The Kembles were one of the greatest English theatrical dynasties. Sarah Siddons (1755–1831), sister of John Philip and Charles Kemble, was the greatest tragic actress of her day, famously commemorated in a portrait by Reynolds as 'The Tragic Muse'. After a disastrous first appearance with Garrick, she learned her trade on the Yorkshire circuit and returned triumphant. She and her brother were virtually the founders of the English Classical style, heroic, monumental, yet passionate. Magnificently imposing, she conveyed both nobility and tenderness, and critics adored her. Highly intelligent – she was a friend of Samuel Johnson – she declined to play comedy, and was famous above all for her Lady Macbeth. Her niece, Fanny Kemble, was widely regarded as her outstanding successor.

The French tragic muse

The French answer to Mrs Siddons's Lady Macbeth was the Phèdre of Elisa Rachel (1820–58), described by the theatre scholar Michael Booth as 'an incandescent performance, one of the greatest in the history of acting'. A contemporary described her first entry: 'You felt that she was wasting away under the fire within, that she was standing on the verge of the grave with pallid face, hot eyes, emaciated frame – an awful ghastly apparition.' Others paid tribute to her panther-like grace and manifest emotional tension. Coming from a destitute Jewish family, her training was cut short by a grasping father, but her first appearance at the Comédie-Française, in Corneille's Horace, was a sensation. Although she also played contemporary roles, Rachel was chiefly responsible for the revival of French classicism in the 1840s. She died at 38, worn out by overwork, frenetic affairs and tuberculosis stemming from her wretched childhood.

Duse and Bernhardt

Eleonora Duse (1858–1924) was born into an Italian theatrical family and first appeared on stage aged four. Her technique was formidable. She was noted for her beauty of gesture, and was reputed to be able to change the colour of her complexion at will. Although primarily a tragedienne, she played in the new naturalistic drama of Ibsen and others, and may have been the inspira-

tion for Mme Arkadina in *The Seagull*, Chekhov having seen her as Shakespeare's Cleopatra. From the 1890s she was heavily committed to the plays of the proto-fascist poet Gabriele D'Annunzio, her lover. By coincidence, she appeared in London in 1895 as Magda in Hermann Sudermann's *Heimat*, at the same time as Sarah Bernhardt (1845–1923) in a rival production. Critics were divided, but Bernard Shaw preferred Duse's performance.

'The divine Sarah' was probably the most famous, perhaps greatest, actress of all time. The illegitimate daughter of a prostitute, she first appeared at the Comédie-Française in 1862, in Racine. Although she was at her sensational peak in *Phèdre*, she was equally famous for the Romantic heroines of Hugo, and in Beaumarchais and other contemporaries – also as Hamlet. Scratchy recordings do little credit to Bernhardt's famously beautiful voice, but photographs confirm her striking beauty and the 'slim figure and dark eyes [that] made her especially suited for roles requiring seductiveness'. A world-famous actress and idol – she toured the U.S.A. nine times – she wrote and produced her own plays and was a gifted poet, painter and sculptor. Highly unconventional (reputed to sleep in a coffin), she never adapted to the rigid conventions of the Comédie-Française, and was probably at her best abroad or, from 1899, at her own Théâtre Sarah Bernhardt. Nothing stopped her, not even the loss of a leg in 1915 after an accident.

Terry

Ellen Terry (1847–1928) was the most famous member of a theatrical dynasty stretching from her father to Sir John Gielgud, her great-nephew. When she celebrated her jubilee in 1906, she appeared with 28 of her relations. She first made her name with the Keans, but was probably at her best when, after a long absence, including a brief marriage to the painter G. F. Watts, she joined Sir Henry Irving at the Lyceum in 1878, later becoming his lover. In spite of highly praised performances as Cordelia and Desdemona, she was not at her best in tragedy – unlike most great actresses. On stage she had a special gift of fresh, joyful, seemingly spontaneous luminosity, and the priceless ability to inspire others to match her. From 1902 she managed several theatres and lectured on Shakespeare – she was an astute critic of the drama.

Judaism was traditionally hostile to the theatre, which smacked of false idols, but, as with Christianity, that did not prevent the growth of a popular dramatic tradition. It probably originated in the responses of the synagogue service, much as Christian religious drama emerged from the liturgy. There are records of Jewish actors in ancient Rome, and a Jewish dramatist, Ezekiel of Alexandria, wrote a tragedy in Greek on the subject of the Exodus. Since Jews were not identified with a nation until recently, Jewish drama, unlike other 'national' dramas, is defined not by political or geographical boundaries, but simply by language. Originally this was Hebrew, but of particular interest is the Yiddish theatre of the 19th and 20th centuries. Yiddish is a blend of Germanic dialects, with borrowings from Hebrew and other languages, which originated in the medieval ghettos of central Europe, becoming the everyday language of most Jewish communities in Europe. There was also a dramatic tradition in Ladino, the language of the Sephardic Jews of the Mediterranean and the Middle East, which was exclusively read, not performed.

Jewish
drama

Above: Maurice Schwartz with his wife leaving America, late in life, for Israel. He was the leading figure in the lively though short renaissance of Yiddish theatre between the world wars.

Purim plays

The Jewish festival of Purim, on the 24th Adar (March in the Christian calendar), commemorates the salvation of the Jews in Persia, as related in the Book of Esther. A minor festival, it had from the late Middle Ages a carnival atmosphere, including a play, originally extemporized, based on the story of Queen Esther and the Persian vizier Haman. The performances, which eventually came to embrace other Old Testament stories, included song and dance and the kind of rough humour associated with the mystery plays. They constantly risked offending the religious authorities, and in the 17th century there was a partially successful movement to rid the Purim plays of some of their coarseness. The tradition was strongest in rural areas, surviving until the 19th century in eastern Europe. It was at least distantly related to the tradition of Italian comedy, some of the stock characters resembling those of the commedia dell'arte, while one version in German is known from the 16th- and 17th-century English troupes of actors in Europe. The rise of a permanent, professional, Yiddish theatre finally brought the tradition to a close.

Yiddish theatre

The Haskalah or Enlightenment movement, which had attempted to reform the Purim plays, was largely responsible for encouraging Hebrew writers to adopt Yiddish, the vernacular of the masses. One of the first permanent Yiddish theatres was founded in Russia by the playwright Abraham Goldfaden (1840–1908), the author of about 400 plays, popular in nature, with song and dance, racy humour and satire, and some borrowing from other European traditions. Goldfaden was also responsible for the appearance of female actors. After the anti-Semitic repression of the 1880s and 90s, he, with many others,

Above: A scene from a New
York production of *Two
Hundred Thousand*, adapted
from a story by Sholom
Aleichem.

left the country. In 1903 he settled in the U.S.A. where a Yiddish theatre had
been founded in New York, 20 years earlier. It served an important social
function, entertaining the intensely poor, non-English-speaking Jewish immi-
grants with its comical or sentimental plays about life in the communities
from which they had been driven by persecution.

The 20th century

Later writers, such as Jacob Gordin (1853–1909) and Halper Leivick
(1888–1962), revivified the old-fashioned Yiddish theatre and brought it up to
date. Gordin took much of his material from non-Jewish sources (including
Shakespeare and Goethe), recasting it in a Jewish context. He put an end to
the persistent custom of improvisation and in dramatic terms his work represents a marked advance over the more traditional material.

A number of other Yiddish theatres were established in Europe and
America, including the Moscow State Jewish Theatre, originally founded in St
Petersburg in 1919. It survived until 1948 and greatly influenced Maurice
Schwartz (1889–1960) and others. Schwartz, an actor-director born in the
Ukraine, was a major figure in the New World, founding the Yiddish Art
Theatre, the prototype of several others, in 1926. At about that time the
Yiddish theatre approached its peak, with companies flourishing in London (in
Whitechapel), Paris and Buenos Aires, as well as the traditional centres of
Jewish culture. There were no fewer than twelve Yiddish theatres in New York
alone. Schwartz broadened the repertoire, encouraged new writers, and discovered Sholom Aleichem (1859–1916), probably the best-known Yiddish
writer, if only for the play *Tevye the Milkman*, based on his short story, which
became a hit as a musical on Broadway and the West End in the 1960s as
Fiddler on the Roof. As assimilation continued, Jewish immigration diminished,
and American Jews all spoke English, the Yiddish theatre as a popular institution inevitably fell into decline and most of the theatres closed. At the
end of his life Schwartz moved to Israel, hoping to found a new Yiddish
Theatre there.

For theatre in general, the dominant preoccupation of the last half of the 19th century was the effort, shortly to be challenged by the cinema, towards amazingly realistic effects.

The Meininger Company was a leading influence here, leading to the theatres of Antoine and Stanislavsky, while in England, Irving and his successor, Herbert Beerbohm Tree (1853–1917), brought stage realism to a peak. A review of Irving's production of *Romeo and Juliet* devotes more space to the scenic artistry, effects and lighting than to the acting, and the critic Joseph Knight, discussing Irving's *Hamlet*, remarked that 'to the majority of the audience the play is wholly spectacle, and Shakespeare's words . . . a species of incidental music'. But, probably, the most masterly effects, the most stunning stage spectacles, were provided by David Belasco.

popular drama
in the 1890s

Actor-directors

It is misleading to think of either Duke George of Saxe-Meiningen or of Irving as directors in the modern sense. The term was often used, but there was really no such individual, although many of the functions of the modern director were carried out one way or another. The general organization of rehearsals, stage movement, and more, was often in the hands of one person. Some sense of unity was thus imposed, but he or she was essentially a manager, usually also the leading actor, sometimes the playwright. He did not tell an actor how a part should be played, and owing to the conventions of Classical acting, it was probably familiar to audience and performers alike: since actors were usually playing the type of role in which they specialized, it was perhaps not necessary to do so. Another, more practical reason was that long runs were exceptional or non-existent. Most theatres operated on something close to the repertory system, which meant that rehearsal time was strictly limited and actors had to play many different parts in quick succession (Irving played 428 different parts in 30 months). The situation varied in different countries. In Germany there was an official called the Dramaturg, who oversaw text and context, but did not conduct rehearsals. A director who works with the actors on the interpretation of the play and its individual characters was unknown until the last years of the century.

Belasco

David Belasco (1859–1931) was a huge personality in American theatre and the man who demonstrated the potential of the long run (*The Music Master* ran for four years). He was a child actor, but gave up acting as an adult to become a dextrous playwright, taking much of his material from novels, reworking old plays and above all staging spectacular melodramas. From 1886 he was at the New York Lyceum, where his most popular plays included *The Girl I Left Behind Me* (1893) and *Madame Butterfly* (1900), based on a story, and the basis of Puccini's opera. He took over his own theatre on West 42nd Street in 1902 (the present Belasco Theater opened under that name in 1910), where he produced *The Music Master*, the play that made the reputation of the actor David Warfield, and *The Girl of the Golden West*.

Although he had a long and fruitful association with Warfield, Belasco's technicians were possibly more important than his actors. He taught himself the techniques of stagecraft and brought the powerful effects of melodrama to the more everyday setting of his own plays. Like Irving, he was intent on realism, and the Indians v. Cavalry fights of Davy Crockett were described as 'an exact copy of such a scene' by a contemporary, who noted that the cavalry were 'covered with alkali dust'. In this play Belasco divided the stage in three and kept three stories going (Indians, settlers, cavalry) until they joined up in the climax. In a way, Belasco was teaching Hollywood its business (Cecil B. de Mille was his assistant). Nothing was beyond him: snow storms, real horses, effects the infant cinema could not compete with. However, Belasco's production costs were enormous, making long runs vital.

Oscar Wilde

The various forms of popular entertainment (see page 112) were still going strong into the new century, farce was at its peak, and there was still a place for the 'well-made play' and the aristocratic comedy. Oscar Wilde (1854–1900) is probably most familiar today because of his striking persona and miserable decline – imprisoned and ruined for homosexuality. However, he was the author of one of the most enjoyable comedies of the British (Wilde was Irish) theatre, *The Importance of Being Earnest* (1895), in which the brilliantly witty, fast-moving dialogue does not obscure deft plotting and characterisation. Wilde had three earlier successes in this vein, notably *Lady Windermere's Fan*, slightly marred by sentimentality. He wrote other plays, little remembered now, except perhaps his last, a poetic drama in one act, *Salomé*, written in French, banned in England, but produced in Paris by Bernhardt in 1896.

music hall

Besides drama, in the late 19th century many types of popular performance, collectively described by the highly appropriate word 'variety', kept ordinary people amused. Variety appealed especially to the managers, increasingly businessmen outside the theatrical tradition, who controlled the big theatres. They were not much interested in drama as an art. Rather, they sought to provide sure-fire, popular, i.e. commercially profitable, entertainment predominantly for the lower classes – although nearly everyone patronized the music halls, from royalty downwards.

The halls

In Ireland, singing is still frequently part of pub life. Early in the 19th century, some English taverns and, later, 'song-and-supper' clubs provided entertainment in the form of comic songs and monologues while customers ate and drank. It was generally informal, with plenty of interplay between performers, spectators, and the 'chairman' who was host and compère. This type of performance proved so popular that, after the Theatre Regulation Act (1843) banned drinking in theatres, special buildings, music halls, were created for it, providing more highly organized entertainment. The first music hall was the Canterbury in London, which opened in 1852. Soon, they sprang up everywhere, with grand names such as the Alhambra, the Coliseum or the Hippodrome, often later described as a 'Palace of Variety'. At first the entertainment was predominantly songs and music, but comedy soon assumed a greater role, along with various other acts allied to circus. Among famous performers in this area were the acrobat Jules Léotard (1830–70), the original 'Daring Young Man on the Flying Trapeze' whose name is commemorated in the garment he wore, the German-born juggler Paul Cinquevalli (1858–1918), and the famous clown Grock (Karl Wettach, 1880–1959). Mesmerists (hypnotists) were popular for a time.

Stars

The stars of the music halls such as 'Champagne Charlie' (George Laybourn) and the diminutive Jenny Hill ('the Vital Spark') became immensely popular, with corresponding earning capacity, outclassing even the most popular actors of the day, who (even the great Bernhardt), like their successors in television comedy, were prepared to appear on music-hall stages themselves. The old cellars and supper clubs were exclusively male preserves, but the music halls not only encouraged families, but also employed women as comedians as well as singers. There was space for 'promenading' (eyeing up girls) and drinking at the rear of the auditorium. The typical bill consisted of twenty or more different 'turns', in swift succession, calculated to maintain the interest of working people tired after a long day, so that music-hall stars on tour could get by with relatively little material. Most of them were also famous in seasonal pantomime.

Although there are many candidates, perhaps the most successful, or most famous, of Victorian stars were Dan Leno (1860–1904) and Marie Lloyd (1870–1922). Dan Leno, a tiny man who delivered his monologues at break-neck speed, was universally declared by his audience as the funniest they had ever seen. He died insane at 44. A lot of Victorian music-hall entertain-ment would today be adjudged politically incorrect – jingoistic (a handsome baritone in uniform singing a patriotic song was a popular item in most bills), racist or sexist. Marie Lloyd, 'the Queen of the Music Halls', was decidedly risqué by Victorian standards, and her performance on the stage as well as her reputation off it pre-vented her appearance at the annual Royal Command Performance. She specialized in the double entendre and, when told she could not perform a song 'She Sits Among the Cabbages and Peas', changed it to 'She Sits Among the Cabbages and Leeks'. Harry Lauder's guying of his Scottishness would not go down well today, but he was funny ('Here comes my true love –' warbled Harry in the glen, 'no, it's a rabbut') and gained a knight-hood. The music hall tradition, vulgar or not, provided the basis for the best British broad comedy until the arrival of the television age, but most of the music halls themselves disap-peared long before then. Music hall provided great comfort during the First World War, but began to decline immediately afterwards. Only a few 'palaces of variety' survived television's dominance of the entertainment industry.

Revue

Revue, developing in the 1890s, outlasted, and to some extent replaced, music hall in popular-ity. The revue was more akin to continental cabaret (a French invention) and café-spectacle (variously represented by the Moulin Rouge, the Chat Noir or the Folies-Bergère) was in style gen-erally a more intimate entertainment. It too contained a series of short 'acts', but they usually featured some or all the same performers. It appealed to less unso-phisticated tastes, and audiences before 1914 generally wore evening dress. Famous examples included Ziegfeld's Follies in New York and the revues of C.B. Cochran at the London Pavilion in the 1920s. Revue was the natural element for such writers and performers as Noel Coward (1899–1973) and Hermione Gingold (1897–1987), and it enjoyed a revival in the 1960s, sparked by the phenomenally successful *Beyond the Fringe*, originally the work of four Oxford and Cambridge students (Jonathan Miller, Peter Cook, Alan Bennett, Dudley Moore).

Opposite: Marie Lloyd (born Matilda Alice Victoria Wood, original stage name Bella Delmere) with her third husband, a jockey, at home in Golders Green. With her vivacity and broad humour, she was the spirit of cockney comedy.

Below: The recording industry was in its infancy in the days of music hall, but song sheets sold in large numbers to a public who made much of their own entertainment at home.

vaudeville

The American equivalent of the music hall was known as vaudeville, a word adopted from the French and applied to different types of entertainment in the late 19th century. Many British stars of the music hall and much British material crossed the Atlantic, and there was equivalent traffic in the other direction, not to mention several successful Australian acts. Variety in America, however, included distinctive native forms, notably the minstrel show.

Vaudeville

American vaudeville was largely invented by one man. In the post-Civil War period, variety was an affair of sleazy bars and beer halls frequented by drunks and prostitutes. Tony Pastor (1837–1908), a professional clown who had appeared in circus as well as variety, decided to clean it up. In 1865, he opened his first show in a Broadway theatre and by 1881 he was established in the Fourteenth Street Theatre downtown, where vaudeville is said to have originated. He was a performer, not an entrepreneur, always appearing in his own shows (he was also a good singer and songwriter) and never attempting to form an empire, unlike successors such as Edward Albee (1857–1930), grandfather by adoption of the contemporary playwright. Pastor wanted to attract respectable people: lewd acts were rejected, drinking and smoking banned from the auditorium. Vaudeville acts included short sketches (often with big-name actors), animal acts, male impersonators, magicians, 'spectacles', as well as humour and songs. It gave birth to great comedians, such as W. C. Fields and 'Bojangles' (Bill Robinson, a black American) and singers such as Lillian Russell, Marie Dressler (her 'Heaven Will Protect the Working Girl' was a great favourite), Eddie Cantor and Sophie Tucker, 'Last of the Red-Hot Mommas'. At its peak between 1900 and 1920, by the 1930s vaudeville was in decline due to competition from radio and film.

Burlesque

Originally, 'burlesque' referred to a play that aped contemporary drama in a satirical manner, and can be traced to Buckingham's *The Rehearsal* (1671), which mocked the heroic drama of Dryden and others. From the 1860s in America, the term was often used interchangeably with 'vaudeville', and it employed many of the same acts. It sometimes included a sketch roughly in line with the original meaning of the word, and there was also a more or less spicy ingredient. With the advent of films, burlesque deviated from the family-entertainment business and sought an exclusively male audience by including striptease as a major ingredient. Gypsy Rose Lee was the most famous exponent of this dubious art, and the burlesque house, notoriously unbuttoned, acquired an increasingly unsavoury reputation. It was finally banned in New York in 1942.

Minstrel shows

Why acts in which white men blacked their faces with burnt cork and sang songs pretending to be Negro slaves should be so popular with (white) audiences is hard to say, but they certainly were. They predated vaudeville, and were probably originated, in Kentucky in the 1820s, by T. D. Rice (1806–60), the original 'Jim Crow' in a song-and-dance act. His success in New York encouraged the formation of similar groups of blacked-up singers and dancers, together with comic-patter dialogues throughout the U.S.A. They were the most popular amusement throughout the middle decades of the century, unaffected by the interruption of the Civil War, and were no less popular in Britain. Even more than music hall, they provided 'family entertainment', suitable for children as well as adults. The 'nigger minstrels' played banjos, sang Stephen Foster songs ('Old Folks at Home', etc.), and wore striped trousers and waistcoat, with tall white topper or a straw boater. Unlike other forms of popular entertainment, they survived the pressure from films, playing the seaside resorts in summer, and lasted into the television age. 'The Black and White Minstrel Show' was popular on British screens in the 1950s, until growing racial sensitivity finally put an end to the whole phenomenon.

Wild West shows

William F. Cody, 'Buffalo Bill' (died 1917), was a genuine pioneer of westward expansion, once a rider with the Pony Express, who later slaughtered bison to feed the railroad construction gangs and 'Indians' to make life safe for homesteaders – with equal efficiency. In 1869, a novel based on his exploits made him famous, and he cashed in by becoming, first, a star of melodrama, then, for 20 years from 1883, a showman. His Wild West show staged episodes from the pioneer West , stage-coach robberies, Indian fights, round-ups, buffalo hunts, etc. It was hugely popular, drawing immense crowds at Queen Victoria's Jubilee (1887) and the Chicago World's Fair (1893). It made stars of others, including Annie Oakley, a lady sharp-shooter, and included native American chiefs such as the Sioux warrior Sitting Bull, who made a few dollars in return for the extinction of their cultural heritage. There were other, similar shows, and the rodeo, strictly speaking a sport, which features cowboy skills, remains a popular entertainment today.

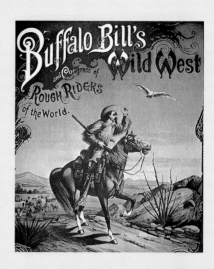

Above: The glamour of the frontier, once it had ceased to exist, sent writers to the West in search of heroes. William Cody was thus transformed into 'Buffalo Bill', and the overdressed frontiersman, seeing a (fictional) play about himself, was smitten by the lure of the footlights.

Below: The figure at the centre of the crowded stage in this New York theatre in 1833 is T. D. Rice, who first became famous in Kentucky in 1828 with a song-and-dance act in which he impersonated an Afro-American, 'Jim Crow' (not yet an abusive name), blacking his face and starting the craze for 'nigger minstrel' shows.

the modern era

chap

The Abbey Theatre, Dublin.

Scandinavians

In the late 19th century change was in the air. Occasional voices were heard calling for theatre to resume its place as commentator on and critic of contemporary society, and demanding that the cultural significance of the drama as a source of profound intellectual and emotional delight should be restored in place of the theatre of 'laughs, glitter and maudlin sentimentality', the 'massage of the masses', then provided by vapid comedies and melodrama. What was required was something similar to the theatre that Wagner had espoused.

Social changes

Huge changes had taken place in Western society during the 19th century. Fundamental assumptions about human beings, society and the universe had been thrown into question by Darwin and Marx, by the discoveries of science, the breakneck advance of technology on many fronts, and the dramatic speeding-up of communications. The arts were being transformed. A few apparently nondescript painters had thrown the visual arts into increasing turmoil, which ultimately spawned the multi-faceted revolution of Modernism. The unsparing Realism of Zola and the soul-searching poetry of Baudelaire had shaken long-accepted literary conventions. In drama, which according to Zola was 'dying of its extravagancies, lies and platitudes', change was overdue, but when it came, it was no less revolutionary than in other arts. 'The time is come', Zola proclaimed, 'to create works of truth.'

He was not ignored. The woods were filling up with idealistic young dissidents. Moreover, Naturalism appealed to a new audience, as demonstrated by the Freie Volksbühne ('Free People's Theatre'), founded in Berlin in 1889. It was not quite 'free' economically, but a seat cost only 50 pfennigs, and it succeeded in its aim of attracting a working-class audience.

Left: Ibsen was one of those writers, like James Joyce, who writes best about his homeland when far removed from it. He lived abroad for nearly 30 years, returning to Norway for only two brief visits.

Right: 'I detest humanity', said Strindberg (right), 'but I cannot live alone.' Tortured by insoluble conflicts, his life was miserable, his work intense, powerful, glaringly uncompromising. Ibsen, latterly, kept Strindberg's photograph on his wall, claiming that it helped him to have 'that madman staring down at me'.

A play, in Zola's view, should be 'a slice of life', and the 'well-made play' of Scribe and his like filled him with scathing contempt. Antoine's Théâtre Libre established Naturalism in the theatre, and the Frei Bühne ('Free Stage'), a theatre club in Berlin, was founded in 1899 as a German equivalent of Antoine's theatre. The outstanding Naturalistic dramatists included Strindberg in Sweden, Gorky in Russia, Jacinto Benavente (1866–1954) in Spain (though not all of his large output can be called Naturalistic), and O'Neill in America. Stanislavsky's productions of Gorky around the turn-of-the-century confirmed its international reputation, although Naturalism was never quite so influential in the British theatre.

Symbolism

Symbolism of some sort is a common feature of virtually all forms of literature in all ages, but in the sense of a specific art form it was a movement in the drama at the end of the 19th century which, though comparatively minor in terms of plays that can be exclusively consigned to it, had a wide-ranging international influence. It embraced literary figures such as Yeats and Hauptmann, ironically the chief German playwright of Naturalism, not to mention novelists such as Virginia Woolf. Symbolism was largely a reaction – not the only one – against the new drama. It arose under the influence of the poet Stephane Mallarmé (1842–98), who advocated a drama that depicted the world of the mind rather than the feelings. Art, to the Symbolists, was a means of understanding rather than feeling, and as a result Symbolist drama, of which Maurice Maeterlinck (1862–1949) was perhaps the leading exponent, tended to be intellectually interesting but static.

The 'headquarters' of Symbolist drama was the Théâtre (Théâtre d'Art) founded by an enterprising young poet, Paul Fort (1872–1960), who challenged most of the tenets of Realism, attacking it for ignoring imagination and fantasy and opting for minimal, stylized scenery that was evocative rather than representational. Besides Maeterlinck, works by Hugo von Hoffmannsthal (1874–1929), Paul Claudel (1869–1955) and the young Yeats were produced in Fort's theatre. The torch was taken up in 1893 by the actor-producer A. F. Lugné-Poë (1869–1940), and his Théâtre de l'Oeuvre. As the original name suggests, the Théâtre Mixte was eclectic, open to anything worthwhile, and its repertoire, still more that of the Théâtre de l'Oeuvre, extended beyond Symbolism.

Above: Edward Rigby as Bread in Maeterlinck's *L'Oiseau bleu* (The Blue Bird, 1909), the most popular of his plays in its day, first produced by Stanislavsky in Moscow. He is now, perhaps, chiefly remembered for *Pelléas et Mélisande* (1892), partly thanks to Debussy's opera (1902).

the theatre of ideas

Disregarding the importance of the 'new drama' initiated by Ibsen and others, not all 19th-century plays were lurid melodramas, frothy operettas and the like. The dramatists we now regard as the giants of Modernism did not attract the audiences for a more conventional drama, represented by the tradition of the 'well-made play', which has continued, through the 'drawing-room drama', into present times.

The 'well-made play'

When this rather uninspiring phrase, from the French *une pièce bien faite*, came into use in the early 19th century, it was as a favourable comment, but two or three generations later it had become, at least in the mouths of the proponents of Naturalistic drama, thoroughly derogatory. 'Well-made' meant 'well-plotted'. It implied a good story, but one mechanically contrived at the expense of psychological Realism. Still, not all the practitioners of the 'well-made play' were artistically or socially worthless and, even if they did set their sights firmly on filling seats – and tills – they were hardly the first, or last, writers whose ambition was to give the audience what it liked.

The outstanding example of this practical approach was the work of Eugène Scribe (1791–1861). He was a thorough professional, in all senses, good and bad. In the first place he was hugely productive, writing, alone or with collaborators, some 400 plays of every kind, from tragedies to operetta librettos. For audiences he provided a welcome antidote to the excesses of Romanticism, with his logical plots and neat resolutions, just as Arthur Wing Pinero (1855–1934) later provided for audiences unable or unwilling to cope with Ibsen. It might be true that, as Dumas said, Scribe's plays 'dissolve . . . into thin air' because he wrote without heart, 'without sincerity', and only one of his plays still holds the stage (the collaborative *Adrienne Lecouvreur*, 1849, the rewarding lead role being played by Rachel and Bernhardt among others), but Scribe nevertheless demonstrated that sheer craftsmanship is not to be ignored and his influence was international. He knew, no less than Chekhov, that 'if there is a gun hanging on the wall in the first act, it must be fired in the last act'.

Naturalism

Naturalism was basically an extension of the Realism for which most 19th-century playwrights in different ways strove. Its approach was supposedly more 'scientific' than the Realism of, say, Ibsen, being concerned with contemporary ideas about heredity and environment. Émile Zola (1840–1902), who dramatized his novel *Thérèse Raquin* – hissed off the stage on its first performance in 1873 – to create what is regarded as the first consciously Naturalistic drama, saw his work as akin to that of an experimental scientist, taking characters of distinctive temperament, usually of lowish social class, placing them in appropriate social circumstances and 'observing' the results.

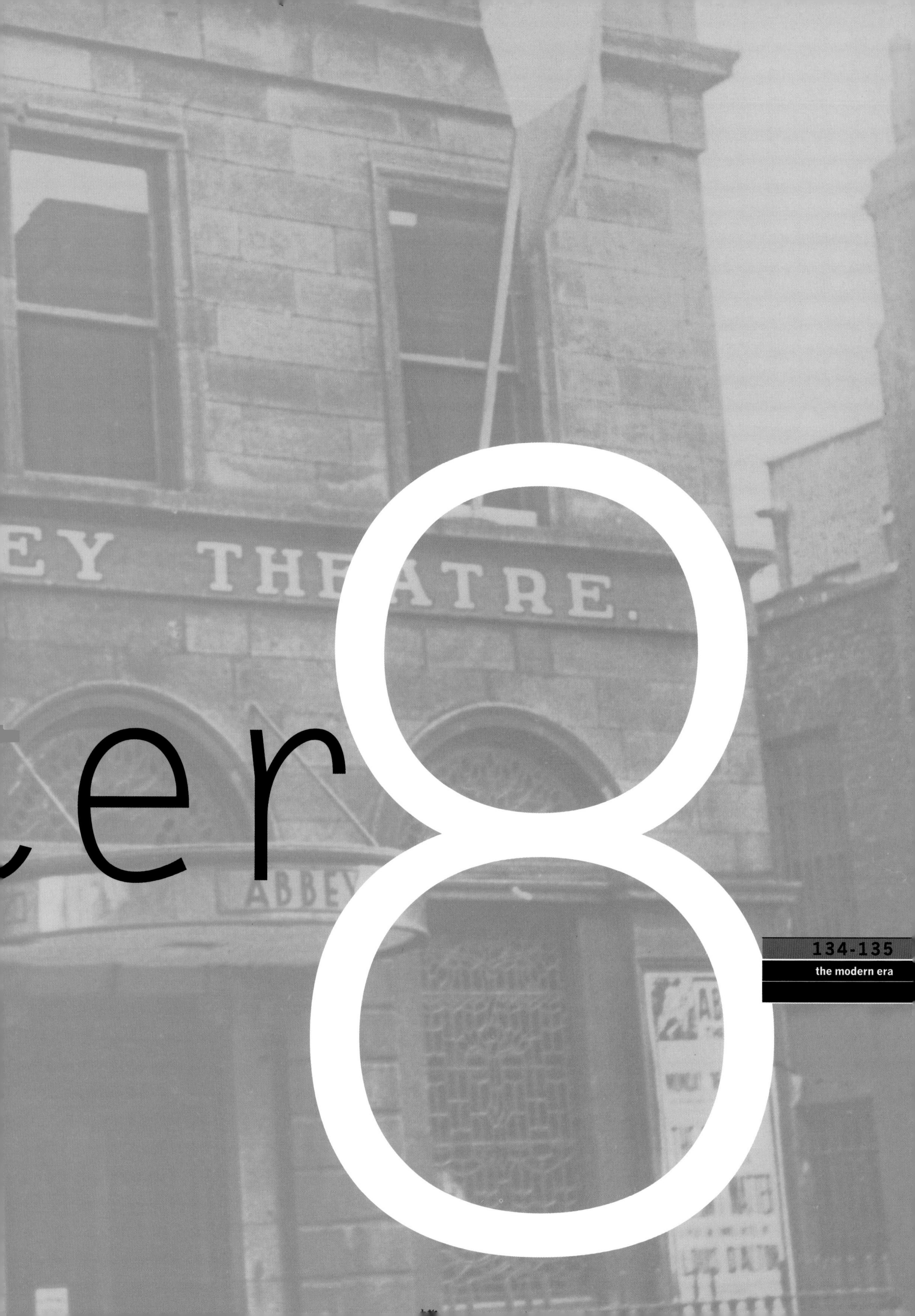

er 8

Ibsen

The man whose plays can be said to have transformed European drama was the Norwegian Henrik Ibsen (1828–1906), probably the greatest dramatist since Shakespeare. He worked in the Bergen theatre and, after a shaky beginning with heroic dramas based on the Scandinavian sagas, he produced a string of works now acknowledged as masterpieces. Ibsen was possessed of a tragic, poetic spirit. His plays were based on insignificant small-town life, depicted with passion and unsparing Realism, occasionally touched by Symbolism (notably in *The Wild Duck*, perhaps his finest drama), but assuming universal meaning – his late plays were much admired by Freud. At the same time, Ibsen had the humbler dramatic gifts of skilful plotting and structure and he wrote in everyday language.

Though he received a pension from an enlightened government after the poetic drama *Brand*, Ibsen's plays did not readily find audiences. When shown in commercial theatres, critical reaction was universally hostile, though many plays, notably *A Doll's House*, were successful with the public. *Ghosts*, which dared to deal with hereditary syphilis, was described by one critic as 'an open drain, a loathsome sore'. But Ibsen had powerful supporters, in England, his translator William Archer (1856–1924) and Archer's friend, the formidable young critic Bernard Shaw (who was also a devotee of Wagner), and in Germany, Otto Brahm (1856–1912), founder of the Freie Volksbühne. It was in such private theatres, including the Théâtre Libre, London's Independent Theatre in Soho (all three chose to open with *Ghosts*), and the Moscow Arts Theatre, that Ibsen could be seen. Commercial productions, when they occurred, were often watered down.

Strindberg

The second great Scandinavian master was the Swede, August Strindberg (1849–1912). Like Ibsen he was an unhappy youth, and never overcame it. His three marriages were disastrous, he was tried (but acquitted) for blasphemy, he suffered a mental breakdown (1894–7), and his life was dogged by despair, reflected in his work's concentration on crime, evil, mental torment and sexual conflict. His early plays, beginning with *Master Olof* (1872) were failures, and in 1889, always intensely concerned with production – and under the stimulus of André Antoine – he opened an experimental theatre in Stockholm, where *Miss Julie* (1888), the first masterpiece of Naturalism and one of the few Strindberg plays now frequently revived, was to have been one of the opening plays. Banned there and nearly everywhere, it was not seen in London until 1927 (a private production) and in New York in 1956. In his later work, Strindberg moved away from Naturalism towards a more subjective, semi-mystical, though still predominantly Realist, drama, in which the seeds of Expressionism – and many other modernisms – can be detected. His last plays, written in 1907–9, such as *The Ghost Sonata*, *The Storm* and *The Great Highway*, were produced at the Intima Theatre in Stockholm that he co-founded. Despite mental strife, Strindberg was an amazingly prolific writer on almost every conceivable subject, and his output, understandably uneven in quality, included much fiction, verse, a nine-volume autobiography and about 60 plays. The best of these represent his greatest work; besides those already mentioned, they include the Naturalistic *The Father* (1887), the *Vasa* trilogy (1899), *The Dance of Death* (1901) and *A Dream Play* (1902). His influence on 20th-century drama, both through his drama and his theoretical writings, was deep and wide-ranging.

Plays
date of first performance or approximate year of writing

1850 *Catalina*
1850 *The Warrior's Barrow*
1853 *Midsummer Eve*
1855 *Lady Inger of Ostraat*
1856 *The Feast of Solhoug*
1857 *Olaf Liljekrans*
1858 *The Vikings at Helgeland*
1860 *Love's Comedy*
1863 *The Pretenders*
1866 *Brand*
1867 *Peer Gynt*
1869 *The League of Youth*
1873 *Emperor and Galilean*
1877 *Pillars of Society*
1879 *A Doll's House*
1881 *Ghosts*
1882 *An Enemy of the People*
1884 *The Wild Duck*
1886 *Rosmersholm*
1888 *The Lady from the Sea*
1890 *Hedda Gabler*
1892 *The Master Builder*
1894 *Little Eyolf*
1896 *John Gabriel Borkman*
1899 *When We Dead Awaken*

Other works

1871 *Poems*
Other verse, articles and miscellaneous writings

Quotes

It's not just what we inherit from our mothers and fathers that haunts us. It's all kinds of old defunct theories, all sorts of old defunct beliefs, and things like that. It's not that they actually live on in us; they are simply lodged there, and we cannot get rid of them. I've only to pick up a newspaper and I seem to see ghosts gliding between the lines.
Ghosts, Act 2

The worst enemy of truth and freedom in our society is the compact majority. Yes, the damned, compact, liberal majority.
An Enemy of the People, Act 4

Take the life-lie away from the average man and straight away you take away his happiness.
The Wild Duck, Act 5

Russians

The revolution in European drama in the late 19th century was led not from established theatrical nations such as France or Great Britain but from the northern fringe, Scandinavia and Russia. Russian literature had blossomed since the time of Pushkin, and by about 1850 Realism, as expounded by the critic V. Belinsky, was in the ascendant. It was represented in the theatre by the prolific Aleksandr Ostrovsky (1823–86), best known abroad for *The Storm* (1860), at the Maly Theatre in Moscow, which had also staged Gogol's classic satire, *The Government Inspector* (1836). The movement peaked under Alexander II (1853–81), whose early reign was a period of relative liberalism and reform. By the end of the century, Symbolism was replacing Realism as the dominant literary current.

Turgenev

Ivan Sergeivich Turgenev (1818–83) wrote his first play as a student in Berlin. Although best known for his novels and short stories, he wrote several more, little known now, culminating in his masterpiece *A Month in the Country* (1855). Set among the rural gentry, it was one of the first psychological dramas, a clear forerunner of Chekhov, but was not performed for some years. Censorship and temporary banishment (for praising Gogol) were Turgenev's reward. He sought refuge in the West and wrote no more plays.

Chekhov

Anton Pavlovich Chekhov (1860–1904) was a physician who, though not in constant practice, regarded himself as a doctor first and a writer second. He made his name with his short stories, and his mature plays might never have been performed, or even written, but for his mutually beneficial partnership with the Moscow Arts Theatre (he also married one of its leading actresses). Chekhov was unique, with few discernible influences and no true successors. His plays depend largely on mood and atmosphere, being concerned with inner feelings not outward actions. Little actually appears to happen, yet audiences' hearts are wrung over the fate of some cherry trees.

Chekhov's plays were little known outside Russia before the 1920s, although the Glasgow Repertory Theatre produced *The Seagull* in 1909. At one time, Western directors tended to overemphasize the Slavic gloom and overlook the subtle but exhilarating humour, perhaps taking their lead from Stanislavsky, who burst into tears on first reading *The Cherry Orchard*. Lately, some directors have overcompensated for that tendency. Though lost or disappointed illusions form much of Chekhov's subject matter, he remains hopeful. Today he is established as the greatest of the Russian dramatists, and his

Plays

1887 *Ivanov*
1888 *The Bear**
1889 *The Proposal**
1889 *The Wood Demon*
1890 *The Wedding* (or *The Marriage Proposal*)*
1896 *The Seagull*
1899 *Uncle Vanya* (a revision of *The Wood Demon*)
1901 *Three Sisters*
1904 *The Cherry Orchard*
Also: *Platonov* (unfinished)
*comedy in one act

Other writings

About 60 short stories, published 1888–1904), including:
The Duel, Ward No. 6, My Life, Three Years, The Butterfly, Neighbours, Terror, The Black Monk, The Russian Master, Ariadne, The Artist's Story, Peasants, Doctor Startsev, The Lady with the Little Dog

Quotes

Nina: Your play's hard to act, there are no living people in it.
Treplev: Living people! We should show life neither as it is nor as it ought to be, but as we see it in our dreams.
The Seagull, *Act I*

Man has been endowed with reason, with the power to create, so that he can add to what he's been given. But up to now he hasn't been a creator, only a destroyer. Forests keep disappearing, rivers dry up, wild life's become extinct, the climate's ruined and the land grows poorer and uglier every day.
Uncle Vanya, *Act I*

When a lot of remedies are suggested for a disease, that means it can't be cured.
The Cherry Orchard, *Act II*

sadly few plays – he died of tuberculosis at 44 – are frequently performed in many languages around the world.

Gorky

The real name of Maxim Gorky (1868–1936) was Peshkovsky; 'Gorky', not inappropriately, means 'bitter'. He had a harsh upbringing, memorably described in his three-volume autobiography, went to work aged eight and became a social dropout, gaining the experience on which he drew for his stories and plays about the poorest classes. Gorky's stories brought some success, and his first play, *Scenes in the House of Bersemenov* (1902) was produced at the Moscow Art Theatre at the urging of Chekhov, whom Gorky admired. In trouble for his radical politics, he was imprisoned after the 1905 Revolution, but released in response to international pressure resulting from the success of his most famous play, *The Lower Depths* (1902). It is set in a dosshouse among the misfits and no-hopers whom Gorky championed. Tolstoy's powerful Naturalistic drama of the peasantry, *The Power of Darkness*, though written in 1886, was censored in Russia and had not yet been produced there. Gorky's later plays, including *Summerfolk* (1904), *Children of the Sun* (1905), *Enemies* (1906) and *The Zykovs* (1913), are largely concerned with the class conflict.

Sympathetic to the Bolsheviks, after the October Revolution of 1917, Gorky helped to save writers, artists and works of art from destruction. Under Stalin, his Naturalism was converted to 'Socialist Realism' and, as the chronicler of the proletariat, he was the Soviet Union's chief literary hero. His home town of Nizhny-Novgorod was renamed Gorky. But Gorky was never entirely in Stalin's pocket. He continued to use his influence to protect less favoured writers, and some suspect that his sudden death was hastened by Stalin's assassins.

Top: A production of *The Cherry Orchard* at the Lyric Theatre, Hammersmith (London), in 1994. Chekhov complained of the directors of the Moscow Arts Theatre's original production: 'They either make me into a cry-baby or into a bore.' Historically, Chekhov has proved a deceptively difficult problem for directors.

Opposite: Maxim Gorky (right) chatting to Stalin on the steps of the Lenin Mausoleum, about 1930.

Many of the major figures in English drama were Irish, including Wilde and Shaw. At the end of the 19th century there was a revival in drama in Ireland, in both the English and Irish languages, connected with the struggle to establish Irish cultural and national autonomy after centuries of English dominance.

Irish theatre

Above: As a playwright Shaw (above) has often been criticized for treating the stage as a soapbox. However, unlike many later propagandizing playwrights, he never forgot the need to entertain, and his serious concerns never suppressed his wit.

Shaw

George Bernard Shaw (1856–1950), critic, dramatist and social reformer, arrived in London from Dublin in 1876 and became, first, a music critic then, from 1895, a drama critic of rare quality. He had no illusions about the contemporary theatre, but was a powerful and tireless supporter of the new drama, especially Ibsen. In 1885 he began writing plays himself. Phenomenally intelligent and brilliantly witty, Shaw eventually became a figure of Johnsonian stature in England, the all-purpose wise man of the Left. His plays have a unique flavour, and only fall short of the highest class because Shaw was generally more interested in ideas than people. His early plays were produced privately because of censorship problems. The first to receive public performance was *Arms and the Man* (1894), a sparkling anti-militaristic satire. His popularity was established in 1904–7 when ten of his plays ran in repertory at the (Royal) Court Theatre in Chelsea, produced by his friend Harley Granville-Barker (1877–1946). The best of Shaw's large output is probably *Saint Joan* (1923). Among the most notable are *Man and Superman* (1903), *Major Barbara* (1905), *The Doctor's Dilemma* (1906), *Pygmalion* (1913, the source of the musical *My Fair Lady*), *Heartbreak House* (1919) and, though seldom performed, *Back to Methuselah* (1921).

Yeats and the Abbey Theatre

The poet and nationalist William Butler Yeats (1865–1939) was a founder of the Irish Literary Society in Dublin in 1899 and of the Abbey Theatre (1904), which had some funding from the philanthropist Annie Horniman (1860–1937). She had subsidized the Avenue Theatre in London that produced Shaw's *Arms and the Man*. The Abbey was beset by political and other disputes, but it rapidly became the centre of the Irish renaissance in drama and home to a tradition of fine, realistic acting, but it moved away from the style of Yeats's early poetic dramas. These included *Cathleen ni Houlihan* (1902), written in collaboration with Lady Augusta Gregory (a co-director of the Abbey), with its heroine a kind of personification of Ireland. Yeats was essentially a poet rather than a dramatist, even when he was writing plays (in *The King's Threshold*, 1904, the function of poetry is the subject of the play), and his greatest gift to the theatre was his support for the Abbey and encouragement to other dramatists.

Synge

John Millington Synge (1871–1909), also a founding director of the Abbey, was probably the most talented Irish playwright of this exciting era. Like many leaders of the cultural revival, he was a Protestant, from a middle-class family.

Above: *The Playboy of the Western World*
at the Almeida Theatre, London, 1994.
The original production at the Abbey in
Dublin made Synge famous, though not
altogether for the best reasons. Touring
America, the entire company was
arrested, prompting G. B. Shaw's
comment: 'All decent people are
arrested in the United States.'

At Yeats's prompting, he spent long periods in the Aran Islands, off the coast
of Galway, where he listened to the idioms and cadences of everyday speech
and evolved his own distinctive, rhetorical form of dialogue. His one-act plays,
Shadow of the Glen (1903) and the intense, poetic tragedy *Riders to the Sea*
(1904) were among the early productions of the Abbey. (An earlier play, *When
the Moon Has Set*, was rejected by Yeats and published after Synge's early
death.) They were followed by *The Well of the Saints* (1905) and his masterpiece, *The Playboy of the Western World* (1907). The plot concerns a young
fugitive who confesses that he has killed his father and gains the sympathy of
the villagers until his father turns up with only a bump on the head, where-
upon they turn against him. This somewhat cynical view of the morality of
Irish peasants, plus a frank attitude to sex, caused great offence. There was a
riot at the Abbey and the play was taken off. Synge's final play, *The Tinker's
Wedding*, which was disrespectful to the clergy, was staged in London (1909),
not Dublin.

O'Casey

Sean O'Casey (1880–1964) proved equally unacceptable to the fragile propri-
eties of Dublin in a fraught and dangerous time. He was a difficult man himself, and ultimately fell out with the Abbey when his *The Silver Tassie* was
rejected in 1928. But by then, his best work had been done. Unlike the Abbey
establishment, O'Casey came from a poor background and worked as a
labourer until, after several rejections, *The Shadow of a Gunman* (1923) was
accepted. His two great tragi-comedies, *Juno and the Paycock* (1924) and *The
Plough and the Stars* (1926), are set among the Dublin poor during the era of
the civil wars. The second in particular, taking a critical view of nationalist
heroics, infuriated the public and provoked riots at the Abbey, and O'Casey, a
Communist sympathizer hostile to the Church, moved to England. In his later
plays he experimented with Expressionism. They have never achieved the
status of his Naturalistic masterpieces.

German drama
and expressionism

The most important development in the drama in Germany and central Europe at the beginning of the 20th century was the movement known as Expressionism. However, the outstanding dramatist at that time belonged to an earlier generation, and was perhaps the theatre's finest exponent of Naturalism.

Above: A sketch made at the dress rehearsal of *Winterballade* at the Deutsches Theater in Berlin in 1917, towards the end of Max Reinhardt's period there. From the left: Reinhardt, Hauptmann, Rilke, Margarete Hauptmann.

Hauptmann

Gerhart Hauptmann (1862–1946), winner of the Nobel Prize for Literature in 1912 and compared in his own time with Goethe, was a poet and novelist, although most famous as a dramatist. His first great, but controversial, success, produced by the Freie Bühne in 1889, was *Vor Sonnenaufgang* ('Before Sunset'), a sympathetic but unrelenting study of a peasant family destroyed by alcohol and sexual irregularity. His masterpiece in the same genre was *Die Weber* ('The Weavers', 1892), set during a rebellion by the weavers of Silesia (Hauptmann's native land) in 1844, which has no 'hero', the protagonist being a group rather than an individual. But Hauptmann, whose career was long and productive, encompassed many different styles and subject matter. His first play after *Die Weber* was the once very popular comedy *Der Biberpelz* ('The Beaver Pelt', 1893), and it was followed by *Hanneles Himmelfahrt* ('The Assumption of Hannele', 1893), strongly influenced by Symbolism.

Expressionism

The term Expressionism was first used soon after 1900 when it was applied to painting (it was to have a powerful influence on stage design and on early cinema). It was in part a reaction against the authorial objectivity of Naturalism. Expressionist drama was consciously revolutionary and marked the increasing involvement of theatre with politics. It was a young man's movement – women scarcely figured – and was hostile to contemporary social conventions, not least to the institution of the family. It tended to be extravagantly emotional, even violent, and the hero, a representative of the 'New Man', was usually to be identified with the author, subsidiary characters tending to be little more than ciphers called 'The Father', 'The Boss', etc., without an individual name. Expressionist dramatists were often poets, and employed high-flown poetic language in their crusade for the rejuvenation of society.

The most notable precursors of Expressionism were the later plays of Strindberg (see page 139) and the German actor-playwright Frank Wedekind (1864–1918) who frequently appeared in his own plays. His most famous con-temporary play, *Frühlings Erwachen* ('Spring Awakening', 1889), concerns two teenage lovers destroyed by the moral hypocrisy of their parents. Its sexual candour kept if off the public stage in Britain until the 1960s. Two of Wedekind's later plays, written in the 1890s, were later combined as *Lulu*, which made a profound impression in London and New York in 1970. Berg's opera (1937) based on the two plays, with libretto by the composer, had first been seen in London some years earlier.

Expressionist dramatists

Expressionist drama at its peak commanded the German stage for scarcely a decade, before dying of its own excesses. A leading dramatist was Georg Kaiser (1878–1945), whose best-known play (among many) is *Von morgens bis mitternachts* ('From Morning to Midnight', 1913). It concerns a bank clerk whose desperate efforts to escape the suffocating restrictions of his existence lead to his suicide.

No less highly regarded than Kaiser is the idealistic Ernst Toller (1893–1939). In prison after he refused to return to the trenches in 1916, he wrote the pacifist drama *Die Wandlung* ('Transfiguration', 1919), which trans-formed him and his leading actor, Fritz Kortner (1892–1970), into cultural heroes, at least in some circles. His plays of the early 1920s, including *Masse-Mensche* ('Man and the Masses', 1921) and *Die Maschinenstürmer* ('The Machine Wreckers', 1922) which deals with the English Luddites, are his best-known plays outside Germany. The latter is relatively hopeful in spirit, but from *Hoppla!* (1927) onwards he became increasingly pessimistic. He left Germany just before Hitler came to power and committed suicide in New York as the outbreak of the Second World War loomed.

Expressionist influences

In its character as a revolutionary drama calling for a new spiritual awakening, Expressionism lost momentum in the 1920s as the dramatic political events of 1919 gave way to the flabbiness of the Weimar Republic, but its influence, though diffuse, was widely spread. In the drama, besides Brecht, it strongly influenced O'Neill in the 1920s – and also a later generation of American play-wrights, notably Tennessee Williams – but it had less effect in western Europe. Its influence on production was arguably greater than on the form of the drama. The great director and impresario Max Reinhardt (1873–1943) who, as director of the Deutsches Theater in Berlin, founded the smaller Kammerspiele next door for contemporary drama and sponsored the Berlin Volksbühne after 1914, was one of the first to evolve an Expressionist style for an Expressionist play, a trend further developed by Erwin Piscator, whose famous production of Toller's *Hoppla!* in 1927 included a revolving set on several levels and the use of projected film.

Above: A characteristically lavish set in a Reinhardt production of *Helen* at the Adelphi Theatre, London, in 1932.

American drama

At the beginning of the 20th century the United States, the land of 'show-biz' and razzmatazz, had many good theatres, actors and designers; but there was little serious drama, in particular, no truly American drama, until the emergence of Eugene O'Neill.

The Provincetown Players

The impact of Modernism was first felt through European imports, such as Dublin's Abbey Theatre, whose Naturalistic style impressed the 23-year-old O'Neill. In 1916, he joined the newly formed Provincetown Players in Massachusetts, who produced his play, *Bound East for Cardiff*, based on his experiences as a merchant seaman. The company moved to Greenwich Village, taking a converted warehouse in Macdougal Street named, at O'Neill's suggestion, the Playwrights' Theatre. There O'Neill had freedom to experiment, and many of his early plays were staged there, including *The Emperor Jones*. His first full-length play to be produced on Broadway, *Beyond the Horizon*, won the first of his four Pulitzer prizes (the others were *Anna Christie*, *Strange Interlude* and *Long Day's Journey Into Night*).

Life

The writer's private life is of particular relevance to O'Neill. Most of his 40-odd plays are autobiographical, and *Long Day's Journey Into Night* (which was produced posthumously in 1956) is very closely based on his family life, a source of torment which he fashioned into a hugely powerful drama that many consider his masterpiece.

Eugene was the third son of an Irish immigrant who became a hugely popular romantic actor. His mother, who disliked the theatrical milieu, was a morphine addict for 25 years, and both he and his surviving brother were tortured by guilt. He was a rebellious young man, already suffering from a lifelong sense of not belonging anywhere, who rejected his parents' Catholicism (the source, nevertheless, of O'Neill's intense spirituality) and lived an aimless, knockabout existence. In 1912, a year of personal crisis, he attempted suicide. He lasted one year at Princeton (1906), where he discovered Nietzsche and Strindberg, and attended a famous playwriting course at Harvard (1914), having resolved to be a playwright while in a sanatorium recovering from tuberculosis in 1913. He had three marriages, the first two stormy. Of his children: one committed suicide, another was psychologically unstable, and his daughter Oona alienated him by marrying Charlie Chaplin, a man his own age. In his last decade he was physically unable to write and reluctant to countenance production of his later plays. *Long Day's Journey* was not even published during his lifetime.

Left: Scene from *Long Day's Journey Into Night*, O'Neill's powerful drama of the mutually destructive relationships in a family very like his own.

Right: O'Neill in the good years, not long before he was awarded the Nobel Prize (1936). Later he was overtaken by bad health and depression and became in his final years a recluse who saw only his third wife and various medical attendants.

Major Plays

1916 *Bound East for Cardiff*
1917 *The Long Voyage Home*
1918 *The Moon of the Caribbees*
1918 *Beyond the Horizon*
1920 *Anna Christie*
1920 *The Emperor Jones*
1921 *The Hairy Ape*
1924 *All God's Chillun Got Wings*
1924 *Desire Under the Elms*
1925 *The Great God Brown*
1928 *Strange Interlude*
1931 *Mourning Becomes Electra*
1934 *Days Without End*
1946* *The Iceman Cometh* (written c.1939)
1947* *A Moon for the Misbegotten* (written c.1943)
1956* *Long Day's Journey into Night* (written c.1941)
1958* *Hughie* (written c.1941)
*Date of first production

Quotes

Orin [viewing his dead father]: Death becomes the Mannions! You were always like the statue of an eminent dead man – sitting on a chair in the park or straddling a horse in a town square – looking over the head of life without a sign of recognition – cutting it dead for the impropriety of living!
Mourning Becomes Electra, Part 2, Act I

Jamie: ...Got to take revenge. On everyone else. Especially you. Oscar Wilde's 'Reading Gaol' has the dope twisted. The man was dead, and so he had to kill the thing he loved. That's what it ought to be. The dead part of me hopes you won't get well. Maybe he's even glad the game has got Mama again! He wants company, he doesn't want to be the only corpse around the house!
Long Day's Journey into Night, Act IV

...it is only by means of some form of 'super-naturalism' that we may express in the theater what we comprehend intuitively of that self-defeating, self-obsession which is the discourse we moderns have to pay for the loan of life.
Programme note on Strindberg

The playwright

O'Neill was influenced by Ibsen, Strindberg and Expressionism, notably in *The Emperor Jones*, which features a Caribbean dictator, and the symbolic *The Hairy Ape*, two successes among many early failures. But he was an eclectic as well as an inventive playwright who stands solidly in the Classical tradition. *The Great God Brown* makes use of masks, and *Mourning Becomes Electra*, a huge critical success and the spur for his Nobel Prize (1936), is a reworking of Aeschylus' *Oresteia* trilogy set in New England after the Civil War. Among his innovations were the varied settings of *Marco Millions* (1928), a light-hearted satire on philistinism, and the use of asides, notably in the powerful, nine-act *Strange Interlude*, to assist in the probing of character. Though deeply concerned with social problems such as race relations, his greatest plays, *The Iceman Cometh*, technically probably his finest work, concerning the delusions of characters in a seedy bar, and *Long Day's Journey*, are based on family and friends. His last plays, *A Moon for the Misbegotten* and *Hughie*, sprang from his feelings for his dead brother.

O'Neill's contemporaries

Although none measured up to the stature of O'Neill, several of his contemporaries were major dramatists of the second rank. The most prolific was Maxwell Anderson (1888–1959), many of whose plays, notably *Elizabeth the Queen* (1930), are in blank verse. More memorable than his solid, realist dramas was his political satire, especially *Both Your Houses* (1933). Among his most popular plays were *Key Largo* (1939), *Anne of the Thousand Days* (1948) and *The Bad Seed* (1954).

Lillian Hellman (1905–84) had a striking success with *The Children's Hour* (1934) and *The Little Foxes* (1939), though her later plays, except perhaps for *Toys in the Attic* (1960), did not quite live up to expectations. Thornton Wilder, apart from his novel *The Bridge of San Luis Rey*, is remembered for two plays, *Our Town* (1938), a portrait of a New Hampshire community, produced without scenery, and the entertaining survey of human history, *The Skin of Our Teeth* (1942). Elmer Rice (1892–1967) began with the Expressionist fantasy *The Adding Machine* (1923), but otherwise was largely a commentator on his own times, less appealing to later generations. Genial comedy was the forte of Philip Barry (1896–1949), whose most successful play was *Philadelphia Story* (1939).

The reaction against Naturalism, the foundering of conventions under the impact of Modernism and the widespread feeling of disillusionment with contemporary Western culture led to many new, experimental forms of theatre, some of them verging on the grotesque. If nothing more, they acted as an invigorating stimulant, in spite (or because) of the hostility they provoked. A significant role was played by the eclectic Théâtre de l'Oeuvre, which, besides being 'the temple of Symbolism', was also the theatre that staged Jarry's *Ubu roi*, often regarded as the seminal play of the avant-garde, in 1896.

avant-garde

Jarry

Alfred Jarry (1873–1907) was almost as bizarre a character as his creation Père Ubu, arguably the first 'anti-hero'. The play, written when the author was 15, originated as a schoolboy jape, an attack on an unpopular teacher. It is totally amoral, a tin of greasepaint thrown in the face of the public – more particularly, the French bourgeoisie. The loathsome Père Ubu, cruel, cowardly, vain and stupid, and his wife Mère Ubu make themselves rulers of Poland by killing all opponents. The first word of the play is an expletive not heard before on the French stage but a fair sign of what is to come, and pandemonium broke out among the first-night audience, a distinguished one that included Yeats. He confessed himself saddened and bewildered by what he saw as a kind of apocalypse of poetic drama. The play is nevertheless a success because, however nasty, it is also funny. Jarry wrote several more plays featuring Père Ubu but none measured up to the original.

Ubu roi was a kick in the teeth for Western civilization and also for the naturalistic theatre. Jarry insisted on retaining many features reflecting the play's origin as a piece for puppets, including the idea that the characters themselves are puppets. The use of masks, rudimentary sets and props, which merely allude to what they are supposed to represent, while recalling the popular theatre of the Middle Ages, also influenced future directors (and modern movements in the arts from Dada onwards), as did the coarse farce and slapstick.

The Theatre of Cruelty

Jarry was largely neglected until the 1960s, except by the surrealists and other avant-garde groups, but the Théâtre Alfred Jarry was founded in Paris in 1927 by the poet-playwrights Roger Vitrac (1899–1952), a leading Dadaist, and Antonin Artaud. One of its first productions was the surrealist *Les Mystères de l'amour*, written by Vitrac and directed by Artaud. Its sado-erotic fantasies foreshadowed the so-called Theatre of Cruelty, the principles of which were explained in Artaud's *Le Théâtre et son double*, published in 1938 when the author was in a mental institution. Artaud attacked the whole corpus of Western theatre (proclaiming 'No More Masterpieces!') and indeed the whole of Western civilization, purporting to rediscover the 'necessary cruelty' of natural, instinctive behaviour. Although he was also neglected, apart from the explosions of rage that greeted his work initially, until the 1960s, he has been a powerful influence on the modern theatre. In the visionary theatre of Artaud, the audience is, by intention anyway, encompassed in a hallucinatory world, where the rules of time and motion do not exist. Words are less important than action, rhythm, sound and gesture, and behaviour is immune to conventional morality. Artaud selected Shelley's melodramatic verse tragedy *The Cenci*, which had recently received its first performance in Paris, a century after it was written, as the basis for his play of that name (1935) because, he said, it contained 'corporal and moral excess . . . to the extremity of instinct'.

Among later playwrights strongly influenced by Artaud's ideas was Jean Genet (1910–86), who spent much of his life in prison but wrote strikingly poetic dramas full of ceremony and masquerade, which celebrate cruelty and perversion and demonstrate the meaninglessness of 'reality'. In Britain, Joe Orton (1933–67) employed a mixture of conventional dialogue and extreme, violent action in *Entertaining Mr Sloane* (1964) and *Loot* (1966). Outstanding in this period, though, was Peter Brook's English production in 1994 of a play by Peter Weiss (1916–82), known by its shorthand title as *Marat/Sade*, which was not only a critical sensation, but also, unusually for this genre, a commercial success too. Weiss was previously known as a novelist and *Marat/Sade*, which was centred on the events leading up to the death of Marat in the French Revolution as 'Performed by the Inmates of the Charenton [lunatic] asylum under the Direction of the Marquis de Sade', was his first play. His later work belongs to 'Documentary drama' rather than the Theatre of Cruelty.

Above: Scene from Genet's *Le Balcon* (The Balcony), set in a brothel which becomes the centre of extraordinary, ritualistic events.

Left: A gleeful Charlotte Corday prepares to dispatch the Revolutionary leader Marat in his bath (a scene recalling the famous painting of the incident by J.L. David), in Peter Weiss' *Marat/Sade*.

Pirandello
and Brecht

Some scholars have remarked on the radicalism of theatre in countries suffering some kind of social breakdown, especially disasters of war, and this is borne out in the era of the First World War, where revolutionary developments were most marked in defeated and politically disrupted Germany and almost absent in Britain where, in spite of frightful casualties society – and theatre – experienced no momentous changes. France and Italy stood somewhere between the two extremes.

Meyerhold

In Russia, the Revolution of 1917 gave rise to the revolutionary theatre of, in particular, Vsevolod Meyerhold (1874–?1940). Having joined the Moscow Arts Theatre at the beginning (1898), he briefly ran his own touring company before Stanislavsky put him in charge of a studio theatre (1905). Since Meyerhold was totally opposed to the Naturalism of the Moscow Arts, it was soon closed. During the Revolution, Meyerhold adopted the slogan 'Put the October Revolution into the Theatre!' and staged the early, Soviet plays of Vladimir Mayakovsky (1894–1930), until his failure to embrace Socialist Realism resulted in his fall from favour, arrest and disappearance.

Pirandello

Luigi Pirandello (1867–1936) was, almost single-handed, responsible for rescuing Italian drama from its submergence by the ever-popular opera. Although he came late to the theatre as an established novelist and man of letters, theatre was his true métier. In his later years he formed his own company, which toured Europe, and he often appeared as an actor in his own plays. In private life he was cruelly unfortunate. His young wife developed mental illness, and for many years Pirandello looked after her, until she had to be consigned to an asylum. This may have stimulated his work, his refuge from unhappiness, and perhaps encouraged his pessimistic view of contemporary human existence and the impossibility of a person achieving a whole, integrated personality. These concerns characterize his best-known play, *Six Characters in Search of an Author* (1921), produced in London and New York within the year. Among others were *Right You are, If You Think You are* (1917) and *Henry IV* (1922). His anti-Naturalism anticipated Brecht, and his concern with the disintegration of personality is echoed in Samuel Beckett.

Brecht

Of still greater influence was Bertolt Brecht (1898–1956), inventor of a new type of theatre that rejected Realism in favour of stylized 'epic theatre', in which the actors are self-consciously performers. His first play, *Baal*, was written when he was a medical student in Munich in 1918, though not produced until 1923, after

Left: Bertolt Brecht, in the revolutionary's trademark leather jacket, about 1927, before he had achieved his full dramatic stature.

Right: A modern version of Brecht's *Schweyk in the Second World War.*

his second play, *Drums in the Night* (1922), had won the prestigious Kleist Prize. In 1924 he became assistant to Max Reinhardt at the Deutsches Theater in Berlin, where he began to develop his style and from 1927 was also associated with Piscator. Though a Marxist, Brecht's work in general was more affected by Expressionism than by political commitment, though some works are more 'political' than others. The most controversial aspect of his technique was his employment of 'alienation' and other devices to distance the audience from the play and thus encourage a 'new objectivity' (*neue Sachlichkeit*).

Brecht's first big commercial success was *The Threepenny Opera* (produced 1928), loosely based on Gay's *The Beggar's Opera*, with music by Kurt Weill. They co-operated on several other operas, including *The Rise and Fall of the City of Mahagonny* (1930). In 1933 he left Germany to escape the Nazis and eventually settled in the USA (1941). His best plays belong to this period: *Mother Courage and Her Children* (1941), *The Good Person of Setzuan* (1943) and *The Caucasian Chalk Circle* (written 1945).

The Berliner Ensemble

Brecht returned to Communist East Berlin in 1949, after a clash with the Un-American Activities Committee in Washington. That year marked the publication of his theoretical work, *Short Organum for the Theatre*, the foundation – with his wife the actress Helene Weigel – of the Berliner Ensemble, and the beginning of Brecht's international influence. The Berliner Ensemble was originally housed in the old Deutsches Theater, but moved in 1954 to the Theater im Schiffbauerdam, Reinhardt's old theatre. It achieved worldwide fame under the direction of Brecht and, after his death, his wife. Its highly individual style of production was designed in accordance with Brecht's theories to discourage the suspension of disbelief by the audience, and the Berliner Ensemble made a resounding impact in foreign tours, performing both Brecht and plays of other dramatists, such as Büchner, Wedekind, Shakespeare (notably *Coriolanus*) and the politically sympathetic Shaw, though the original plays were sometimes barely recognizable. Brecht remains controversial. Some say that he would have been a better dramatist shorn of some of his theories, but few would deny that his concept of epic theatre is a major contribution to modern drama.

design

The dramatists who, around the turn of the century, reacted against Naturalism and pictorial Realism in various stylistic ways and (like the painters) tried to delve beneath the surface to explore the mysterious and poetic aspects of life, found allies in contemporary directors and designers.

Below: Max Reinhardt in 1911 with the English aristocrat, society beauty and bluestocking, Lady Diana Manners (later Cooper), who played a part in his famous production of Vollmöller's *Miracle* in London's vast Olympia hall.

Directors

As we have seen the régisseur or director ('producer' in Britain until the 1950s) did not exist in the modern sense until the end of the 19th century, and except in a few companies such as the Meininger Company, rehearsals, owing largely to the repertory system, were brief. Longer and more detailed rehearsals were introduced by Mme Vestris (1797–1856) in London, and she influenced Boucicault who, in America, in turn influenced Belasco. The Meininger approach was taken further by such pioneers as Stanislavsky in Russia and Antoine in France, and their methods were adopted by Meyerhold and Reinhardt. The work of the director was further extended by a growing number of innovators, such as Harley Granville Barker (1877–1946) at the Royal Court in London; by Jacques Copeau (1879–1949), whose disciples, including many notable directors of the future, were known as 'les Copiaux', in France, and by Piscator in Germany. Arguably of greater importance than any of these were the designers and theorists Appia and Craig.

Appia

A landmark in stage design was the publication in 1899 of *Die Müsik und die Inscenierung* ('Music and the Art of Theatre') by the Swiss-born Adolphe Appia (1862–1928). A musician by training, Appia was fascinated by Wagner's theories on staging, the subject of his first book in 1895. In this and the later work, Appia rejected realistic painted scenery and advanced his conception of staging based on the use of light (electricity was still novel), which he saw as the – equally versatile – equivalent of music, and of simple, three-dimensional forms integrating actors (who are, after all, three-dimensional objects) and setting. One practical advantage of his designs was that they could be effected quite easily without the need for expensive machinery: Appia did not even require a conventional raised stage.

   Appia's ideas evolved in his head. He was a shy man with a speech impediment, but he was able to test his theories staging opera in a private theatre in Paris after 1903. For many years he worked closely with a fellow-Swiss musician, Emile Dalcroze (1865–1950), the originator of eurythmics, which was based on his belief that the source of rhythm lies within the body, and was a major influence on modern dance. Appia's fame spread widely through his writing and exhibitions of his work, notably his designs for Wagner's *Tristan and Isolde* (1923). Many seemingly novel and imaginative effects of lighting in the theatre today are derived directly from him.

Craig

A friend and disciple of Appia, also famous chiefly through his writing, was Edward Gordon Craig (1872–1966), son of Ellen Terry and originally an actor. He attracted attention with his sets for productions by his uncle, Fred Terry

(1864–1932), and his mother and was soon in demand elsewhere. In 1908 he made his home in Florence, producing a theatre magazine, *The Mask*, and running an acting school. His innovations in stage design were seen at the Abbey Theatre in Dublin, where the famous device of using large movable panels as the basis for an imaginative, non-realistic setting was first employed; at the Moscow Arts Theatre, in a production of *Hamlet* that was the nearest Craig came to fully realizing his advanced ideas; in Ibsen at Copenhagen and in Shakespeare in New York. His theory of the almighty director – one person who would exercise total control over every aspect of the performance, as author, director and designer – seemed extreme at the time. He looked forward to the elimination of the playwright and the conversion of the actor from a subjective interpreter to an *Übermarionette*, 'in such a state of mechanical perfection that the body [is] absolutely the slave of his mind'.

Reinhardt

The man who came nearest to achieving the total control that Craig advocated was Max Reinhardt. Though not a playwright, he was a huge creative force in the theatre over many years. A sample page of his working scripts frequently contains so many stage directions that there is little room for actual text. He was not committed to any particular form of stage or style, nor to any type of drama, and some of his most famous productions were seen in vast halls, such as London's Olympia, ballrooms and other buildings or spaces. He was renowned for his brilliant direction of crowd scenes, and his famous production of Hofmannsthal's *Jedermann* (1911) took place in the streets of Salzburg, the cathedral providing a backdrop. Reinhardt, of Austrian Jewish origin, emigrated to the U.S.A. in 1938 and directed several plays in New York before settling finally, and perhaps appropriately, in Hollywood.

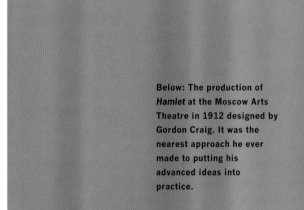

Below: The production of *Hamlet* at the Moscow Arts Theatre in 1912 designed by Gordon Craig. It was the nearest approach he ever made to putting his advanced ideas into practice.

152-153

design

A powerful impact on many aspects of stage design, especially in the expressive use of colour, was made by the Ballets Russes, whose dazzling dance-drama spectacles overwhelmed Europe in the years before the First World War. The Russian ballet had long been outstanding, but the Ballets Russes was something different, and derived from a fortunate conjunction of extraordinary talents assembled and integrated by a master impresario, Diaghilev.

the
Ballets Russes

Above: Diaghilev, a man whose extraordinary personality and ability combined to act as a kind of catalyst to the creation of art.

Diaghilev

As a student in St Petersburg, Serge Pavlovich Diaghilev (1872–1929) abandoned the study of law to pursue his interest in the arts and became an influential figure in artistic circles, joining friends such as the painters Léon Bakst (1866–1924) and Alexandre Benois (1870–1950), to found a new journal of the arts in 1899. In 1905 he mounted a huge and impressive exhibition of Russian painting in Paris, and two years later he was there again presenting concerts of Russian music (including the first production outside Russia of Mussorgsky's *Boris Godunov* with the famous bass Chaliapin). He was thus already a well-known international producer when he brought his Ballets Russes to Paris in 1909. He continued to direct the company until his death in Venice twenty years later, and in that time he presented nearly 70 ballets, many of which are still part of the international repertoire today.

The 'Diaghilev miracle'

The essence of the Ballets Russes, which virtually amounted to a new art form – 'modern ballet' – was a synthesis of dance, design and music. The Russian ballet, like most great national institutions, was highly conservative, and Diaghilev knew that marked deviations from the Classical tradition would not be tolerated in the imperial theatres. His company was therefore a touring company, which performed in London, Berlin and other European and American cities, though not as a company in Russia, and from 1913 made its permanent home in Paris. Diaghilev enlisted the finest modern dancers, choreographers, composers and designers (though sometimes for fairly brief periods), including Fokine, Nijinsky, Pavlova, Ravel, Stravinsky, Bakst (now more famous for his sets and costumes than his paintings), Benois, Goncharova and Picasso. The preference was for relatively short, freshly commissioned works, although the company also produced full-length Classical ballets and works with music not written for the ballet, such as *Les Sylphides*, from music by Chopin.

In every country the Ballets Russes had an immediate dramatic impact as well as longer-term effects, leading to the formation of national ballet companies. Diaghilev's associates subsequently played major roles in this process. Among them were the Irish-born Ninette de Valois (1898–2001), a member of Diaghilev's company in the early 1920s, who founded what became the English Royal Ballet based at Covent Garden, and George Balanchine (1904–83), who was still creating works for his New York City Ballet up to the 1980s.

Opposite: Nijinsky in *L'Après-midi d'un Faune*, 1912.

Fokine and Nijinsky

Mikhail Fokine (1880–1942), who had been influenced by the informal dance style of Isadora Duncan, choreographed *The Dying Swan* for Pavlova at the Maryinski, later Kirov Ballet, in 1907. He taught a more natural style, with more acting or mime, and appropriate costumes. Both subsequently joined Diaghilev, for whom Fokine created *The Firebird* (1910) with a score by Stravinsky.

Vaslav Nijinsky (1886–1950), still regarded, partly because of his intensely expressive acting, as possibly the greatest dancer in the history of ballet, in spite of his sadly brief career, joined the Maryinski in 1907 and was immediately given solo roles. In 1908 he met Diaghilev, who became a powerful influence on him personally. As well as dancing, he choreographed *L'Après-midi d'un Faune* ('The Afternoon of a Faun') in 1912, introducing movements and gestures derived from Greek art. An impetuous marriage in 1913 caused a quarrel with Diaghilev, though Nijinsky returned briefly to the company in 1917 before retiring to Switzerland, increasingly the victim of mental disorder.

Above: Virtually every first-rate artist of the time contributed to the Ballets Russes, notably Léon Bakst who designed costumes and sets for numerous ballets between 1909 and 1921. His exuberant colours and sense of form had huge influence on fashion and decoration.

Later years

The Ballets Russes continued to be experimental and sensational – sometimes controversial. When *Le Sacre du Printemps* ('The Rite of Spring') was performed in 1913, with Stravinsky's almost savage music, weird set designs by Nikolai Roerich and strange, startling choreography by Nijinsky, it caused such a disturbance that the police were summoned, though the performance continued.

Inevitably, French influence increased at the expense of Russian. The scenario for *Parade* (1917) was written by Jean Cocteau, choreographed by Leonid Massine, designed by Picasso, with music (including typewriter keys and street noises) by Erik Satie. Such an assembly of talent would be hard to equal. Choreographers, including Nijinsky's sister Bronislava and, from 1925, Balanchine, remained predominantly Russian, as did the great male dancers – after Nijinsky came Serge Lifar, Diaghilev's last great discovery. The successor to Diaghilev's company was the Ballets Russes de Monte Carlo, founded in 1931 with many of Diaghilev's stars, which carried on the tradition until after the Second World War. But, overtaken by the Ballets Russes's offspring, its bloom was fading long before it finally closed in 1962.

The upheaval in the drama that resulted with the arrival of Modernism around the turn of the century did little to disturb the popular theatre, but a challenge of a different sort appeared shortly before 1900 from the motion picture. The extravagant, spectacular productions of a Belasco appeared vastly superior to the jerky, grainy, black-and-white images flickering on a wobbly screen, but rapid technical advances soon produced a serious threat to the commercial theatre. Live theatre always held some advantages, but no live performance could reproduce the spectacular illusionism of cinematic effects and, in the battle for the mass audience, the theatre was the loser.

rival media

Primitive cinema

Photography was invented before 1850, sound recording (the phonograph) in the 1870s, moving pictures in the 1890s. The earliest films, lasting a minute or less, were understandably preoccupied with the tricks of the new medium, especially the depiction of movement. Many stories are told of the shock experienced by audiences seeing a train racing straight at them from the screen. The object of the first film makers was to astonish the audience, and the next step was illusionistic 'special effects', like the transformation scene in pantomime. They were easier to manage on film than on stage, by editing – simply stopping the camera, altering the scene, then restarting it. The leading figure was George Méliès, a former stage magician, whose *A Trip to the Moon* (1902) was a minor sensation. *The Great Train Robbery* (1903), the first 'western', in the course of telling a story employed freer camera work with action scenes – all on a single reel lasting less than ten minutes.

It was already obvious that motion pictures were moving beyond their early reliance on novelty and cheap tricks. By 1905, they were being shown in the U.S.A. as one of the acts in vaudeville. The first nickelodeon (a ticket cost a nickel – five cents) opened in Philadelphia with *The Great Train Robbery* the same year. These early cinemas were often converted from a shop on Main Street, and seated only a dozen or so people. But expansion was swift, with purpose-built cinemas soon springing up everywhere. As there was no sound, only printed captions, pianists were hired to improvise a suitable musical commentary. Already, cinema was being hailed as 'the drama of the people'. It was not yet, perhaps, an art, but it was attracting large and rapidly increasing numbers. Moreover, a film could be easily transported, and distributed all round the world at little extra cost. You did not have to go to Paris to see Sarah Bernhardt. You could see her in *Queen Elizabeth* (1912) in a shack in the Australian outback, although the quality of the image and the stagey acting might make you wonder what all the fuss was about.

Effects

By the end of the First World War the cinema was established as a serious entertainment. Film premieres acquired the glamour of theatrical first-nights. Hard-headed businessmen invested money in film making. The talkies arrived

CINÉMATOGRAPHE LUMIÈR

in 1927, and were shown in grotesquely grand cinemas ('theaters' in the U.S.A.), in marked contrast to the housing of their patrons. Audiences were massive.

The appeal of Hollywood was as strong as, or stronger than, any of the great centres of theatre. Most stage actors adapted easily to the screen, and some of the most gifted abandoned the stage altogether and consigned themselves to California, where the pay was much higher. Hollywood's isolation from theatre capitals, and the comparatively slow speed of travel, made it difficult for actors to alternate between stage and screen.

The battle for the mass audience was lost. The greatest advantage of cinema was that it was much cheaper, and the price of cinema tickets tended to fall as audiences increased, while theatre tickets rose as audiences declined. Music hall and vaudeville entered a terminal decline. Many theatres closed, or were converted to cinemas, especially in the provinces. Managers went bankrupt, old performers were reduced to poverty. Still, this was not so much a defeat as a major, often painful, readjustment. There was still an audience for the classics and for 'middle-class' drama. The stage musical was thriving. The audience for avant-garde drama, though a mere drop in the bucket of cinema audiences, was growing appreciably.

By 1939 cinema had advanced further, with colour and dubbing of speech for foreign-language audiences. But there were new threats looming. In the 1920s most families had a 'wireless', and could listen to plays in their own home. Television followed, though its development was interrupted by the war. Eventually TV and ensuing developments later in the century, such as videos, posed as great a challenge to cinemas as cinemas had to theatres. In the 1950s they were closing just as fast, and cinema had to make similar kinds of adjustment as the theatre had faced a generation earlier.

chapt

Ben Kingsley as Estragon and Alan Howard as Vladimir in Samuel Beckett's *Waiting for Godot*.

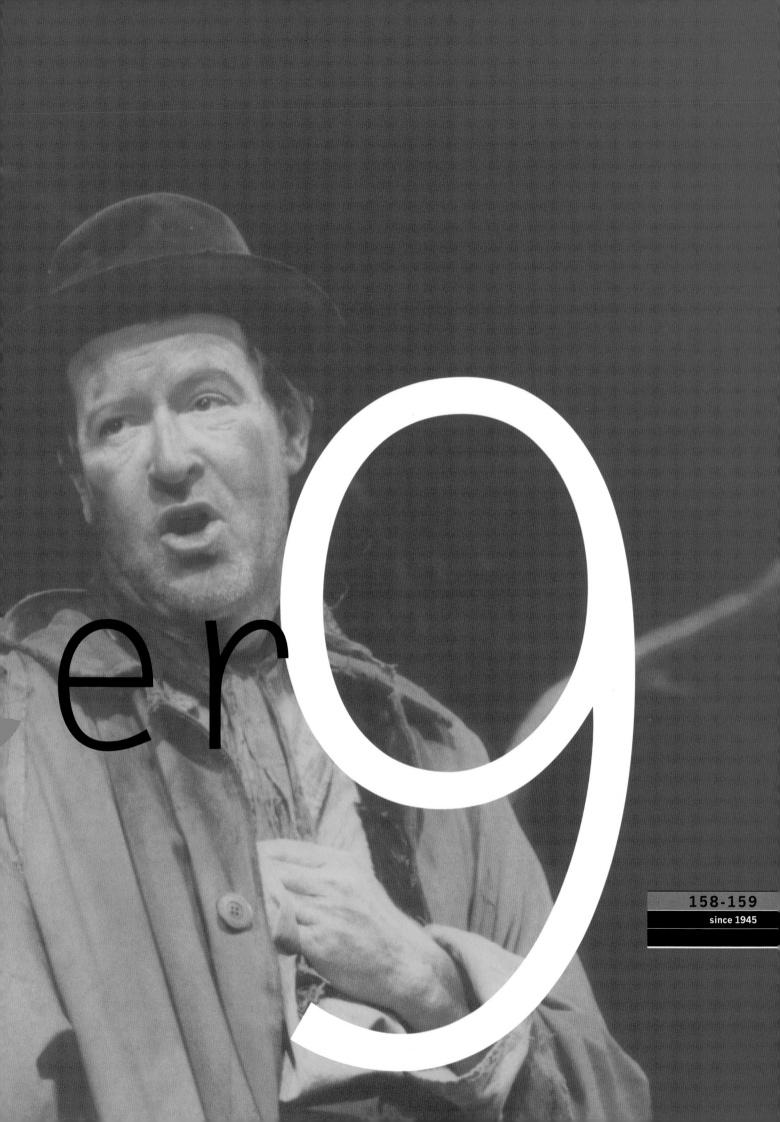

er**g**

In wartime the theatre tends to a variable extent to be taken over by politicians, generals and government propaganda but, even earlier, the rule of the dictators in Europe between the world wars almost destroyed creative drama in those unfortunate countries. Where theatre was not actively involved in encouraging the war effort, it was largely given over to light, escapist entertainment of various kinds. Tired soldiers and workers generally preferred dancing girls to challenging drama. The effects of war, moreover, were prolonged beyond the end of the fighting. Soviet dictatorship, which had long before extinguished the burst of Russian creativity in the Revolutionary period, was extended to the countries of eastern Europe, with similar effect on cultural activities. In Germany, the horrors of Nazism and military defeat encouraged conservative attitudes, while in countries, notably Britain, that had not been directly affected by totalitarian rule, the wartime taste for light and undemanding entertainment continued after 1945 during the era of austerity and the Cold War.

war and
its aftermath

Above: Lorca, one of the earliest victims of the ideologically motivated violence that swept across Europe in the second quarter of the 20th century.

The dictators

The rise of fascist dictatorship and the ensuing six years of international conflict effectively crushed the development of drama, especially avant-garde drama. Fascist dictatorships imposed rigid political censorship, burning books of which they disapproved and closing down theatres. In Spain, the poet-playwright Federico Garcia Lorca (1898–1936) was shot by the fascists at the start of the Civil War. In Germany, all Jewish and Left-wing artists and writers were persecuted. They either fled the country or remained silent, sometimes surviving through reluctant compliance with the Nazi regime, writing historical dramas in which righteous Germans overcame the wicked French or English.

But not all avant-garde movements were crushed by the New Right. Futurism, with its glorification of power and machines, appealed to Mussolini and the fascists, and its leader, Filippo Marinetti (1876–1944), became a fascist hero, guest of honour at a ceremonial banquet in Berlin in 1935. The theatres and art galleries were not simply closed, as happened in Puritan England in the 17th century, but controlled. The purpose of the arts in a fascist state was simply to affirm and support the regime. In fact, with their keen awareness of the potential of propaganda, the Nazis put theatre first among the arts. Goebbels was himself the author of a vaguely Expressionist play, and Mussolini had written a turgid historical drama about Napoleon. In Russia, the Stalinist clamp-down was already in effect, with Meyerhold among the casualties, and it was to continue into the 1960s. In other countries too, the effect of the politically inspired freeze continued to affect the drama some time after the war had ended and the fascist dictators had vanished.

Occupied Europe

Most of Europe was under German occupation in 1940–45, and Nazi censorship was therefore imposed elsewhere. Nevertheless, it was possible to attack the regime indirectly by producing classics, or versions of classics, which apparently offered no threat to a system they predated by centuries, or plays that could be interpreted in the light of the current situation by a native audience in ways that, with luck, eluded the Nazi censors. One example was the *Antigone* of the prolific and popular Jean Anouilh (1910–87), a study of the conflict between personal loyalties and political authority produced in German-occupied Paris in 1944.

Besides America, there were still a few refuges in Europe. Switzerland, though without a great dramatic tradition of its own (Dürenmatt's first play was not produced until 1949), was especially welcoming to Germans. Brecht wrote *Mother Courage* in Zurich, before he moved on to America. Fritz Hochwälder (1911–86), author of distinguished 'Classical' plays dramatizing moral issues, settled permanently in Switzerland after leaving Vienna when Hitler arrived.

Getting away from it

War had scarcely less effect on countries not under German occupation. There also, experimental drama gave way to the needs of the moment – maintaining public morale and entertaining those wanting light relief from suffering, hardship and excessive work. Equivalents of E.N.S.A. (Entertainments National Service Association) existed in all combatant countries. While it presented full-length plays and symphony concerts, broad comedy and 'glamour' were probably more popular in British factories and war regions where E.N.S.A. was active. Noël Coward turned to patriotic drama while enjoying the royalties from his hugely popular comedy *Blithe Spirit* (1941), which ran for a record 1,997 performances.

In the U.S.A., far removed from the combat area, and less lengthily engaged, drama was less affected. Numerous patriotic and anti-Nazi plays were written, of no lasting interest, and light entertainment – farces, musical revues, etc. – provided the bulk of the fare. But *Arsenic and Old Lace* (1941) by Joseph Kesselring proved perennially popular and *The Voice of the Turtle* (1943) of John van Druten was a beautifully crafted comedy. The musical came of age, O'Neill returned to the theatre with *The Iceman Cometh*, and the first plays by Tennessee Williams were produced in the war years.

Above: Noël Coward provided relief. In *Blithe Spirit*, Margaret Rutherford, as the medium Madame Arcati, advises a haunted wife (Fay Compton) on how to get rid of Elvira, a predatory ghost.

censorship

Until comparatively recently, practically all governments have maintained some form of censorship of the printed word and the public performance, and some still do. Governments were especially sensitive to theatre, because of its social involvement and tradition of political satire and social criticism. Moreover, theatres gathered a number of people in one place, and governments without an efficient police force were nervous of crowds, whatever the reason for their assembly. A performance in a theatre could, and sometimes did, provoke public disturbance, something unlikely to happen as a result of scattered individuals reading a book (although pamphlets and news-papers had greater potential for causing a riot).

The theatre and the state

Censorship is obviously much harder to impose where there is no written script. Hence, popular forms of theatre, which usually incorporated tempor-ized dialogue, were at an advantage. At the least, plays could not be censored in advance, although their progenitors might be arrested later. Censorship was scarcely either practicable or necessary until the invention of printing in the late 15th century, which vastly facilitated subversion. Governments quickly introduced laws and proclamations designed to keep the press under control.

The object of censorship in earlier times was quite different from today. What governments were worried about were political rebellion and religious heresy, not sex and violence, the main preoccupation now. The change began in England in the late 17th century, with an outcry against the licentiousness of Restoration theatre, and reached its height in the rigid society of the 19th century. Governments in the 16th century required all books to be licensed. Since there was at first no public, professional theatre, and most plays were actually produced under the aegis of political and religious authorities, the likelihood of subversion from that quarter was much less threatening than it soon became. Nevertheless, plays too were licensed in various – often ineffi-cient – ways, sometimes by local authorities, who were generally unsympa-thetic towards travelling companies of actors independent of princely or aristocratic patronage.

Prejudice

Censorship in the age of 'absolute' monarchy was often highly arbitrary. James I of England (VI of Scotland), for example, was highly sensitive to derogatory portrayals of pampered Scots. Molière could get away with more than another dramatist might expect because of the favour of Louis XIV, but Louis XVI listened to a reading of Beaumarchais's *The Marriage of Figaro* with obvious disquiet, muttering remarks like 'This will never do!'. On that occa-sion, though, he did not prevent the play's performance, but signified his dis-approval by his absence. Similarly, Gogol's *The Government Inspector* would never have reached the Russian stage if the Tsar had not liked it so much. As it was, it caused such a fuss that Gogol left the country for a decade.

State censorship and theatre clubs

In some European countries in the 19th century, notably Russia and Prussia, authoritarian rule imposed censorship so strict as to inhibit the development of the drama. The advent of the 'new drama' led by Ibsen heightened the problem, not only in those countries but in states with more liberal regimes. In many centres, including London, censorship of dramatists widely admired by the intelligentsia, such as Ibsen himself, Bernard Shaw and others, caused an outcry. The difficulties over censorship encouraged the establishing of pri-vate theatres, or theatre clubs, including the Théâtre Libre, the Freie Bühne and the Moscow Arts Theatre. The censorship of even tsarist Russia, however, was mild compared with the oppression of the arts under the Soviet regime.

The Lord Chamberlain

In Shakespeare's time, all plays had to be licensed by a court official called
the Master of The Queen's Revels, later by his superior, the Lord Chamberlain.
His powers tended to grow subsequently, and the Licensing Act of 1737
required not only that all publicly performed plays should be licensed, but
also that a copy of the script should be submitted to him in advance. The
Bulwer-Lytton Act of 1843 in effect reinforced the Lord Chamberlain's powers
and has resulted in much criticism owing to the fact that, although generally
the powers were used leniently and comparatively few plays were banned out-
right, there was no appeal against his decision. In 1909 a Parliamentary committee recommended that licensing plays should be optional, and no penalty
imposed on unlicensed plays (unless, of course, they infringed the laws, a
matter for the Director of Public Prosecutions). No action followed, and in fact
the Lord Chamberlain's powers remained intact until finally abolished in
1968. Other democratic countries had abolished censorship of the theatre
years earlier (in the U.S.A. it had never existed). In general, self-censorship
has worked well in the modern theatre, and there is little temptation to
infringe the laws against obscenity, slander, racial incitement, etc.

Above: Shaw's *Mrs Warren's Profession* (1893) was an example of a play that was automatically barred from public performance since the profession concerned was prostitution, a subject not to be mentioned. (Above, the National Theatre production of 1986.)

Below: Howard Brenton's *The Romans in Britain* (1980) featured nudity, plenty of bloodshed and homosexual rape. It drew a parallel between the Roman occupation of Britain and the British occupation of Northern Ireland, but the political import was lost in the controversy over the sex and violence.

In North America, the cultural chasm of the war period was less evident, continuity was hardly interrupted, and theatre was vigorous and increasingly diverse. The early plays of Tennessee Williams and Arthur Miller appeared before the last of O'Neill's; Lillian Hellman, Maxwell Anderson and Thornton Wilder were all active; lesser dramatists such as Robert Anderson and William Inge were represented on Broadway before O'Neill's death in 1953. In Canada, though without major dramatists, theatre was increasingly lively after the war, largely through the work of semi-professional companies, and it gained new solidity with the founding of the Shakespeare Festival at Stratford, Ontario, under Tyrone Guthrie's direction in 1952.

American drama
after O'Neill

Above: Arthur Miller oversees a rehearsal in 1965.

Tennessee Williams

Tennessee (Thomas Lanier) Williams (1911–83), a Southerner who had a tough youth but managed to graduate from the University of Iowa, won a prize from the Theater Guild (see page 168) in 1939 for four one-act plays later published as *American Blues*. His first professional production was a failure, but in 1945 he gained sudden fame with *The Glass Menagerie*, imaginatively staged under Elia Kazan's direction. It also established the theme that characterised his best plays, which are compassionate, unblinking explorations of the frustrations and failures of psychologically troubled or inadequate individuals, frequently women, usually in a Southern setting and often, at the time, shocking in their candour. Perhaps the best is *A Streetcar Named Desire* (1947), in which the clash between the fading spinster Blanche, clinging to outdated but civilized dreams, and the loutish Stanley, representing a new, brutish culture, admits a wider social dimension. The young Marlon Brando gave a now-legendary performance as Stanley. Almost equally successful was *Cat on a Hot Tin Roof* (1955), an intense drama of family relationships set in a Mississippi plantation.

Tennessee Williams' plays, especially *The Glass Menagerie*, sometimes suggested an autobiographical basis, and Williams's personal struggle with drugs and alcohol accounts for a falling-off in quality after *Night of the Iguana* (1961). Besides those mentioned, the best of his plays include: *Summer and Smoke* (1948), another study of a Southern spinster undone by sexual desire; *The Rose Tattoo* (1951), a sexual comedy about an older woman; the controversial *Camino Real* (1953); and the trilogy based on the myth of Orpheus, transferred to a modern setting and marked by violence and perversion – *Orpheus Descending* (1957), *Suddenly, Last Summer* (1958) and *Sweet Bird of Youth* (1959).

Arthur Miller

As with Williams, the best plays of his near contemporary, Arthur Miller (born 1915), are his earliest, and like Williams (with whom he shared a student drama prize), Miller gained international fame with early success on Broadway. Both would have a liberating effect for their successors, such as

Sam Shepard (born 1943) and David Mamet (born 1947), through their stylistic experiments, and both are superficially naturalistic, but in other respects, the two writers are not very similar. Williams is concerned primarily with individual psychology, while Miller, though no less concerned with the individual, is the more intensely concerned with contemporary society, the pressures it exerts and the conflicts it causes.

Miller's first Broadway play closed within days, but his second, *All My Sons* (1947), established his reputation as a skilful dramatist and formidable critic of contemporary society. It concerns a war profiteer who sells faulty equipment to the government, causing the death of American pilots, and is then exposed by his son. His third established his international reputation; *Death of a Salesman* (1949), like *The Glass Menagerie*, benefited from an imaginative set and, like *All My Sons*, from Kazan's direction. It has become a kind of talisman of American drama and perhaps the most famous play of the century. Through the decline and death of a small-time commercial traveller, ruined by the materialist values he has loyally espoused, it mounts a compelling attack on the American capitalist system. In *The Crucible* (1953), Miller exploited the Salem witch trials in early colonial Massachusetts to launch a passionate attack on intolerance and repression in the era of McCarthyite 'Red-baiting' (also attacked, more obliquely, in Robert Anderson's *Tea and Sympathy* the same year). The scarcely less powerful *A View From the Bridge* (1955), set among immigrant workers in the Brooklyn Docks, was a one-act play later expanded to three acts, and was seen in London in a club production because of its allusions to homosexuality.

Thereafter Arthur Miller abandoned Broadway theatre, disgusted at its commercialism, and his return with *After the Fall* (1964), allegedly based on his sensational, short-lived marriage to Marilyn Monroe, was not well received. Among later plays, some produced first in England where Miller has been perhaps even more highly regarded than in America, the best is probably *The Price* (1968), returning to the theme of a family destroyed by society's materialistic values, followed by the plays of the 1990s, *Ride Down Mount Morgan* (1991) and *Broken Glass* (1994), when Miller had become the Grand Old Man of the theatre.

Above left: *The Crucible*, Miller's political parable about the dangers of ignorance and dogma.

Above: A scene from a rather rare revival of Tennessee Williams's Southern Gothic melodrama, *Cat on a Hot Tin Roof*.

Broadway
and the musical

Broadway is the long street running aslant Manhattan's grid pattern and forming Times Square where it meets Seventh Avenue. It is also a generic name, like London's 'West End', for New York commercial theatre. The major theatres are grouped in a relatively small area adjacent to Broadway (few are actually on it) immediately north of Times Square, the 'Great White Way'. The association has existed since the early days of American theatre, but the theatre district was then farther south. It moved gradually north as Manhattan itself expanded.

Commercialism

The concept of Broadway arouses mixed feelings. It has been the scene of great theatrical events, both triumphs and disasters, it commands a mass of talent and technological expertise, and it is certainly glamorous – in a uniquely American way. It is also very expensive. In the 1940s, experimental drama could find a foothold there, but the high cost of production has placed a premium on commercial success, and few shows appear that are not seen as potential hits, at least by those investing money in them. Although ticket prices are generally higher than in other centres, full or nearly full houses are vital, and at the first sign of lagging ticket sales, plays are taken off to minimize losses, or cancelled during their provincial trial run. This situation contributes to the influence of a small handful of critics, whose first-night reviews can make or break a production.

Serious dramatists are seldom admirers of Broadway. As Arthur Miller remarked in 1996, 'I can't think of a [serious] writer who liked Broadway.' Like O'Neill before him, Miller withdrew from it for a long period. Broadway, as he observed, 'is a place of sheer entertainment, one or another version of the Folies Bergères and all that. [It] . . . has always been suspicious of art when it was not openly hostile.' Still, as a place of sheer entertainment – and, to be fair, occasionally for serious plays (even if a large proportion of them are imported) – Broadway reigns supreme. Perhaps the most notable ingredient of its success in the period since the war was a succession of productions of what is generally seen as a characteristically American genre, the musical.

The musical

The term originated as an abbreviation of 'musical comedy', implying a mixture of song and spoken dialogue, and is related to earlier forms such as 18th-century ballad opera, operetta, Gilbert and Sullivan, revue and so on. Early examples of 'musical comedy', from the end of the 19th century, were English as well as American. Plots were slight, the music often an add-on, with little dramatic relevance. The first major landmark was *Show Boat* (1927), music by Jerome Kern, libretto (or 'book') and lyrics by Oscar Hammerstein II (1895–1960). Though produced at the Ziegfeld Theater, it opened not with leg-flashing chorus girls but weary black cotton workers singing 'Ol' Man

River'. In short, it was a serious play, dealing with human problems – a 'musical', rather than a 'comedy', in which the songs grew out of the action.

Rodgers and Hammerstein

After *Show Boat*, Hammerstein was associated with a long succession of flops,
before the American musical reached maturity overnight with the premiere of
Oklahoma!. It originated in a straight play produced by the Theater Guild (see
page 168), which had also produced Gershwin's *Porgy and Bess* (1935), an
opera rather than a musical. Legend relates that Jerome Kern turned down
the projected musical on the grounds that 'Westerns don't make money',
leading to Hammerstein's partnership with the composer Richard Rodgers
(1902–79), who had previously worked with lyricist Lorenz Hart on such
shows as *Pal Joey* (1940). Rodgers and Hammerstein continued to work
together until Hammerstein's death, their most notable works being *Carousel*
(1945), *South Pacific* (1948), *The King and I* (1951) and *The Sound of Music*
(1959), all great international successes on stage and film. The partnership of
Lerner and Loewe produced similar hits, especially *My Fair Lady* (1956), a
musical version of Shaw's *Pygmalion*.

Refinements

Oklahoma! contained all the elements of the musical, most of which had
appeared before, but never in a single, integrated whole. Agnes de Mille's balletic choreography signalled the importance of dance in various forms, and
future choreographers such as Jerome Robbins and Bob Fosse were often
directors as well. The plot of *Oklahoma!* was fairly lightweight, but serious
subject matter was no longer taboo for the musical. The outstanding example,
and one of the best of the genre, was the versatile Leonard Bernstein's *West
Side Story* (1957), a version of Shakespeare's *Romeo and Juliet* transferred to
the contemporary youth gangs of New York. The lyrics were by Stephen
Sondheim who, as composer and lyricist, became the outstanding exponent of
the musical in the 1960s and 70s, and extended the genre further, at times
moving close to opera. Otherwise, a decline in the American musical became
apparent, although others, such as the English composer Andrew Lloyd
Webber, achieved great commercial success.

off-Broadway

Arthur Miller complained of the persistence of 'the myth that Broadway is where American theatre lives'. It is certainly true – although it could be said of other countries too – that many of the most interesting developments have taken place elsewhere.

The Theater Guild

The Theater Guild arose from the work of a group called the Washington Square Players (1914–18) who specialized in contemporary, non-commercial drama. In the 1920s it produced contemporary plays, mainly by European dramatists, Shaw especially, but also O'Neill's *Mourning Becomes Electra* and Gershwin's *Porgy and Bess*. The Guild built its own Broadway theatre (now the Virginia) in 1925, but ran into trouble during the Depression, being saved by the success of *Oklahoma!*. The Guild's greatest contribution lay in, so to speak, its spin-offs, and the subsequent careers of leading figures, such as Elia Kazan, the outstanding director of the post-war period, and Lee Strasberg. Politically committed members, including Strasberg, formed the democratically run Group Theatre in 1931, producing plays of social criticism on a repertory basis. Another member was Clifford Odets (1906–63) who, after the militant *Waiting for Lefty* (1935), became virtually its resident playwright. Other dramatists associated with the Guild, including Maxwell Anderson, Elmer Rice and Robert E. Sherwood, formed the Playwrights' Company (1938). The Group's concept of political theatre influenced The Federal Theater Project (1935–9), one of the enlightened cultural programmes of Roosevelt's New Deal government (and a rather rare – in America – example of government subsidy).

The Method

The style of acting known as the Method was first adopted by the Group in reaction against the conventional, externalized acting of Broadway and proselytized by the Actors' Studio, founded in 1947 by Kazan and others. Strasberg became its leading figure. The Method was based on the theories of Stanislavsky, requiring the actor to identify emotionally with the character, building the part from within and including unscripted details of performance – pauses, gestures, even exclamations – prompted by the actor's intuition. This approach was to have wide-ranging influence, and the Method as exemplified by Marlon Brando in *A Streetcar Named Desire* had a powerful impact. But Brando subsequently moved into film, a medium to which, in general, the Method is perhaps better suited.

Off-Broadway

The exorbitant costs of Broadway production and a resulting unwillingness to take risks were responsible for the growth of small 'off-Broadway' theatres, tending to congregate in Greenwich Village but found almost anywhere. At first, off-Broadway productions hoped to transfer to Broadway, and many did. Actors and directors moved freely from one to the other, and many playwrights began their careers off-Broadway, among them Edward Albee, until he shot to Broadway fame in 1962 with *Who's Afraid of Virginia Woolf?* (though he later moved out again). In time the division tended to harden as particular companies or directors established a niche, such as Jose Quintero and the Loft Players at the Circle-in-the-Square (1951), the first New York theatre designed for theatre-in-the-round. In the 1960s, off-Broadway spawned another fringe, off-off-Broadway, centred largely in the unsavoury Lower East Side, and mainly concerned with experimental work often incompatible with a normal stage and produced in old lofts or cellars.

Outside New York

There were also developments beyond New York, which from small beginnings developed into major provincial theatres. The oldest is the Cleveland Playhouse, which traces its origins to an amateur group performing in an old church in 1915. It became fully professional in the 1930s, with two auditoriums, adding a third on another site in 1949. The Alley Theater in Houston, Texas, run for over 30 years by Nina Vance, began in 1947 as a largely amateur group renting a smallish dance hall, then a disused factory, but within ten years had become a fully professional resident company, playing a varied international repertory for nine months of the year. Its new theatre, opened in 1968, one of the architectural sights of Houston, contains two versatile auditoriums, the smaller one based on the arena stage of the old factory. The Arena Stage in Washington D.C. began in 1950 in a cinema, then a disused brewery, before building its arena stage. A second theatre, with a thrust stage and seats in curved tiers in the classical manner, opened in the 1970s.

Many of the original Arena Stage Company were local drama students, and the universities played an important part in the development of theatre outside New York, often supported by private benefactors, philanthropic organisations or government subsidy. The University of Washington in Seattle had the first theatre-in-the-round (1940); Harvard had the first automated theatre, which could adjust to provide any type of stage (1960). Although drama at Yale can be traced back to colonial times, the Yale Repertory Theater was founded by the critic Robert Brustein, then head of the Drama School, in 1966. It later moved off campus and its buildings include four auditoriums, two for the Drama School exclusively. In 1980 Brustein became director of a professional company at Harvard. Yale and Harvard each have famous theatre-history collections.

Bottom: Marlon Brando as the slobbish Stanley Kowalski in the original Broadway production of *A Streetcar Named Desire*, one of the most famous stage performances in history.

Below: Lee Strasberg (1901–82), the leading figure in the Actors' Studio and chief proponent of the Method.

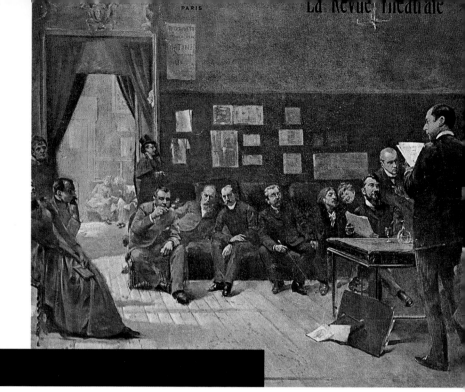

directors

At different times theatre has been dominated by the actor, the manager or even the writer, but the 20th century will probably be seen by future generations as pre-eminently the era of the director's theatre, although actors have never been reduced to the puppets that Gordon Craig wanted them to be and, at times, 20th-century theatre was writer- rather than director-driven. As we have seen, the rise of the director was based on late 19th-century innovations in form, on the ideas of innovators such as Antoine in France, Brahm in Germany and Stanislavsky in Russia manifested in the work of such as Reinhardt and Meyerhold.

Director's theatre

The disaster of the First World War, which discredited old conventions and prompted hopes of a fresh start, helped to facilitate change in theatre as in other arts, so the 1920s became a decade of artistic experiment and radical change. There was also a good practical reason for the rise of director's theatre, in that the complications of staging a play had become so numerous and so various, the technology so complicated, that there was an obvious need for one controlling intelligence to forge the various elements into a coherent whole. This was also evidently necessary, almost from the first, in the rival medium of cinema. 'Director's theatre', almost by definition, reduced the significance of the writer. Erwin Piscator (1893–1966), a major influence on Brecht, was one of the first directors to move away from a rigid script and to employ film along with live actors, while developing highly complex, technically ambitious staging.

The creativity of directors was sometimes taken to such extremes that it provoked antagonistic reactions. Shakespeare in modern dress (for example) was nothing new, and some very strange versions of his plays, stranger than any modern production, were produced in the 18th–19th centuries. One of the reasons for Shakespeare's continuing appeal is his adaptability, but the question arises how far a director is entitled to change or ignore a dramatist's specific instructions or artistic intent, and even alter the text. Ronald Harwood quoted the example of a production of *The Seagull* by the Moscow Arts Theatre in the 1970s. Some lines from the first act were repeated, appropriately in the eyes of the director, but presumably not in the eyes of Chekhov, after the suicide of Konstantin, which, in Chekhov's script, is the final incident in the play. More extreme examples of the director's ego superimposing itself on the intentions of the playwright could be quoted. Perhaps we should remember too that Chekhov himself strongly disliked Stanislavsky's original productions of his plays. But Stanislavsky would not have taken such liberties with the text.

Guthrie

The career of Tyrone Guthrie (1900–71) spanned the Second World War. In 1937, he directed Olivier's *Hamlet* in London, and later *Elsinore*, but achieved international prominence at the Old Vic in London and was the virtual creator

of the Stratford Festival theatre in Canada and founder of the Minneapolis (now Guthrie) Theater. He was by nature experimental, though not a radical, perhaps at his best with Shakespeare and Chekhov, often staged in modern dress. He was renowned for his handling of crowd scenes, frequently the hallmark of an outstanding director.

Barrault

A student of mime, Jean-Louis Barrault (1910–94) was perhaps the outstanding figure in modern French theatre. He was with the Comédie-Française in the 1940s but was happier in an independent theatre. He worked with his wife, the brilliant actress Madeleine Renaud, at the Théâtre Marigny and later with the Théâtre des Nations, sponsored by U.N.E.S.C.O., until his dismissal after the '68 student riots. He directed his own adaptations of Rabelais and Jarry in an old wrestling hall, briefly occupied a circus tent in the defunct Gare d'Orsay, and finally adapted a former skating rink. As well as an innovative director, whose long and somewhat chequered career included many ground-breaking productions, Barrault was an extraordinary actor, with a mime-born mastery of expression in the slightest gesture.

Brook

Along with Kazan, Strasberg and a few other Americans, the populist Joseph Papp is fondly remembered for Shakespeare in the (Central) Park (1954), where admission was free. He later founded the Off-Broadway Public Theater, with several auditoriums, staging new plays, American and foreign, and was director of the Lincoln Center theatres. Artistically, however, probably the most influential director of the era was the British Peter Brook, who attracted attention directing Shakespeare in his teens. His most famous production in England was his *A Midsummer Night's Dream* (1971), utilizing elements from circus. He then left England and, influenced by Barrault and the Polish actor-oriented, minimalist director Jerzy Grotowski, founded his International Centre of Theatre Research in Paris. He took his company to African and Asian countries where theatre was unknown, besides lecturing, writing, filming and researching, demanding much and inspiring many. His nine-hour version of the Hindu *Mahabharata* was seen in an English version in 1987.

Opposite: The innovative and influential French director André Antoine (1858–1943) lecturing in a Paris theatre. He staged the first performance of *Ghosts* in 1890, playing the part of Oswald himself.

Above: Guthrie directing George Grizzard in *Hamlet*, for the inaugural production of the Guthrie Theater in Minneapolis, May 1963.

protest
theatre

Since the dawn of Modernism, adherents of this or that cultural trend have applied their theories to the theatre, and attempts to categorize them have produced a confusing number of labels, many of them hard to justify. Their profusion suggests simply that 20th-century theatre has been extraordinarily diverse and lacking in any powerful, cohesive cultural influence or predominant style.

Political drama

The term 'protest drama' encompasses all plays, and there are a great number, that attack generally accepted conventions. It is associated especially with the politicization of drama since about 1920, when the catchphrase 'Theatre is a weapon' was first heard. This was an aspect of the increasingly close connection between theatre and society which largely arose from the cataclysmic events of world war and revolution. It was often this kind of theatre that manifested the greatest creative energy.

Some dramatists were actively engaged in politics, invariably left-wing. Brecht sang ballads, in his rough, proletarian voice, in workers' clubs, and Toller was elected president of the revolutionary soviet republic in Bavaria, an achievement only equalled by the Czech playwright Vaclav Havel, who after a heroic career of resistance to communist totalitarianism became Czech president in 1989, a longer-lasting position than Toller's. The Dadaists and their successors, the Surrealists, endeavoured to shatter cultural conventions and, although their effect on theatre was transitory, a performance of Tristan Tzara's *Gas Heart* in 1923 caused one of the many theatre riots of the period, ending with the closing-down of the theatre – perhaps the aim of the exercise. Pirandello mocked, among other things, theatrical conventions, and the Russian Revolution unleashed briefly a rash of experimental theatre, with Meyerhold a leading figure. A notable feature was the vast celebrations of the working class, such as *The Storming of the Winter Palace* (1920), with, literally, a cast of thousands. 'Agit-prop' (agitation/propaganda) arose through efforts to popularize the Revolution and instil socialist views by crude sketches performed in street and factory, largely by amateurs. It was soon suppressed by the dead hand of Socialist Realism, but had some effects abroad, notably on Piscator in Germany and on Odets in the U.S.A., whose *Waiting for Lefty* represented the one enduring dramatic achievement of agit-prop.

Documentary drama

Protest had some effect too on the development of 'documentary drama' or
'Theatre of Fact', along with the productions of the Living Newspaper, a unit of
the Federal Theater Project in America. The form is regarded as originating
with Piscator, who employed it in the service of socialist ideals. His high-tech
productions also featured actors made up to look exactly like the real people
they represented. Weiss's *The Investigator* (1965), directed by Piscator,
included genuine testimony of concentration-camp guards. The same technique was employed by Hochhuth in plays such as *The Deputy* and *The
Soldiers*, again directed by Piscator, and some of the plays of the 1970s tackled political topics by similar means.

Theatre of the Absurd

In spite of the influence of Brecht and the Berliner Ensemble, the sharp political edge of protest drama was largely absent after 1945, though it returned in
the late 1950s with the rise of radical black drama, the 'theatre laboratories'
such as Guerrilla Theatre, and Sondheim's politicization of the musical. But
Dürenmatt declared that in the post-Fascist age of the atom bomb, 'comedy
alone is appropriate to us'. Another response to the impossibility of dealing
with the meaninglessness of contemporary civilization was the so-called
Theatre of the Absurd, a critics' term that now seems rather inappropriate,
especially when applied to the leading representatives of the genre, Beckett
and Pinter (see page 176). Otherwise, the leading Absurdist influence was the
surrealistic, nihilistic farce of Romanian-born Eugene Ionescu (1912–94),
beginning with The Bald Soprano (1950). In America, the early one-act plays
of Edward Albee were classed as Absurdist. His *The Zoo Story* appeared in
London in the same year (1960) as Ionesco's *Rhinoceros* (with Laurence
Olivier). *Tiny Alice* (1964) totally puzzled the New York critics, and Albee is
now considered at his best in his savage dissections of family relationships,
beginning with *Who's Afraid of Virginia Woolf?*.

Africa

Western civilization also came under attack from without. Wole Soyinka, the
outstanding African dramatist, blended contemporary Western trends and
techniques with traditional African dance-drama, but, although his plays are
partly non-naturalistic, he attacked both Western values and African social ills
such as tribal hostility and bureaucratic corruption. In South Africa, Athol
Fugard's plays, such as *Boesman and Lena* (1969), attacked racism and the
apartheid system as destructive of individual morality. He worked closely with
his actors, starting with a rough draft from which a script emerged in the
process of creative rehearsal. They toured the townships, performing in the
sort of places that emphasized the grimness of his message.

theatre in Britain

After a slow start, the theatre in Great Britain in the past half-century has been as varied, at times more vigorous than anywhere else, and probably more various than in any other period. It has also suffered many of the problems that have afflicted the traditional European theatre generally in recent times.

Public subsidy

A major influence after 1945 was the willingness of government to subsidize the theatre. In addition to local government funding, many enterprises benefited from grants from the Arts Council (founded in 1946). Initially, this probably had the greatest effect in the provinces, though by the 1970s it was felt, with some reason, that the capital had disproportionate advantage. New theatres were proudly erected in provincial cities, sometimes radical in form, such as Manchester's Royal Exchange, a suspended glass module for theatre-in-the-round. Distinctive local theatre cultures developed in some towns, and local theatres, such as the Citizens' Theatre in Glasgow or Joan Littlewood's Theatre Workshop in London's East End, maintained close touch with the community, patronizing local playwrights. Alan Ayckbourn's plays were mostly written for the Stephen Joseph Theatre-in-the-Round in Scarborough, where he became director of production in 1970, although they usually transferred in due course to the West End.

State theatre

Willingness to subsidize drama permitted the long-delayed creation of the state-subsidized National Theatre. France had had such an institution since the 17th century, and efforts to start an English equivalent dated from the time of Garrick. A plan to establish it for the tercentenary of Shakespeare's death in 1916 was scotched by the outbreak of war, and a second attempt foundered, after Bernard Shaw had laid the foundation stone in 1938, for the same reason. The third attempt succeeded. A National Theatre company was formed in 1961 under the aegis of the great actor Laurence Olivier (1907–89). It appeared at the famous, but unpretentious, Old Vic Theatre from 1963, until its own building on the South Bank of the Thames near Waterloo was ready in the early 1970s. The theatre was able to call on the finest talents available, the company was outstandingly successful both at home and, from 1989, on regular tours.

What in effect was a second state theatre, the Royal Shakespeare Company, was also formed in 1961, at the Royal Shakespeare Theatre, Stratford-upon-Avon, directed by Peter Hall, who later succeeded Olivier at the National. Its London base was the Aldwych, until it moved to the Barbican Centre in 1982. It too established a peerless reputation, but its position became precarious in

Left: Kenneth Haigh in the lead role in the original production of *Look Back in Anger*. Its effect on serious English theatre was enormous, though perhaps more for social than dramatic reasons.

Right: Edward Bond's *Saved* at the Royal Court in 1965. The characters were largely inarticulate, and the scene of a baby stoned in its pram caused a minor uproar.

the cost-cutting 1970s, when there was talk of closing it altogether. By that time regional theatres, receiving a decreasing slice of the reduced subsidy cake, were under strain, and commercial theatres also languished.

Dramatists

The most successful contemporary playwright after the war was Terence Rattigan (1911–77), an outstanding exponent of the 'well-made play', but the rather conventional British theatre was challenged in 1956 by John Osborne's *Look Back in Anger*, first of the so-called 'kitchen sink' school. It was not in fact revolutionary in form, much less so than *Waiting for Godot*, which predated it, but being less problematic, it created more fuss. It was produced by George Devine's English Stage Company at the Royal Court Theatre, Sloane Square, which became the leading force in contemporary drama, at least until restricted by financial problems in the 1980s. This was also a boom period for musicals, heralded by 'rock' musicals of which the most famous was *Hair*, a celebration of sixties youth culture. *Jesus Christ Superstar* (1972), words by Tim Rice, music by Andrew Lloyd Webber, was the first step to the creation of an international industry based on Lloyd Webber's work.

Above: Sir Peter Hall in 1976 outside the National Theatre, where he succeeded Olivier as director in 1973. He became the most influential man of the English theatre in recent years, and a fierce battler for decent funding.

Fringe theatre

The annual Edinburgh Festival (founded 1947), besides heavyweight, international productions, spawned a phenomenal 'fringe', sparked partly by the lively, local Traverse Theatre (since 1963). By the early 1990s, the fringe involved about 500 groups from every continent, involving nearly 10,000 performances (a large proportion being new works) in 150 diverse locales. The name was adopted as a general description for the growing number of small, experimental or specialist companies in London and elsewhere. There were about 70 'fringe' theatres in London in the 1990s, often located in pubs, abandoned factories, etc., though some acquired their own theatres while, in the provinces, they found a home in the new 'civic centres' and cultural complexes. Several, such as the Bush Theatre in Shepherds Bush, the Gate in Notting Hill, and the Orange Tree in Richmond, became well-established institutions in the London theatre world, notable for their unusual repertory or production qualities.

Once seen as a fringe figure, the reputation of Beckett has risen steadily over the course of half-a-century to classic status, although his full-length plays were few in number and – perhaps following the logic of a view of the world as absurd and pointless – became ever less substantial. Pinter, influenced by Beckett and famous for his ability to suggest much while saying little, apparently gave up writing plays altogether at a relatively early age.

'minimal' theatre:
Beckett and Pinter

Above: A production of Pinter's *No Man's Land*, with Paul Eddington (left) and the author himself (right) in the parts played in the original production by John Gielgud and Ralph Richardson.

Beckett

The Irish playwright was born near Dublin, brought up a Protestant, and studied languages at Trinity College. He first went to Paris at 22 to teach English at the École Normale Supérieure. He became friends with the novelist James Joyce, whose work was the subject of his first publication in 1929. He returned to lecture at Trinity College in 1930, but soon resigned and, after several years wandering and writing poetry, stories and a study of Proust, settled permanently in France. Thereafter he wrote mainly in French. By the time *Waiting for Godot* (or *En attendant Godot*) was first produced by Roger Blin (1907–84) at the tiny Théâtre de Babylone in Paris in 1953, Beckett had published several novels and was well known in literary circles. The English version of *Godot*, translated by the author, was first seen at Cambridge in 1955.

Waiting for Godot

The play was seen as a major contribution to the Theatre of the Absurd, and made Beckett internationally famous. Two clown-like tramps wait, in a desolate spot, for the mysterious Godot, unsure when or where he will arrive. Little happens. Two other characters appear, one driving the other at the end of a rope. A boy announces Godot's imminent arrival, but he never arrives. There is some grimly witty, inconsequential talk:

> Vladimir: That passed the time.
> Estragon: It would have passed in any case.
> Vladimir: Yes, but not so rapidly.

Both acts end with the same exchange: 'Well, shall we go?' 'Yes, let's go', followed by the stage direction: They do not move.

The play has been performed in many languages and many countries and varying interpretations, showing that, while a summary or even a reading do it no justice, it is marvellously theatrical. None of Beckett's late plays has had such appeal, although they maintain Beckett's unique tone of voice. His bleak and desolate view of the human condition is laced with a kind of gallows humour, and, somehow, the whole experience is exhilarating rather than depressing. In *Endgame*, two old people inhabit dustbins throughout, *Happy Days* has a single character buried at increasing depths in a mound, *Play* has three heads emerging from urns. *Krapp's Last Tape* is a monologue, written for the Irish actor Patrick Magee, of an old man listening to, but not

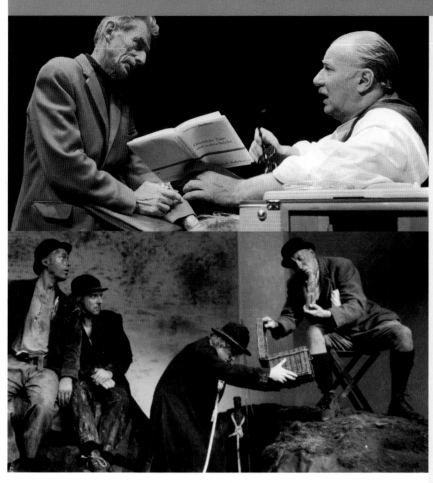

Plays

1953 *Waiting for Godot*
1957 *Endgame*
1958 *Krapp's Last Tape*
1961 *Happy Days*
1963 *Play*
1966 *Come and Go*
1967 *Breath*
1971 *Not I*
1975 *Footfalls*
1981 *Rockaby*

Novels

1938 *Murphy*
1951 *Molloy*
1953 *Watt*
1958 *Malone Dies*
1960 *The Unnameable*

Other works

Radio plays, poems, short stories

Quote

1. Faint light on stage littered with miscellaneous rubbish. Hold about five seconds.
2. Faint brief cry and immediately inspiration and slow increase of light together reaching maximum together in about ten seconds. Silence and hold about five seconds.
3. Expiration and slow decrease of light together reaching minimum together (light as in 1) in about ten seconds and immediately cry as before. Silence and hold about five seconds.
Breath (complete script)

Top: Beckett (left) discussing *Krapp's Last Tape* with Martin Held at the Schiller Theater in 1969.

Above: A revival of *Waiting For Godot* in London in 1991. Beckett's first play 'works' extremely well, though it is hard to say why. Nothing that he wrote afterwards is quite as effective, and in his late work Beckett marginalized his genius.

comprehending, recordings made in his youth. Beckett was notably loyal to favoured interpreters, such as the actress Billie Whitelaw, for whom he wrote two plays, and his American director for thirty years, Alan Schneider. Beckett's later plays are remote from conventional theatre. *Come and Go* has only 120 words, *Breath* has none, *Not I* is a 'monologue for mouth', delivered by an actor, of either sex, whose mouth alone is visible.

Pinter

Harold Pinter (born 1930), son of a Jewish tailor, was an actor in his early career, later a screenwriter and then a stage director, notably of Simon Gray's plays. His plays were first seen between the late 1950s and late '70s. His second play, *The Birthday Party* (1958), established his characteristic tone of quiet, inexplicable menace, and his extraordinary ability to suggest layers of meaning with minimal, colloquial dialogue – qualities that are expressed by the term 'Pinteresque'. However, few critics could make anything of *The Birthday Party*, and Pinter was not generally recognized as an outstanding contemporary dramatist until *The Caretaker* (1960), concerning the relationship between two brothers and a tramp in a dingy London flat, in which nothing is certain and all the characters are psychologically damaged in some way: one of the brothers suffers from headaches resulting from the electric-shock treatment he received for his – unspecified – 'complaint'.

It was followed by several one-act plays, which Pinter also directed, and *The Homecoming* (1965), a family drama with Freudian overtones, admired by Beckett and perhaps Pinter's best play, in which his gift for combining the shocking with the commonplace was exploited to great effect. Among his later plays, perhaps the best are *Old Times* (1971), *No Man's Land* (1975) and *Betrayal* (1978).

Any list of the writers today who are most likely to feature in a future history of the theatre is bound to prove unreliable. Posterity makes its own judgements. Nor is it possible to pick out the most significant trends among so large and so various a group, although there is one trend that in itself partly explains the difficulty. That is the increasing merging of the media. Most of today's most successful writers are also associated with film, television and other arts (including the novel), and they are often better known for their work in the more obviously 'popular' media. They are also, though this is not new, sometimes intimately involved with particular companies, like the Nobel prize-winner Dario Fo in Italy.

contemporary playwrights

Britain

In England, the Royal Court continued to be the cradle of innovative new drama, in particular the work of Arnold Wesker, David Storey, Christopher Hampton, resident dramatist in the late 1960s, and David Hare, a powerful social critic whose plays have usually been staged by the National Theatre. Edward Bond's *Saved* (1965) offended the Lord Chamberlain and is credited with expediting the end of his censorship. The Lord Chamberlain would certainly have objected to works of Howard Brenton, notably *The Romans In Britain* (1980) at the National which prompted an unsuccessful private prosecution, to the black farces of Joe Orton, whose chief purpose was to shock the middle class, and to Irving Welsh, whose *You'll Have Had Your Hole* (1998) was 'an orgy of drug-taking, torture and homosexual rape'. But the most acclaimed of contemporary playwrights tended to be less overtly antagonistic. They included Alan Ayckbourn, whose comedies often had subversive, disturbing, even nightmarish – for example *Woman in Mind*, 1986 – effects; Simon Gray, a subtle satirist; and Caryl Churchill, another Royal Court protégée. Her biggest commercial success was *Serious Money* (1987), an exuberant satire of the financial world written partly in rhyming verse. Probably the outstanding talent was that of the Czech-born Tom Stoppard, an intellectual with scintillating verbal dexterity and a highly developed sense of fun, as well as infinite dramatic scope. Among a newer generation, Jonathan Harvey and Patrick Marbler shed light on aspects of contemporary sexuality, and Terry Johnson presented new insights into the nature of comedy. In Ireland, Brian Friel consistently produced admirable plays such as *Dancing at Lughnesa* (1990), about five spinsters coping with poverty and frustration in the 1930s.

Europe

German theatre in the 1980s and 1990s produced a surge of new and provocative drama, including the tour de force of septuagenarian George Tabori, *Mein Kampf* (1987), set in the Viennese flophouse frequented by the young Hitler. Klaus Pohl tackled xenophobia in *Beautiful Stranger* (1991), and Georg Seidel dealt with social alienation in *Carmen Kittel* (1987). Others in the German van-

guard included Botho Strauss, a fierce critic of modern materialism who worked with the famous director Peter Stein at the Schaubühne in Berlin, and the East German Heiner Müller, who skilfully employed historical situations to comment on the present in, for example, *Quartet* (1982), which sites the characters of an 18th-century novel in a future world. The French playwright most widely esteemed, especially abroad, between about 1950 and 1980 was probably the fertile Jean Anouilh (1910–87), a brilliant craftsman in the tradition of Molière whose dominant theme was the corruption of human nature in a decadent society. Among European plays produced in English-speaking countries, one of the biggest commercial successes of the 1990s was *Art*, a comedy on the superficially unlikely theme of the nature of art, by the French writer Yasmina Reza.

U.S.A.

Among the most successful American playwrights of the 1960s–1980s was the witty and socially observant Neil Simon, who once had four plays on Broadway simultaneously. The equally prolific Lanford Wilson was one of the founders of the Circle Repertory Company in New York, associated with many first productions of modern American plays. Among a profusion of talented American writers, two whose future reputation looked secure in the 1990s were Sam Shepard and David Mamet. The plays of the prolific Shepard, also an actor and screenwriter, reflect popular culture, and his dominant theme is the corrupt effect of industrialization on early American idealism. *The Tooth of Crime* (1972), one of his best plays, written while he was living in London, concerned the decline and death of an ageing rock star. His Pulitzer-Prize-winning *Buried Child* (1978) depicted the disintegration of a poor farming family. Mamet, whose career began in his native Chicago, is an entirely different, more cerebral playwright, whose style, though contemporary and colloquial, is essentially literary, and whose subject matter is varied. In general, he may be at his best on a small scale – one-act plays and small casts. Some of his most successful plays tended to satirize easy targets, such as property dealers (*Glengarry Glen Ross*, 1984) and Hollywood producers (*Speed-the-Plow*, 1985). John Guare has displayed a gift for savage farce, notably in *Six Degrees of Separation* (1990).

contemporary theatre

Theatre in the 20th century has survived cinema, television and the information technology revolution. It has had to adapt, but then it has adapted to changing times before, and its capacity for doing so seems to be unlimited. We can be certain that theatre will exist into the foreseeable future, but we cannot say what forms it will take, even a short time ahead.

Cash crisis

A major problem for subsidized theatre in recent years has been the widening gap between resources and performance. As we have seen, the problem was arguably worst in Britain, but recently it has been looming larger in other European countries, where subsidies are generally higher, and in the U.S.A., where state subsidy has been insignificant but private subsidy, facilitated by tax concessions, has been far greater. At the end of the 20th century these problems remained unsolved. There was widespread acknowledgement that costs must be reduced, but no painless way of reducing them – without sacrificing artistic concerns to economic priorities – had been found.

Art and technology

Paradoxically, one answer to adverse balance sheets was greater expenditure. More money was invested in so-called 'blockbuster' musicals in order to achieve spectacular visual effects, an enterprise that, as in movies, seemed bound to be ultimately self-defeating but proved to have more mileage than might have been expected. A good seat for a Broadway musical cost over $50 in the 1990s, so it was nice to know that the show's producers had also splashed out. For the sake of a more authentic and versatile set, New York's Majestic Theater, with seating capacity of 1,655, was partly rebuilt for Lloyd Webber's *The Phantom of the Opera* as a complex, automated machine, handling tons of props and scenery and providing no less than 96 traps for the Phantom to make his ghostly entrances and exits. The big subsidized theatres, such as the Royal Shakespeare Company, followed suit, employing cutting-edge technology to achieve extraordinary, and often highly imaginative, visual effects of a kind familiar from TV and video but on a far greater scale – and live!

Another characteristic of theatre towards the end of the century has been increasing novelty and experiment, often in fringe theatres where production costs were less oppressive. A bewildering number of small groups arose, often temporary, sometimes held together by one inspired individual – Peter Brook is a famous example – sometimes incorporating a team of independent artists of various kinds, and frequently exploiting other media, especially film and recorded sound but also visual arts, journalism, etc. A powerful driving force was the urge to investigate the roots and reassess the nature of theatre.

'Collective creation'

The idea of a communal endeavour became influential during the 1960s. As the term suggests, 'collective creation' was the fruit of a group of people working together from no more than a concept through discussion, improvisation, and rehearsal, for months, even years, until the final performance. A striking international success of this kind was the Paris-based Théâtre de Soleil's evocation of the French Revolution, 1789, in 1970. Other notable collectives were the Performance Group founded by Richard Schechner in New York and the People Show in England. The concept was, of course, not wholly new. The Living Theatre and its derivative, the Open Theatre (1963–73) were run on similar lines, which seem not so far removed from the commedia dell'arte or even, perhaps, Burbage's company in Elizabethan London.

East and West

The Théâtre de Soleil was also prominent in another trend, the cross-fertilization of Eastern and Western theatre. For sheer variety, Tokyo was probably the world's biggest centre of theatre, packed with mostly young, imaginative companies playing to full houses. The Asian emphasis on acting (rather than script) was particularly influential through, among others, Suzuki Tadashi's company, which took its inspiration from the ancient Noh drama and, through the expressive power of the actors, essayed a drama not dependent on language (Japanese, after all, is not spoken by many foreigners). In different ways, many of the most innovative and intelligent Western directors focused on the relationship between actor and audience. 'Theatre ought to be the encounter of human beings with human beings, and nothing more', declared Ingmar Bergman. The use of small studio theatres concentrated attention, and, together with the collapse of social conventions, the demands made on actors greatly increased. Innovation, however, was made easier.

In much of Asia, as in eastern Europe, the theatre remained highly political, often operating in the teeth of censorship. In Czechoslovakia, Havel continued to write plays that could not then be publicly performed. Radical drama also existed in the West, though handicapped by the need for subsidies from the kind of regime it sought to overthrow. Minority theatre – feminist, black, 'gay', etc, – expanded, especially in North America, and the sheer number of writers, actors and designers, now moving more easily between different media, multiplied. The theatre continues to attract talented, creative and energetic artists, and to provide profuse variety of entertainment, stimulation and instruction. It remains the liveliest of arts.

Opposite: Characteristically inventive light and sound effects in the Cirque du Soleil's *Saltimbango*, 1997.

Above: Many theatres are unsuitable for contemporary theatrical productions: *De la Guarda* running across a vertical surface in the Round House, an old engine shed in north London, 1999.

timeline

c. 526–456 BC	**AESCHYLUS**		1652–1685	**OTWAY,** *Thomas*
496–406 BC	**SOPHOCLES**		1668–1747	**LE SAGE,** *Alain René*
c. 484–406 BC	**EURIPIDES**		1668–1777	**CONGREVE,** *William*
c. 448–380 BC	**ARISTOPHANES**		1684–1754	**HOLBERG,** *Ludvig*
c. 342–293 BC	**MENANDER**		1688–1763	**MARIVAUX,** *Pierre*
c. 330 BC	**ARISTOTLE:** *Poetics*		1694–1778	**VOLTAIRE**
c. 254–1284BC	**PLAUTUS**		1720–1806	**GOZZI,** *Carlo*
c. 4 BC–65 AD	**SENECA**		1709–1793	**GOLDONI,** *Carlo*
10th century	**HROSWITHA**		1717–1779	**GARRICK,** *David*
from late 10th century	LITURGICAL DRAMA		1718–1777	**SUMAROKOV,** *Alexei*
from c. 1150	NOH DRAMA		1729–1781	**LESSING,** *Gotthold Ephraim*
from c. 1250	MYSTERY PLAYS		1730–1774	**GOLDSMITH,** *Oliver*
1350	MORALITY PLAYS		d. 1732	**GAY,** *John*
c. 1460	INVENTION OF PRINTING		1732–1799	**BEAUMARCHAIS,** *Pierre Augustin Caron de*
1469–1527	**MACHIAVELLI,** *Niccolo*		1749–1832	**GOETHE,** *Johann Wolfgang von*
1474–1533	**ARIOSTO,** *Ludovico*		1751–1816	**SHERIDAN,** *Richard Brinsley*
c. 1505–1565	**LOPE DE RUEDA**		1759–1805	**SCHILLER,** *Friederich von*
from c. 1550	COMMEDIA DELL'ARTE		1791–1861	**SCRIBE,** *Eugene*
1558–1594	**KYD,** *Thomas*		1808–1850	**TYL,** *Josef*
1562–1635	**LOPE DE VEGA**		1810–1857	**MUSSET,** *Alfred de*
1564–1616	**SHAKESPEARE,** *William*		1813–1883	**WAGNER,** *Richard*
1564–1593	**MARLOWE,** *Christopher*		1818–1883	**TURGENEV,** *Ivan Sergeevich*
1572–1637	**JONSON,** *Ben*		1819–1880	**OFFENBACH,** *Jacques*
1580–1627	**MIDDLETON,** *Thomas*		1823–1886	**OSTROVSKY,** *Alexander Nikolaevich*
c. 1580–1634	**WEBSTER,** *John*		1825–1899	**STRAUSS,** *Johann, the younger*
1600–1681	**CALDERÓN DE LA BARCA,** *Pedro*		1826–1914	**SAXE–MEININGEN,** *Duke of*
1606–1668	**D'AVENANT,** *Sir William*		1828–1906	**IBSEN,** *Henrik*
1606–1684	**CORNEILLE,** *Pierre*		1833	BULWER–LYTTON ACT
1622–1673	**MOLIÈRE,** *Jean–Baptiste Poquelin*		1836–1911	**GILBERT,** *Sir William Schwenck*
1631–1700	**DRYDEN,** *John*		1838–1905	**IRVING,** *Sir Henry*
1639–1699	**RACINE,** *Jean*		1840–1902	**ZOLA,** *Émile*
1640–1715	**WYCHERLEY,** *William*		1840–1908	**GOLDFADEN,** *Abraham*

1842–1898 **MALLARMÉ,** *Stéphane*	1896 BERNE CONVENTION
1845–1923 **BERNHARDT,** *Sarah*	1896–1948 **ARTAUD,** *Antonin*
1849–1912 **STRINDBERG,** *August*	1897–1975 **WILDER,** *Thornton Niven*
1854–1900 **WILDE,** *Oscar*	1898–1956 **BRECHT,** *Bertolt*
1855–1934 **PINERO,** *Sir Arthur Wing*	1905–1984 **HELLMAN,** *Lillian*
1856–1912 **BRAHM,** *Otto*	1906–1963 **ODETS,** *Clifford*
1856–1950 **SHAW,** *George Bernard*	1906–1963 **BECKETT,** *Samuel*
1858–1943 **ANTOINE,** *André*	1907–1989 **OLIVIER,** *Laurence*
1859–1931 **ALEICHEM,** *Sholom*	1910–1986 **GENET,** *Jean*
1859–1931 **BELASCO,** *David*	1910–1987 **ANOUILH,** *Jean*
1859–1943 **STANISLAVSKY,** *Konstantin Alexeyev*	1910–1994 **BARRAULT,** *Jean–Louis*
1860–1904 **CHEKHOV,** *Anton*	1911–1983 **WILLIAMS,** *Tennessee*
1862–1921 **FEYDEAU,** *Georges*	1912–1994 **IONESCU,** *Eugène*
1862–1946 **HAUPTMANN,** *Gerhart*	born 1915 **MILLER,** *Arthur*
1862–1949 **MAETERLINCK,** *Maurice*	1916–1982 **WEISS,** *Peter*
1864–1918 **WEDEKIND,** *Frank*	1921–1990 **DÜRRENMATT,** *Friedrich*
1865–1939 **YEATS,** *William Butler*	born 1926 **FO,** *Dario*
1866–1954 **BENAVENTE Y MARTÍNEZ**	born 1928 **ALBEE,** *Edward*
1867–1936 **PIRANDELLO,** *Luigi*	1929–1994 **OSBORNE,** *John*
1868–1936 **GORKY,** *Maxim*	born 1930 **PINTER,** *Harold*
1870–1948 **LEHÁR,** *Franz*	born 1932 **FUGARD,** *Athol*
1871–1909 **SYNGE,** *John Millington*	born 1934 **SOYINKA,** *Wole*
1872–1929 **DIAGHILEV,** *Serge Pavlovich*	born 1934 **BOND,** *Edward*
1872–1966 **GORDON CRAIG,** *Edward*	born 1937 **WILSON,** *Lanford*
1873–1907 **JARRY,** *Alfred*	born 1938 **CHURCHILL,** *Caryl*
1873–1943 **REINHARDT,** *Max*	born 1938 **GUARE,** *John*
1874–1929 **HOFFMANNSTHAL,** *Hugo von*	born 1943 **SHEPARD,** *Sam*
1874–1940 **MEYERHOLD,** *Vsevolod*	born 1947 **HARE,** *David*
1880–1964 **O'CASEY,** *Sean*	born 1947 **MAMET,** *David*
1888–1953 **O'NEILL,** *Eugene*	
1888–1959 **ANDERSON,** *Maxwell*	
1893–1966 **PISCATOR,** *Erwin*	

glossary

Act
A major division of a play, in classical drama one of five

Ad lib
Latin *ad libitum*, 'as you like', an unscripted remark by an actor, often made to conceal an error, fill in for a memory lapse, etc.

Agit-prop
Theatre designed as revolutionary propaganda, derived from the 'Agitation and Propaganda' department in the Soviet Union in the 1920s

Alienation
Also known as *Verfremdungseffekt*, the technique employed by Brecht to encourage a detached, critical view of the action by the audience; for the actor, a technique opposed to Stanislavksky's method

Alternative Theatre
The great variety of more or less unconventional theatre since the 1950s, often with radical or reforming intent

Antihero
A protagonist who lacks the characteristics expected of a conventional 'hero', sometimes parodying those characteristics

Apron stage
A thrust stage projecting into the auditorium, associated with 16th-century theatres; later the forestage in front of the proscenium arch

Archon
The official in charge of drama festivals in ancient Greece

Arena stage
A thrust or open stage; also applied to theatre-in-the-round

Asphaleian system
The use of hydraulic pistons to raise, lower or tilt the stage, named after the Austrian company that developed it

Atellan farce
Rustic comedy characteristic of southern Italy in Roman times, a distant ancestor of the commedia dell'arte

Auditorium
The space in a theatre occupied by the audience

Backcloth
Or backdrop, a painted cloth at the back of the stage used, together with wings, to suggest perspective

Backstage
The whole area behind the stage, including dressing rooms, etc.

Blocking
Working out the actors' stance and movements in the course of rehearsal

Box office
The ticket office in a theatre: in Shakespeare's time spectators put their money in a box as they entered

Box set
A realistic set representing three walls and ceiling of a room by an arrangement of flats; it superceded the perspective arrangement of wings and backcloth

Breeches role
The part of a (romantic) male played by a woman, popular in Restoration England

Burlesque
A type of comedy mocking a particular style, fashion, writer, etc.; also, a type of US variety entertainment in the late 19th–20th century

'Business'
Of a performance, suggestive activity of various kinds, often unscripted and sometimes involving props, to augment the impact

Carpenter's scene
A scene played on the forestage before a curtain, to allow for elaborate scene changes, e.g. in pantomime

Catharsis
'Purging', Aristotle's term for the emotional release experienced by the spectator at a tragedy

Clouding
A means of disguising the top of the set by a border suggesting clouds in the 17th–early 18th centuries

Constructivism
Russian art movement of the 1920s, influenced by cubism and technological forms, an important influence on design

Corpus Christi Plays
Mystery plays, which were performed at the feast of Corpus Christi

Cue
The words or incident that warn an actor that speech or action from him is due

Dénouement
The final resolution of the plot

Dithyramb
Song sung at festivals of Dionysus, said to have been the origin of Greek tragedy

Downstage
The part of the stage nearest the audience, in contrast to 'upstage'

Dramatis personae
The characters in a play

Ensemble
A permanent company of actors with individual style, technique, etc.; e.g. Brecht's Berliner Ensemble

Epilogue
A speech at the end of the play, after conclusion of the action, sometimes spoken direct to the audience

Equity
Name of the actors' trade union in Britain, Canada and the USA

Exit (plural exeunt), Latin, 'he/she (they) leave', a stage direction; hence, a way out

Flat
A piece of scenery consisting of painted canvas stretched on a wooden frame, forming the wings in 17th-century and later theatres

Flies
The space above the stage, out of sight of the audience, to or from which scenery can be 'flown' by a system of ropes

Footlights
Stage lights at the front of and level with the stage

Front of house
The area of the theatre in front of the stage, including the auditorium

Grand Guignol
One-act melodramas in 19th-century Parisian cabaret; named after 'Guignol', a Punch-like, 18th-century French puppet

Green room
A backstage common room for the actors

Ham
Of an actor's perfomance, exaggerated, phoney

Improvisation
Unscripted and unrehearsed performance figuring in many theatre traditions, important in actor training

Leitmotif
A recurring theme, image or form of words (first applied to Wagner's works)

Libretto
The written text in an opera, musical, etc.

Limelight
The intense white light used like a spotlight in early 19th-century theatres

Masque
Court entertainment featuring song, dance, drama and spectacle, originating in Renaissance Italy

Melodrama
'Music drama', the heightened, popular drama of the 19th century, using much incidental music, with plot, characters and moral conventions simplified and exaggerated.

Melpomene: *see* Muses

Miracle Plays: *see* Mystery Plays

Mise-en-scène
The scene or setting of a play, in the most comprehensive sense

Morality Plays
Late medieval didactic religious plays about the relations between the individual and personified virtues and vices

Muses
Greek goddesses of the arts, including Melpomene, muse of tragedy, and Thalia, muse of comedy

Mystery Plays
Cycles of medieval religious plays based on Biblical themes, performed in open spaces in towns, often by trade guilds

Offstage
In the wings, where an event may be heard but not seen by the audience

Orchestra
The 'dancing place', or acting area, in Classical theatres

Pageant
A waggon on which an episode of a mystery play was performed; hence a temporary stage for a ceremony and, eventually, a ceremonial procession

Passion Play
Traditional religious play about the Christian Passion – Crucifixion and Resurrection

Peking Opera
Traditional Chinese theatre incorporating music, song, speech, dance and acrobatics

Perspective
Representation of three dimensions on two-dimensional (flat) surfaces, which led to narrow and rectangular, rather than broad and curved, auditoriums

Picture-frame: *see* Proscenium arch

Pit
The area, before seats were introduced, now called the stalls

Principal boy
The leading male role in a pantomime performed by an actress

Prologue
A speech that precedes the main action of the play; see also Epilogue

Prompter
The person, usually seated inconspicuously at stage left, who follows the performance from a script and if necessary 'prompts' an actor who mometarily forgets a line

Props
Short for 'properties', all objects other than scenery that are required for a scene

Proscenium arch
A frame-like structure that divides stage from audience and helps to create the illusion of a different environment

Purim plays
One-act plays associated with the Jewish Purim festival, based on the Book of Esther but including popular folk elements

Raisonneur
A character who is relatively detached from the action and represents a neutral or authorial point of view

Repertory theatre
A programme of plays each presented for a short, fixed time by a permanent company

Ritterdrama
Popular, late 18th-century, German melodramas about medieval knights

Run
Consecutive performances of the same production, its length usually depending on ticket sales

Safety curtain
A fireproof curtain that can separate stage from auditorium in the event of fire

Satyr play
A form of Greek burlesque featuring satyrs – crude, goat-like creatures associated with Dionysus – which often presented a derisive parody of events in the preceding tragedy

Scene
A subdivision of an act

Script
The complete text of a play, including dialogue and stage directions

Set
The stage environment, in particular a three-dimensional environment composed of solid props rather than painted scenery

Skene
The building at the back of the orchestra in Classical Greek theatres

Stage directions
The playwright's instructions regarding action and appearance, usually brief (as in Shakespeare) sometimes long and detailed (as in G. B. Shaw)

Stock company
A regular company at a particular theatre, as distinct from a touring company, performing plays in repertory

Thalia: *see* Muses

Theatre in the round
A theatre in which the performing area is surrounded by the audience on all sides

Thrust stage
A stage that projects into the audience, creating more intimate relations between actor and audience

Thunder sheet
Suspended sheet of thin metal which, when agitated, sounds like thunder

Tiring house
Dressing room in an Elizabethan theatre, the front of which formed the back of the stage; it also gave access to an upper gallery the 'hut', on top, containing devices for sound effects

Tragic carpet
Green baize spread on the stage during tragedies in 17th-century theatres to protect costly costumes in death scenes

Trap
A trap door in stage or scenery through which actors or props can suddenly appear

Tree border
Similar in function to clouding, but with leaves rather than clouds

Troupe
A company of actors; hence, an 'old trouper', an experienced actor

University wits
A group of Oxford- and (especially) Cambridge-educated Elizabethan playwrights, rivals to professionals such as Shakespeare

Upstage: *see* Downstage

Wind machine
A drum attached to loose canvas which makes a sound like wind when rotated

Wings
The invisible areas at each side of the stage; formerly, the painted flats that masked these areas

Zarzuela
A popular form of musical play in Spain

acknowledgements

Aisa,Barcelona 37, 68, 142

AKG, London 31, 35, 39, 46, 125 Top Left, 133 Top, 150, 154 Top, 155, 177 Top, Accademia Rossini, Bologna 82, Bibliotheque Nationale, Paris 75, Jaques Callot (1592/93-1635) "Balli di sfessania" 42-43, Herzog August Bibliothek Anton Graff (1736 - 1813) "Portarit of Gotthold Ephraim" Lessing 90, Kunsthalle, Hamburg Sir Lawrence Alma-Tadema (1836 - 1912) " A dedication to Bacchus" 12 Bottom, Ferdinand Leeke "Seiglindes Flucht" 1895 115, Jean Lepautre " Le Malade Imaginaire comedie represente dans le jardin de Versailles devant la Grotte 1676" 62-63, Eric Lessing/ Musee Conde, Chantilly Pierre Mignard (1612 - 1695) "Portrait of Moliere" 70, Eric Lessing/ Musee du Louvre, Paris Claude Gillot (1673 - 1723) "The two coaches scene from the comedy Foire St Germaine from 1695" 49, Emil Orlick 144, Private Collection "Laska von Zeitgenossisch Nach Scluss der Vorstellung" 114-115, Sammlungen der Universitat Leonhard Schorer (1715-1777) "Portrait of Johann Christoph Gottsched" 91, State Russian Museum Leon Baskt (1866 - 1924) "Diaghilew und seine Mutter 1906" 154 Bottom, Stiftung Weimarer Klassik Georg Melcior Kraus (1737 - 1806) " Portrait of Johann Wolfgang Goethe" 93 Top, Stiftung Weimarer Klassik, Weimar Georg Melchior Kraus (1737- 1806)" portrait of Johann Wolfgang Goethe" 63, Uinversitatsbibliothek, Heidelberg 40

Bridgeman Art Library, London/New York Bibliotheque de L'Opera, Paris/Lauros-Giraudon French School (16th c) Balthazar de Beaujoyeux "Ballet comique de la reine" 1581 engraving 64, Bibliotheque Nationale, Paris France Attic red-figure vase depicting Dionysus playing a lyre, 5th century BC 12, Bibliotheque Nationale, Paris/Lauros-Giraudon " Title Page from 'Autos Sacramentales' by Pedro Calderon de La Barca (1600 - 81) edited Juan Garcia Infanzon" 1690 69 Top, Bonhmas, London Tosa School 1800 "Scenes of urban life under the 'Bakufu' government from a performance of Noh Drama Japanese, (detail from six fold screen, see 67712) (colour woodblock print) 29, British Library, London engraving by Droeshurt 1623 G11631.B.L "Title Page with a portrait of Shakespeare, from Mr William Shakespeare's Comedies, Histories and Tragedies, edited by J Heminge and H. Condell" 58 Bottom, British Museum, London Okumura Masanobu (1686 - 1764)" Interior of a Kabuki Theatre"c.1745 (woodblock print) 28, British Museum, London "The Sage Begawan Bisma and a maid servant" Indonesia 19th century (puppets of painted hide) 22-23, Burgtheatre, Vienna Franz von Matsch (1861 - 1942) "The Greek Theatre at Tormina, Sicily from a series on the History of Theatre" (ceiling painting) 14, Chartes Cathedral, France "Capital frieze depicting Scenes from the Passion from the south door of the Royal Portal, west facade" mid 12th century (stone) photo by Peter Willi 36, Chateau de Versailles, France/Lauros-Giraudon Nicolas Gosse (1787 - 1878) A. Dauzats (1804 -68) "Production of 'Richard Lionheart' by Gretry for Queen Victoria at Chateau d'Eu September 1843" 96-97, Dougga, Tunisia View of Roman Theatre, 168-169AD photo Ali Meyer 21, Guildhall Library, Corporation Of London T. Rowlandson (1756 - 1827) & Pugin A. (1762- 1832) " Interior of Drury Lane 1808" 87 Top, Hermitage, St.Petersburg John Hoppner (1758 - 1810) "Portrait of Richard Brinsley Sheridan (1751 - 1816) 89, Kunsthistoriches Museum , Vienna Jean Fouquet (1425- 80) " Gonella, The Ferrara court jester" c. 1445 (panel) 41, Leeds Museums and Galleries (City Art gallery) Rmeberandt Harmensz Van Rijn (1606 - 69) "Dr Faustus in his Study" (engraving) 60, David Lees, Florence "Interior of the Teatro Olympico, Vicenza designed by Andrea Palladio (1580 - 80) and stage set designed by Vincenzo Scamozzi (1552 - 1616)" 53, Louvre, Paris, France "Statuettes of Actors and Actresses, Hellenistic, c.325-50BC" (terracotta) photo Peter Willi 19 Top, Philip Mould Historical Portraits Ltd., London Jonathon Richardson (1665 - 1745) "Sir Robert Walpole (1676-1745) 122, Philip Mould Historical Portraits Ltd. Moses Houghton (1772 - 1848) "Mrs Siddons(1755 - 1834) as the Tragic Muse, after Reynolds portrait in the Dulwich Picture Gallery"124, Musee Carnvalet Jean Beraud (1849 - 1936) "In the Wings of the Opera House 1899" (oil on canvas) 105, Museo Archeologico Nazionale, Naples, Italy "Strolling masked muscians, scene from a comedy play by Dioskourides of Samos (2nd centuryBC) found in Villa of Cicero Pompeii" (mosaic) 20, Museo di San Marco dell'Angelico, Florence, Italy Fra Angelico (Guido di Pietro) (c. 1387 - 1455) "Scenes from the Passion of Christ and the Last Judgement, orginally drawers from a chest storing silver" (tempera on panel) 32-33, Museo di Storia della Fotografia Fratelli alinari, Florence E Hadler(fl. 1883) "Portrait of Goldoni"84, Museo Lazare Galdiano, Madrid Eugenio Caxes (1577 - 1642) attr to 506 131 -0795275/1"Portrait of Lope Felix de Vega Caprio(1562 - 1635)" c.1630 oil on canvas 69, Museum of the City of New York American School (19th century) "American theatre, Bowery, New York, depicting the 57th Night of Mr.T.D. Jim Crow Rice (1808 - 60) November 25th, 1833" (oil on canvas) 133 Bottom, Philip Mould, Historical portraits Ltd. London Sir Pter Lely (1618 - 80) "Nell Gwynn(1650-87), mistress of Charles II" 76, Phillips, the International Fine Art Auctioners Philippe Mercier (1689 - 1760) " Pierrot and Harlequin" 48, Private Collection "Cinematographe Lumiere" 157 Top, Private Collection Cornelius de Visscher (1619/29 - 62) "View of London with the Swan, the Rose and the Globe Theatres and St.Paul's after the removal of the spire by Inigo Jones" 58-59, Private Collection engraved by Joseph Swain (1820 - 1909) "A play in a London Inn Yard in the time of Queen Elizabeth" hby English School (19th century) 57, Private Collection/Roger -Viollet, Paris French School (19th century)"Louis XIV (1638 - 1715) of France in the costume of the Sun King in the Ballet 'La Nuit' c.1665 (litho) 47, Private Collection/Stapleton Collection Thomas Allom (1804 - 72) " Scene from the Specatacle the Sun and Moon from 'China in a series of Views' by George Newham wright (c.1790 - 1877) 1843 coloured engraving 27, Royal Cornwall Museum, Truro Dirck Hals (1591 - 1656) attr to "Queen Elizabeth I and the Earl of Leicester at Kenilworth" (panel) 54, Somerset Maugham Theatre Collection, London Sir Joshua Reynolds (1732- 92) "David Garrick (1717-79) between the Muses of Tragedy and Comedy "86, Stapleton Collection "Interior of the Theatre Royal, Drury Lane, viewed from the stage - altered and decorated in 1775 by R. and J. Adam" 80-81, Victoria and Albert Museum, London Anonymous "Scene from Tartuffe by Moliere" 1850 70-71, Victoria and Albert Museum, London Charles Robert Leslie (1794 - 1859) " Jourdain fences his maid, Nicole with his wife looking on Scene from 'Le Bourgeois Gentilhomme' Act III Scene 3" (oil on canvas) 77, Woburn Abbey, Bedfordshire John the Elder Decritz (1552 - 1642) " Lucy Harrington, Countess Of Bedford, in a masque designed by Inigo Jones 1606" 65, Christopher Wood Gallery, London UK John WatkinsChapman (1832 - 1903) "The Gallery, Drury Lane" Back Cover bottom

Jean-Loup Charmet 35 Bottom, 101, 136, 170-171, Musee Conde Chantilly Jean Fouquet (1420 - 1480) "Le Martyr de St AppolineHeures d'Etienne Chevalier" 39 Top

Z.Chrapek 96

Corbis UK Ltd Front Endpaper, 6, 44, 109, 147, Archivo Iconografico/Galleria Palatina, Palazzo Pi Florence Italy 45, Yann Arthus- Bertrand 11, Austrian Archives 117 Bottom, 153, Bettmann 8-9, 19 Bottom, 93 Centre, 104, 119 Top, 129, 138 left, 169 Bottom, Hulton -Deutsch Collection 88,124 Centre, 130,157 Bottom,164,169 Top,167,175 Bottom, Robbie Jack 172, 177 Bottom, Wolfgang Kaehler 10 Top, Charles&Josette Lenars 26,Michael Nichols 15, Gianni Dagli Orti Bibliotheque des Arts Decoratifs, Paris Prologue frontispiece by Duplessis 72-73, Gianni Dagli Orti 71, 85,Leonard de Selva 116,John Springer 179 Top, Alison Wright 25, Michael S. Yamashita 30,

Culver Pictures Inc. 102, 103, 111, 120, 121, 127, 128

PhotoDisc/PhotoDisc arlin

Mary Evans Picture Library 55, 98-99, 106, 123

Guthrie Theatre, Minneapolis 171

Hulton Getty Picture Collection Back Cover top, 56, 111 Bottom, 138 right, 140, 145, 152, 165 Top Left, 174, Gordon Anthony 161, Keystone 61, 134-135, Rischgitz 92,

Image Bank, London Archive Photos 126,

Mander & Mitchenson 66, 113 Bottom, 137, 148 Top

Oronoz, Madrid 50, 51 Bottom, Delgado Ramos Alvar 160-161

Performing Arts Library, London Henrietta Butler 17,

Photostage Ltd Donald Cooper 16, 24 -25, 67, 78, 79, 140-141, 143, 146, 149 Bottom, 151, 158-159, 163 Top, 163 Bottom, 165 Top Right, 173, 175 Top, 176, 179 Bottom, 180, 181

Tony Stone Images, London Wayne Eastep Front Cover bottom, Spine, Front flap, Back flap, 2,Siegfried Layda 166-167,Rex A Butcher 3,

Theater Institute Nederland 94-95,

Victoria & Albert Museum, London 83, 100, 106 Top, 108, 112, 125 Top Right, 131 Enthoven Collection 117

index

Page numbers in italics refer to captions